is a whopper, but what have we hooked? A journal, an auto-
aphy? Neither net is large enough to land Gary Saunders's
hkeeping, a splendid gathering of stories by this devout family
., artist, forester, environmentalist, and superb storyteller. The
result is what we find here: evocative, inciteful, provocative,
d even fanciful snapshots telling of a rich life incorporating
knowledge and traditions of rural life in fine art and in science.

— DIRK van LOON, founder of *Rural Delivery*

Gary Saunders has the brain of a scientist, the eye of a painter,
and the heart of a poet. Whether describing ticks or dovekies, the
origins of oatmeal or the development of house paint, *Earthkeeping*
will hold your interest with a marvelous balance of personal story
and clearly rendered science. These essays on rural themes are
lovely, intimate conversations between reader and writer, a magical blend of folk art and academic clarity. The writing sings.

— ROBIN McGRATH, author of *Life on the Mista Shipu:
Dispatches from Labrador*

Charming, thoughtful, and highly readable. Each vignette is a
reminder of the richness and meaning contained in our everyday
interactions with the natural world. Together, they're a plea for a
world that's very much worth saving.

— TOM CHENEY, conservationist, ecologist, and award-
winning journalist

Also by GARY SAUNDERS

My Life with Trees: A Sylvan Journey

Free Wind Home: A Childhood Memoir, 1935-1948

*At a Glance: A Guide to Identifying and
Managing Nova Scotia Hardwoods*

*So Much Weather: Facts, Phenomena and
Weather Lore from Atlantic Canada*

Discover Nova Scotia: The Ultimate Nature Guide

Doctor, When You're Sick You're Not Well

Doctor Olds of Twillingate

Wildlife of Atlantic Canada & New England
(with Wayne Barrett)

September Christmas

Alder Music

Rattles and Steadies

GARY SAUNDERS

Earth keeping

love notes
for tough times

GOOSE LANE

Edited by Paula Sarson.
Cover and page design by Julie Scriver.
Cover illustration by Julie Scriver with materials from Freepik.com.
Printed in Canada by Marquis.
10 9 8 7 6 5 4 3 2 1

Library and Archives Canada Cataloguing in Publication

Title: Earthkeeping : love notes for tough times / Gary Saunders.
Names: Saunders, Gary L., author.
Description: Essays.
Identifiers: Canadiana (print) 20220197164 | Canadiana (ebook) 20220197326 |
ISBN 9781773102696 (softcover) | ISBN 9781773102702 (EPUB)
Classification: LCC PS8587.A38658 E27 2022 | DDC C814/.54—dc23

Goose Lane Editions acknowledges the generous support of the Government of Canada, the Canada Council for the Arts, and the Government of New Brunswick.

Goose Lane Editions is located on the traditional unceded territory of the Wəlastəkwiyik whose ancestors along with the Mi'kmaq and Peskotomuhkati Nations signed Peace and Friendship Treaties with the British Crown in the 1700s.

Goose Lane Editions
500 Beaverbrook Court, Suite 330
Fredericton, New Brunswick
CANADA E3B 5X4
gooselane.com

MIX
Paper from
responsible sources
FSC® C103567
www.fsc.org

To Neil Van Nostrand,
Earthkeeper extraordinaire
1930–2016

Contents

Foreword

I've forgotten the exact date, somewhere in the seventies, but I remember well that foggy night on Duckworth Street in St. John's, and the open door of a pub letting in the distant murmur of a foghorn. A group of us, professors, students, and would-be writers, were clustered in a corner listening to Alden Nowlan. He had just completed his poetry reading at the university and was feeling in good spirits about it all, glad to be back in the province, he said. That was the night he mentioned the name Gary Saunders, a multitalented Newfoundlander living in the Maritimes. He told us he was a big fan of Gary's work from day one, praising him for his humane zest for life; his easy, evocative style; and his love for his Newfoundland origins. Up to this time, I was not familiar with Gary but, after that night, I went looking. And I wasn't disappointed.

In the following days, I came across a colour plate reproduction of one of Gary's paintings, an "autumn" composition, a prize-winner in a past Arts and Letters Competition. This was a particular pleasure for me, a free-flowing, semi-abstract, mixed-media piece with lines of glue, raised cords under the vibrant colours; it transported me to a pensive point in our island landscape, somewhere I'd been before—yet far beyond that to a universal realm, the enticing woods of myth and fairy tale. Years later, when I asked Gary about this painting, he described to me how he dribbled "white glue straight from the container onto his horizontal canvas. Free style, yes, but thinking of falling leaves as they loop from side to side on a windless autumn day, taking sometimes several minutes to reach the ground from a tall tree."

—TOM DAWE, St. John's Poet Laureate, 2010-13

Introduction
Nature under Glass?

Every time we take away a technology, we find a gift underneath.
—Minutes of the Lead Pencil Club

Believe it or not, you and I were once citizens of an enchanted land where the sky was never so blue and the grass never so green, and every day was a week long. I mean the land of childhood. And though we've since mislaid our passports, secretly we cherish a moment when Nature's beauty first smote us.

This was brought home to me years ago, when I worked in a sunless basement office with a single upstairs window at sidewalk level — tough for a forester-educator. Though we brightened the place with prints and philodendrons, plus a geranium on a windowsill over the stairs, I grabbed any excuse to escape outdoors, especially when the air began to smell of spring.

One such March day, a child's cry stopped me on the stairs.

"Mommy! Wait!" Outside the window I saw two pairs of snow boots wheel and stop. "Look, Mommy! The red flower!"

What flower, I thought, unaware that our sulky geranium had finally bloomed. Then the window darkened, and a little girl's face hovered in the frame like a Botticelli.

I'd seen that rapt expression before. It was our daughter Gillian, age seven or so, reverently pouring her first catch of live tadpoles into our bathtub. It was our little Matthew gazing up into a huge sugar maple's armature of branches while sap *plinkplonked* from drilled spiles into empty pails beside him. It was our little son Robin, plopped on his belly, watching carpenter ants snip their post-flight nuptial wings.

11

Moments later the window girl was gone. Without ever seeing me she restored my faith in childhood's passion for Nature — even Nature under glass. She also softened a cynical anecdote I'd recently read: Worried mom asks TV-loving, computer-nerd son why he prefers playing indoors. Son replies, "More electrical outlets." The anecdote disturbs me even more today. Thanks to the internet and web, the cathode ray tube has become our favourite window on the natural world — Nature under glass, indeed.

Which may be okay for jaded adults; for small children it is not. True, the tube is unbeatable for sourcing information. A five-year-old can now click on *maple* or *frog* or *ant* and download the whole scoop in seconds. Download everything, that is, but the texture, smell, taste, the weather, the local lore — the joy.

For the tube is cerebral, instant, remote, an electronic dispenser of insipid picture-sound pablum. Nature by contrast is physical, ongoing, *present* — a live provider of hot porridge for *bodymindspirit*. Compared to the wet wriggle of a tadpole through the fingers amid birdsong on a scented May morning, the tube is a poor bargain. One bite of clove, said a Sufi master, tells more than watching a whole spice caravan go by. Young souls need that jolt to really germinate into Nature lovers.

But maybe I needn't fear for our millennial children plugged into the electronic hive, nor fret about a digital future where virtual Nature is all young Canada knows. Maybe the global marketeers won't persuade future voters that clean water really comes from a plastic jug, food from a grocer, wood from a lumberyard, power from a wall plug. But I fear they will — unless we reach them first with the truth.

Dr. Fraser Mustard, renowned Canadian physician and educator, warned that children who don't learn basic coping skills by age six may never master them. (What's more basic than Earthkeeping? Earthkeeping as here intended is stewardship writ large.) For, thanks to modern communications and travel, we've shrunk the globe, while rampant consumerism and population growth are making ever-greater demands on a finite resource. Sure, we now have fine outdoor education centres and greener public school curricula. The trouble is, they all kick in too late for toddlers. No, for them it's up to parents, aunts, uncles, daycare workers.

Luckily the job doesn't demand a doctorate in science, nor a private nature park. Love, common sense, and a vacant lot— even a potted plant—will do. And luckily there are immediate rewards. On a nature walk with Cub Scouts, I challenged them to name one everyday thing that doesn't come from Planet Earth. Eagerly they listed Ninja Turtles, contact lenses, computer chips. Each time, I shook my head.

"I know!" cried one. "Pizza!" (Perhaps he was hungry.) So we ticked off pizza's ingredients. It came out the same. As my Great Truth sank in, you could have heard an acorn drop. "All from the Earth? Cool!"

"Yes, and only from the Earth."

Part One
The Life Rural

GLS/DEC4/'86

A Place in Time

For over half a century now we've lived in an old Nova Scotia farmhouse near the Bay of Fundy's eastern end. Our windows look out on a patchwork quilt of woodlot, field, and salt marsh rich in legend and history: Glooscap, Champlain, Evangeline, the New England Planters of 1760–61. Tourists gawk at our monster tides — "World's Highest!" — and take home photos of black-and-white cows posing on pastures impossibly green.

"What a lovely spot you have!" visitors say. "So peaceful."

Well, not always. The month of May can be noisy as dairy farmers roar up and down the gravel road lugging laden manure-spreaders and seeding the cattle corn or alfalfa that will feed their herds come winter. Same with September and October, as they harvest and store those precious crops. But mostly it's quiet out here. And quiet was what we sought after life in Toronto and St. John's. Quiet, and a place of our own, after renting for several years with a growing family. And since both of us were raised rural, Beth on a New Brunswick farm near the Richibucto River, I on the Gander River estuary in northeast Newfoundland, it was rural we went looking for, and found in 1969. We even found a river, the Salmon that empties into Nova Scotia's Cobequid Bay near Truro. True, its waters are always cloudy with Fundy's pinkish tidal silt — but nothing's perfect. More important, since by now we had three kids under age five and planned to stay, it was far enough from the nasty new shopping malls to tempt them for a decade or so yet.

It was this landscape — rolling pastures and mixed woods enclosing our fifth-hectare of sloping, unkempt lawn and a run-down apple orchard—that greeted us five that June. Across the road was a small pond where tree frogs trilled every evening. To the north lay Acadian dike-lands, and, beyond that, tidal marshes, the bay itself, across the bay more marshland and, behind that, the blue three hundred-metre Cobequid Hills.

As for our century-plus home-to-be, it had stood unpainted for fifteen years. Starlings were breeding in its rain gutters and tree swallows nested atop the hydro power pipe. Otherwise the house was sound, its roof level, and its rooms livable with some work. Five years later we bought what, as a forester, I'd long craved: a nearby woodlot, twenty-five hectares to call our own. All of these, plus our subsequent vegetable and herb gardens and my berry patch, would help me weather a coming cancer ordeal—but that's another story.

Before that we'd rented a vacant house up the road for five years. Unaccountably, it seemed to us then, the nearest village was called Old Barns. (Canada Post later changed our part of it, the Shore Road loop, to Clifton, a more upscale, less odorous handle.) During those years our landlord Carman Forbes and his wife, Viola, lived just up the road. Our monthly rent of only twenty dollars was a lifesaver for a college-broke young family, and possible only because the place lacked an indoor bathroom. Our three kids, familiar with flush toilets, revelled in the outdoor privy, even inviting their friends to use it. Carman later replaced it with an indoor facility, for which we gladly paid an extra fifty dollars a month.

Asked about the village name, Carman smiled; a story was coming. "Well," he began, "many of our ancestors shipped here from New England, Massachusetts in particular. They weren't Loyalists, that was later; this was six years after the Expulsion of the original settlers in 1755, the Acadians. The newcomers were called Planters, brought here to take up vacated Acadian lands.

"The story goes that those ancestors, sailing east up Cobequid Bay to settle, were told to watch on the south shore for two hexagon-shaped French barns, which the soldiers tasked with torching their homesteads had spared to mark the safest route ashore across the treacherous mud flats at low tide. Hence the name."

Those Acadians, he went on, had arrived around 1690 from earlier settlements around Grand Pré, near today's Wolfville. They came from northwestern France to escape the endless squabbles between France and England. This was all news to me. Our Newfoundland school textbooks, though they described France's seasonal Grand Banks cod fishery and the Seven Years' War, focused instead on how France kept trying to capture St. John's. There was scant mention of the Indigenous Beothuk, and as for the Mi'kmaq, who were early present on the southwest coast and later rivals to the Beothuk, their only mention that I recall was of the French using them as allies in their wars.

So I did some research. Seems their place came from the Mi'kmaw word a'kati, meaning "place of," as in Shubenacadie ("the place where wild potatoes grow"). As early as 1604, French explorer Samuel de Champlain had scouted the Bay of Fundy. Anxious to attract royal support for colonization, he played up its supposed mineral wealth. Thus he named the inner part Bason des Mines, and named a prominent nearby headland Cap d'Or (names eventually anglicized to Minas Basin and Cape d'Or), for what seemed like gold glinting from its cliffs. (It turned out to be copper.)

In 1605, after a hard winter at Saint Croix, an island near today's Saint John River, Champlain sailed south across Fundy into today's sheltered Annapolis Basin. There he built a stockade, the first European *habitation* in what is now Canada. Later the British, after several failed attacks, finally took it. They renamed it Fort Anne after their then queen, and the valley and its river became Annapolis.

For settlers a major attraction of the Minas Basin was its wide tidal marshes. Flushed twice daily by the world's highest tides, laden with rich brown silt from Triassic sandstone, diluted by a dozen streams, these marshes abounded in waterfowl and coarse *Spartina* grass for the taking. The Acadians that followed Champlain, familiar with diking techniques back home in Normandy and Brittany, soon set to work with horses and sturdy homemade carts to wall out the high tides with brush-filled earthworks, much like beaver dams only crammed with dried mud and sodded over.

But these sea barriers also trapped in streams and their flash floods. So the builders equipped them with clever wooden culvert-like *aboiteaux* (literally, "water-boxes") with top-hinged doors that opened only outward—valves, in effect—at low tide, thereby letting fresh water escape. Building such dikes before the age of steam shovels, front-end loaders, and dump trucks was brutally hard work. For tools all the Acadians had were homemade wooden spades, horse- or ox-drawn carts, hand-bars, and wheelbarrows. And until all gaps were closed, they could work only when the tide was out, a narrow window of a few hours each day and night.

Still, it was easier than clearing the surrounding woods. In our damp climate such clearings rapidly restocked to aspen and grey birch, then to fir and spruce. Besides, marshland soil was rock-free and very fertile once rain had rinsed the salt away. The Acadians did of course clear some woodland for homes, barns, and kitchen gardens. And they did fell many large trees for bridges, wharves, fencing, farm implements, fish weirs, boats, and ships. Moreover, unless they were able to afford coal from the Louisbourg area of Île Royale (later Cape Breton), they needed year-round firewood for cooking and heating and for making charcoal for blacksmithing.

Once they had walled out the sea and got rid of the brine, Acadian families needed only to fence the family hectares and maintain an allotted section of dike, especially after storms. And marsh mud, carted or wheel-barrowed to their herb and vegetable gardens, made excellent fertilizer.

With those gardens, with a patch of rye for bread and one of oats to feed the hens and oxen, with a field of flax to provide linen for cloth and linseed oil for waterproofing oilskins and for cooking; with a pig or two fed on kitchen scraps for winter ham and bacon; and, above all, with marshland to graze cattle on for beef to eat and sell, the Acadians finally made themselves a good life.

In those decades, continued Carman, our local dikes were fairly short, enclosing a few hectares at the mouths of brooks. But at Grand Pré (Great Prairie) in the eastern Annapolis Valley they eventually encompassed 1,215 hectares (3,000 acres). Apart from the Seven Years' War, fought partly to decide who owned eastern North America, it was a hard but satisfying life. Then in 1755, as noted, came the dreaded Expulsion or *Grand dérangment*. The routine was simple. The Acadian men of each village — imagine their families' misgivings, anticipating what was coming — were herded into a church or other public place and presented with an ultimatum: take the British oath of allegiance or face deportation.

Most Acadians, said Carman, wanting no part in those distant wars (though they gladly sold beef to Louisbourg), naturally refused. The rest is well known, how whole Acadian villages were torched and their occupants crowded onto ships bound for English colonies and elsewhere, even back to France, separating families in the process. This is the tragedy that American poet Longfellow immortalizes in his verse saga *Evangeline*, about the fictional heroine and her lost lover, Gabriel.

However, hundreds of Acadians escaped the Expulsion by hiding out around the Bay of Fundy. One such refuge was Cape Chignecto, where Indigenous allies from the Wabanaki Confederacy helped them survive on clams and seal meat. Then, in the summer of 1758, New England troops finally succeeded, by a brilliant landward attack, in taking the mighty French fortress on Île Royale. "With General Wolfe's capture of Quebec," concluded Carman, "France's overseas empire fell apart."

Later we learned that some Acadians returned from Louisiana and elsewhere to settle in southwest Nova Scotia, on Île Royale (now Prince Edward Island), and in coastal New Brunswick's Cocagne and other villages where their descendants still dwell. Nearly two decades after the New England Planters and others took up their vacated lands hereabouts, came the American Revolution. Thousands of Loyalists, no longer welcome there, plus disbanded soldiers were given land grants here. Finally, the nineteenth century saw thousands of other immigrants arrive from Scotland, Northern Ireland, and Europe.

It was those latter colonists, unfamiliar with diking but used to land clearing, who "let daylight in the swamp," meaning our ancient mixed wood forest. By the late 1800s, roughly two fifths of Maritime old growth would be cleared for agriculture and town lots. Meanwhile the Acadians' neglected seawalls suffered the assaults of tide and storm. Wide swaths of their hard-won hay meadows were reclaimed by salt water. Trees like beech, rock maple, and yellow birch, too big and flinty for the crude axes of the day — the crosscut saw hadn't been invented — were killed by girdling (notching) the trunk. Left to dry for a year or two, they were either burned in piles or junked for firewood. On windless days or in muggy weather a pall of acrid smoke became a harsh summertime reality. Finally, before plowing and seeding, the grey ashes were spread to sweeten the otherwise acidic soil. Tree stumps too huge to be removed were often left to rot. Within a decade the hinterland, then called Cobequid, now Truro ("True Road," originally after a county town of Cornwall, England), was squared off into neat farms and woodlots bounded by roads.

Generations later, New Brunswick's Acadian novelist Antonine Maillet would recount, in her fictional *La Sagouine*, how her "Cajun" ancestors straggled back from Louisiana by ox cart and shank's mare to reclaim what scraps of land and fishing sites the Englishers had not taken in their absence. Anglophone Planter descendants like Carman and later a son and grandson still farm their Holstein dairy cattle here.

And made us late-comers welcome. Whatever ancestral apologies are owed to the Mi'kmaw and the Acadians should come from me, not my spouse, for her ancestors were Scots— Robertson, MacWilliam, MacMichael—who suffered similar evictions, whereas mine hail from medieval Anglo-Saxon usurpers (Gillinghams and Saunderses) on my father's side, seventh-century Anglo-Saxon (Waterman and Layman) on my mother's. First as renters, then as neighbours, finally as friends—we've stayed to this day.

Meditating
in the Country

Visitors to our village near the Bay of Fundy's eastern end, where we've lived for many years, always remark on the peacefulness here. I thought so too — until I tried to meditate. The word "meditate" literally means to "middle" or centre oneself. This never interested me much until I visited a Montréal retreat centre founded in 1977 by the late John Main. A Benedictine monk, Fr. Main revived the lost tradition of Christian meditation — "listening prayer" — and transplanted it to Canada and the world. That weekend, kneeling with others on little pillows in the peaceful meditation hall on Mount Royal's leafy shoulder, I vowed to take his peace home with me. All I had to do was sit still in a quiet place twice a day and mentally chant my word, my mantra, for twenty to thirty minutes.

No problem. I'm an early riser, the kids have grown and flown, we're surrounded by open fields. Isn't it amazing how a fresh viewpoint can alter your take on reality? Join me, then, at dawn on a June morning during my first year of meditation. A waning sickle moon hangs in my open, east-facing window as I sit comfortably erect, muscles relaxed, eyes closed. The only sound is my breathing. Inhale. Exhale. Then, silently, I begin to recite the four-syllable word, *Ma-ra-na-tha*, which means "Come, Lord Jesus" in Aramaic, that quells all distracting thoughts. Slowly the mind's chatter subsides, the heart's drumbeat slows. A tide of peace creeps in.

"Cawww!"

A lone crow in our elm tree announces the sun. Answering calls float up from the far forest. A chorus of robins, white-throats, and warblers chime in. With effort I resume my mantra. Moments later our dog Sidney descends stiffly from his creaky stuffed chair, pads across the porch floor and noisily slurps water. *Say your mantra.*

Then comes the purr of the fridge compressor cutting in, followed by the furnace burner, followed by the furnace fan. Warm, dry air brushes my cheek. *Say the mantra.* A housefly, warmed by the rising sun, revs its motor and blunders about between window curtain and sash. A whiff of new-mown hay tickles my nose. *Never mind, say your word.*

Next a woodpecker (whether downy or hairy I can't tell) starts to jackhammer the nearest sugar maple. Normally this is a cheerful sound, but this morning it annoys me. Across the way a male chickadee whistles his three-note "Sweet weath-err." No one can be annoyed with a chickadee. Around 7:00 a.m. the first car speeds along our gravel road. That would be Glenn, who works flex-time at the sign shop in town. Under his tires the newly graded gravel sounds like cornflakes being crushed, which gives me a hunger pang. *Say your...*

Now Sidney woofs politely under the kitchen door. Sid is nearly eleven—seventy-seven in human years—and his bladder, like mine, isn't what it used to be. *Hold on, Sid.*

A louder racket heralds the passage of McCurdy's manure tanker hauling five thousand litres of ammonia-scented slush to a holding pond. Barrelling close behind comes the school bus. For some years now it has gone by without stopping at our place. A pleasing thought—but not today. *Never mind; try again.*

But it's no use. The commotion will only escalate. Maybe monks in hilltop retreats can do it; I can't. My stomach growling approval, I rise, go downstairs, let Sid out, feed the cats, light the wood stove, fill the tea kettle, do some tai chi, take a shower, start the day.

Maybe I picked the wrong month. For our June countryside pulsates with urgent life. Life is no quiet thing. Were our ears sharp enough, we'd hear the bumping of mitochondria and chloroplast, the kiss of bees from blossom to blossom, the gurgle of sap in a million grass stems, the cosmic *whoosh* of our solar system hurtling toward the distant constellation Vega.

I did struggle on for another two years. Now I pray a different prayer. Not to Nature, who cares not a fig for human piety or wisdom, but to the God beyond. Though for all we know, the morning conversation of crows may hide more wisdom than all the mantras of all the sages of distant Kathmandu.

Robinsong

Recovering at home from cancer surgery one spring, forbidden to lift anything heavier than a book for six weeks, I spent hours resting on our deck, watching the grass grow, listening to the music of tree frogs (aka spring peepers) and songbirds. As the regular frog and toad concerts from a nearby pond faded, so did the winter notes of blue jay, chickadee, and ring-necked pheasant. Next, migrant birds took up the chorus, led by returning male robins. Then came the sparrow tribe, notably the melodious song sparrow with its dark chest patch, whistling sweet variations on a theme known only to them, elixir for my ailing spirit. I don't even count the monotonous cheeping of the introduced "English sparrow" (European weaver finch), which can't sing for beans. But soon afterwards, when our crab-apple tree bloomed, we were treated to a week or two of yellow warbler arias among the pink-and-white blossoms.

Meanwhile, the salt marshes north of us were coming alive with migrant sandpipers, plovers, and other shorebirds, their voices mostly lost to me by distance. As for woodpeckers, our feeder guests of last winter were away to the woods to mate and lay eggs. And as for the noisy, ant-eating yellow-shafted flicker, I was too early. With luck, however, I might see a sapsucker drilling our apple trees.

Back then the monotonous treetop wheezing of starlings—it's called a murmuration—was rare. Introduced from England to New York City in 1890 by a Shakespeare buff intent on importing every bird mentioned in the Bard's plays, including the weaver finch, this intelligent nuisance soon overran the northeast and by 1941 had reached California.

But the avian songster who most delighted my hungering ears that spring was native Robin Redbreast. Migrating early from Mexico and the Gulf coast, clusters of males had arrived with the last snow flurries to select, advertise, and defend chosen territories. One male chose for his soapbox our giant elm. For days on end his quicksilver folderols floated down, no two sounding exactly alike.

Perhaps his brain was addled by multiple mini-concussions? Glimpsing his reflection in our windows, he repeatedly charged the supposed rival, raking the glass with beak and claw. To help my own concussed brain recall those songs, an earlier fall on ice having cost me a tooth filling, I translated them into English. "Cheerily, cheerily, cheer, cheer—cheer!" was his commonest rendition. Years later I would learn that Canadian novelist Kyo Maclear, in her lovely 2017 memoir *Birds Art Life,* used virtually the same wording. But my Maritime songster went further. From my journal:

> Sometimes he does a final exclamation that sounds like "Read it!" Or perhaps "Eat it!" Sometimes there's also a querulous end note that sounds like "See?" And sometimes he changes the order. Meanwhile, far away, nearly out of earshot, an answering male cries, "Hear me? Hear?"

Which calls to mind a Prussian UNB classmate of mine who, on first hearing our native robin sing, judged it inferior to its Old World counterpart. The word Kris used was "undisciplined." He had a point. I've heard the European robin in England, and it *is* hauntingly lovely. And, yes, disciplined. What Kris likely didn't know was that ours isn't a true robin, but one of our several native thrushes. Anyone who has heard the heart-melting threnody of our hermit thrush in dusky woods at sunset or dawn, as I often have under canvas on forest surveys, knows what I mean. Melodic variation is a thrush specialty, and in our spring meadows the redbreast is undisputed king.

I Miss My Barbers

I miss my barbers. Both of them. Not that it takes two to handle my dwindling thatch. These two women happen to own the Truro, Nova Scotia, shop I've gone to since the 1980s. Each has her own cubicle and chair, so phoning ahead for my monthly trim I never know which one I'll get. Nor do I care; both are excellent. Not for nothing did a Canadian literary critic call barbering "the genial profession...whose motto is 'I serve.'"

But thanks to COVID-19, they're now both jobless, their shop shuttered. Calling recently to check, I heard the recorded voice of one saying, huskily I thought, "Hi, valued customers, we've been ordered, as of midnight tonight, to close until further notice. We will miss you all. Hopefully this will pass quickly. Until then, stay safe."

Truth to tell, I miss them as much for the talk as the trim. For no sooner was I seated and caped, no sooner had the ritual question been asked, "Leave some over the ears this time?" than we'd be off and running. Life, Love, Parenting, Politics. You name it, we talked it.

And this wasn't unique. Of the six or so barbers of all genders I'd known over the years, all were great at conversation. They didn't learn that in barber school. It comes with the trade.

Come to think about it, how else could anyone snip or style human hair six days a week, year in, year out, without going dotty? And that's only half the equation. The other half is the clientele with their unique life stories. And let's face it, most of us, in unguarded moments, like on a plane among strangers, tend to tell more than we mean to. With barbershop intimacy it's hard *not* to talk freely.

The difference here is trust. Here, on home ground so to speak, we're communing with someone we feel we know. Indeed, your regular barber or stylist may know as much about you as do your friends or even your kinfolk. What a book they could write! (A local barber nearing retirement once asked me to help with his. Carefully, I declined.)

In some ways one's barber is like a priest-confessor. Or, better—since there's cash involved—like a personal therapist. Mine charged eighteen dollars per cut, including a beard trim—a real bargain. Post-COVID they'll likely charge more. (Tip yours if you can, they deserve it!)

So no wonder I miss those two. Not only did they make me look almost respectable, they helped me face my days. Now, thanks to COVID, I can't even wave to them through their shop window.

Meanwhile, my remaining hair keeps growing. And though I can manage to do a passable *beard* trim, doing the back of my head is, so to speak, beyond me. Besides, hair is so unforgiving. Mis-cuts can't be glued back on. Blunders show for weeks afterwards.

Still, my spouse, braver than I and also barber-less, did her own last winter. Overnight she went from a respectable shoulder-length senior to a spiky-tufted motorcycle moll. Took some getting used to, for both of us. But it turned out to be a smart move. Now she won't need another cut for months.

I'm torn between doing the same or letting mine grow till the lockdown ends, if ever. What that would look like—the hair, I mean—I've no idea. Part of me likes the Mark Twain look—but then Twain, unlike me, had that magnificent silver mane and no beard, just a moustache. Albert Einstein? Same problem. For models that leaves Karl Marx, Walt Whitman, and Charles

Darwin. All three had full beards, but Darwin's dome was bare like mine. Charlie it is.

Foolishness aside, who knows, post-COVID, what "normal" will look like? For all we know, total baldness may be in. If I'm still around then — it could be years — I may try shaving the works, sideburns, beard, and all.

Move over, Captain Picard!

Part Two
Ecology

Peeper Spring

My fingers tingle with cold as I listen in the April dusk, clipboard in hand. Tendrils of Fundy fog climb my waders. *Too early,* I think. *Best try next week.* As I turn to go, a piercingly sweet trill stops me in mid-stride. Excitedly I scribble date and time, air and water temperatures on my Nova Scotia Museum tally sheet. The tree frogs have awakened!

It felt good that spring night, knowing hundreds of volunteers like me were out counting frogs in the rain. For frogs of all sorts are mysteriously declining worldwide. FrogWatch is Nova Scotia's do-it-yourself approach to monitoring our own amphibian populations. For such a new program, the turnout of volunteers was strong. But it's not surprising, because most Nova Scotians care about their environment.

What is surprising is that after three hundred and fifty years of use and abuse, that environment is surprisingly hale. Mixed forests still clothe three-fourths of the peninsula. Eastern cougar and peregrine falcon seem to be coming back.

Moreover, most Bluenosers still lead rural lives. No doubt the province's compact geography, with no place farther away than a five hours' drive from the centre, helps to explain this. So do family ties and nostalgia. But the real reason is love of place.

For me, kinship and nostalgia had nothing to do with moving here in 1965. The Truro job looked interesting; the pay was decent. Once we had a car, we explored. Between us Beth and I had already lived in Newfoundland, Ontario, British Columbia, and the Yukon. Somehow this felt better. Nature on a human scale? Something.

In the ensuing years, my work in natural resources took me all over the province. Slowly its natural assets grew on me. And until the early nineties I thought I knew them well. Then Dorothy Blythe of Nimbus Publishing asked me to write a nature guide to the important roads. Newly retired, restless between books, I agreed. The project opened my eyes. Nova Scotia *is* a naturalist's delight.

There's a big difference between driving to get somewhere and driving back to Nature. Before, I'd viewed the convoluted Atlantic shore from Canso to Yarmouth as foggy and tedious. Now, I saw a folded and faulted slab of Africa welded to North America and flooded by a post-glacial ocean. I saw cozy villages tucked into a filigree of inlets, islets, and capes. I walked clean sand beaches smelling of kelp and salt and fog.

That summer, loons yodelled me awake in western Cape Breton. From that island's Mabou Highlands I gazed *down* on a soaring eagle. At Fox Harbour on the Sunrise Trail I counted eleven herons fishing, still as statues. Not much farther east, a man had just found the tracks of a giant Coal Age amphibian.

Near Grand Pré, I walked where North America's first apple orchards had borne fruit. On Cape Blomidon, home of the Mi'kmaw man-god Glooscap, I hefted black Jurassic basalt that had gushed red-hot when the North Atlantic was no wider than Lake Michigan and dinosaurs sprinted along the future Bay of Fundy. It made one think.

Ghosts of wooden wind ships and vanished shipyards whispered from every tidal creek along Fundy's Glooscap Trail. The falling tide bared miles of satiny pink mud flats alive with amphipods, the crustacean that fuels eastern North America's diminutive sandpipers on their non-stop autumn flight to Suriname.

At Cape d'Or our family watched the equivalent of forty St. Lawrence Rivers surge through a 10-kilometre gap, lifting every moored ship like a teacup, reversing the flow of every stream clear back to Minudie and Truro. Nova Scotia's new wilderness park near Cape Chignecto was still being developed, but we hiked its cobble beaches past echoing sea caves and shouted to seals that sported in the green surf.

Once the book I'd been writing was nearly done, I asked myself where else in Canada could one find such natural diversity so close to home. The answer is, nowhere. And with that realization comes gratitude and a challenge.

For if FrogWatch tells us anything, if the Ice Ages tell us anything, if NASA's famous photo of Planet Earth turning like a turquoise jewel in the starry void tells us anything, it is that life is vulnerable. For example, we know that a single autumn oil spill in the upper Bay of Fundy could snuff out most of the world's semipalmated sandpipers. And we suspect that a few more tatters in the ozone layer could silence the peepers forever.

There's no lack of information anymore. The internet will see to that. What is needed is more FrogWatchers, more people who not only enjoy the landscape, but who work to maintain it.

At dusk one overcast November afternoon I parked at Mickey Hill's interpretive trail on Route 8 near Annapolis Royal. The trail crossed a chasm on a rope bridge and wandered through old pines and oaks down to a frozen cattail swamp. Kneeling to photograph a glacial boulder the size of a bus, I heard a rustle coming through the silent forest. White grains came pattering across the frost-crisped moss, the curled oak leaves, the polypody ferns.

First snow always gets me. Confetti for the bride of winter. When reality sets in a few weeks later, it's comforting to know that underneath the frozen moss and mud the little frogs lie sleeping, dreaming April dreams.

Cornsequences

Back when Britain ruled the waves, some wag said the nation's power depended not on warships but on the number of old ladies living in the country. His reasoning? Most such women kept a cat or two. Cats catch mice, leaving more grain to feed more steers, which meant more good red English beef for the Royal Navy. In other words, everything connects.

Last winter, the first time in twenty years, our home had rats. Night after night their gnawing woke us. Naturally I looked for a cause, a connection. Was it because I banked our farmhouse with eelgrass for the first time? Was it the death of our dog of fourteen years? My forgetting to close the basement hatch for two weeks in November? The soybeans drying in the basement? My basement worm farm for making compost? All of these?

I decided it was none of these. When we had rats years before, we kept hens. Rats love hen feed. We don't keep hens anymore. But last summer, for the first time ever, cattle corn replaced alfalfa and timothy in the fields around us. Rats love corn too. I blamed the corn. Anyhow, our rats are gone — for now. Took me six weeks of nightly trapping with cheese for bait. When the gnawing stopped, we breathed a sigh of relief. A person has enough problems without hosting rats!

Still, the switch to cattle corn had grimmer consequences. One day, walking the fields, I saw something I'd never seen here before. A sudden thaw plus heavy rain had melted most of our snow, and there, between two drumlins, was a gully half a metre deep and nearly seventy metres long, paved with pebbles like a streambed. Downhill, red Fundy topsoil fanned out on the snow like dried blood. Had the subsoil not been frozen, I'm sure the gully would have been much deeper.

I'd seen erosion here before, sheet erosion after fall plowing for example, or wind erosion staining snowbanks brown. That happens even with the best of farming practices—and my neighbours are good farmers. But real gulleying? After three decades of living here, it shook me up. And many local cornfields, especially those on sandy soils like ours, had the same problem.

To be fair, the previous crop on that particular field had been soybeans, not corn. And stubble had been left to hold the soil. The previous dry summer had so stunted those plants that nearly half the crop couldn't be harvested because the cutter bar couldn't be set low enough. Soybean stubble is sparse at best and breaks down quickly. So frost and rain played havoc. Since soybeans are part of the corn rotation here, I still blame corn.

Rats and severe erosion the same winter…was there a link?

Zea mays (hence corn's real name, maize) is a native North American grass no longer found in the wild. Botanists call it a cultigen, that is, a human creation. Mexicans were cultivating the original at least seven thousand years ago. By the time Columbus arrived, Amerindian farmers had already perfected many of today's varieties—though with smaller cobs.

Today, through repeated cross-breeding and hybridizing, this species can no longer seed itself without human help. And since 1988, when the first foreign gene was successfully implanted in maize, the species has been losing even the ability to replicate its original genes. From now on, its fate may lie in the hands of genetic engineers. Moreover, the companies for whom they work can legally file "genetic copyrights." Monsanto and others have already done so, thereby controlling the future seed supply worldwide.

But genetic tinkering isn't all bad. Geneticists have made great strides in developing hardier, more productive corn varieties. Which is one reason why this plant has become one of the world's four human food staples (the others being wheat, rice, and potatoes). Worldwide, there are over 132 million hectares under corn cultivation, of which 40 per cent is in the US, nearly half for fodder. What brought cattle corn to the northeast was the development of hardier strains. For many dairy farmers, tired of trying to make hay in our fickle climate, it seemed a godsend. And when the weather obliged with two, three warm, dry summers in a row — Corn Belt weather almost — corn's allure increased.

Farmers able to rent or buy the necessary choppers, able to afford a silo or two, or to buy huge sheets of storage plastic, plus the extra fertilizer and herbicides, made the switch. And they produced more and better fodder with less work and time. (Today's US growers claim they average three minutes' labour per bushel of corn, a tenfold increase in sixty years.) Who can blame our hard-pressed Maritime dairy farmers for buying into that? Nobody. Just as nobody blamed our East Coast fishers for buying bigger boats and high-tech gear in the eighties so they could compete with the Russians and the Spaniards catching cod.

Some of the ecological side effects of our new dependence on corn are obvious, and not all bad, for example the change in local wildlife populations. When we moved here in 1965, Canada geese were seldom seen. Oh, we might hear them honking high overhead, but they rarely landed on our side of the bay. Now it's nothing to see a whole field bobbing with them. And they stick around for weeks, even braving the first snows.

Blackbirds are increasing too. Last October we saw at least a thousand in a single flock. They hung around the corn stubble for days, pecking fallen seed, refuelling. A hungry pigeon hawk dive-bombed them, but in the hubbub got nothing. When the flock passed by it was like a black blizzard and roared like surf. Settling into the giant elm beside our house, they actually dragged its branches down. Put me in mind of Alfred Hitchcock's movie *The Birds*. Luckily, none came down our chimney.

Crow numbers are up too, their dawn choruses louder. Residents of Kentville in Nova Scotia's Annapolis Valley know all about that. A few years back, some thirty-five thousand crows began roosting on a nearby ridge of elms every spring and fall. The cause may have been a disturbance in their traditional roost on nearby Boot Island. But that alone wouldn't account for the huge numbers. Did bigger acreages of cattle corn play a part there too? It takes a lot to feed thirty-five thousand crows. Consider the Valley's overwintering bald eagle population. Before the 1970s, it was low. Now it's one of the highest in North America. Biologists credit the abundance of poultry farm offal. Eagles aren't stupid. Why hunt elsewhere when you can get meals-on-wheels? And crows are far smarter than eagles.

Well, at least crows and eagles are native. Here in central Nova Scotia we're also seeing not only more English sparrows, but also more starlings and pigeons. The first two, nesting earlier than our native sparrows and blackbirds, often hog the best spots. Our pigeon or rock dove—that hardy, fecund import from Europe and Asia—is fanning out from urban areas. Every farm seems to have its resident flock. How this will affect our shy native mourning dove is hard to say. Ring-necked pheasants, introduced decades ago for hunters, seem to be on the rise too.

Most farmers don't mind. The extra birds mostly feed on gleanings anyway, and the extra manure is a plus. So is the natural pest control. Nesting birds, seed-eaters included, constantly stuff their voracious young with high-protein grubs and worms to get them airborne by fall. Many "good" bugs get eaten too, but the net effect is likely positive.

What about corn's impact on wild mammals? Well, nobody begrudges the tiny deer mouse or meadow vole a few kernels of corn. Some people even think house mice—one or two—are cute. Same with raccoons. But nobody, except maybe medical researchers and behavioural scientists, really likes rats. Even avid environmentalists draw the line at them—though rats are said to make good pets.

The ones that invaded our house were *Rattus norvegicus*, the common Norway or brown rat. Originally from the Far East, they arrived on the eastern seaboard around 1775 as stowaways from Britain and Europe. (They've recently shown up on America's west coast.) The other common rat is *R. rattus*, infamous carrier of flea-borne bubonic plague that killed a fourth of Europeans in the 1300s. In America this rat fortunately occupies only a narrow strip on both coasts. That's because the fiercer Norway rat, which forms packs and likes meat, generally kills and eats the interlopers. Even so, in 1998 one of the latter was trapped on the Halifax waterfront, Nova Scotia's first record in a century.

By the way, Norway rats likewise spread diseases: typhus, trichinosis, rabies, and salmonella food poisoning. Together these two rodents, by spreading microbes and gobbling half the grain humans grow, have taken a greater toll on humans than all the wars and revolutions in history.

Does corn encourage rats? It must. Not in the fields perhaps, where birds clean every husk. Anyway, rats hate being in the open, day or night. No, smart rats head for the storage sites, especially ground silos, those great mounds of silage covered with black plastic. Why not? In there, it's dark and dry and almost warm, with life's three essentials — food, shelter, and water (from nearby rain or snow) — all under one roof. Far better than a drafty barn, dodging poison, pitchforks, cows' hooves, and hungry cats. And far better than living in a tall, chilly silo of hard-to-chew concrete, menaced by lethal gas and churning augers.

Whatever, once settled in, a single pair producing *six to eight litters of four to eight young a year* wouldn't take long to populate this area. In fact, swarms of rats once forced a dairy farmer to abandon his new ground silo. And when he switched back to his old tower silo, the refugee rodents climbed 25 metres up its inside walls to lunch under the dome.

Anyway, my guess is that as our next-door ground silo rats multiplied, they so depleted the farmer's winter fodder that the boss rats must have called an urgent meeting, after which some of the colony lit out for the next nearest home — ours.

What about corn's role in erosion? Wisely, Maritime growers quickly adapted their traditional grass/alfalfa/clover rotation to a corn/soybean/sod rotation with little or no plowing between. No-till farming, using uncut stubble to hold the soil, definitely reduces erosion, especially on level land and short slopes, and on clay soils. However, on long gentle grades it often fails. That's because the runoff has room to gain momentum, increasing its gouging power exponentially.

Another casualty of intensive corn production is the hedgerow. Hedges, shelterbelts, and stream-side copses are routinely cleared and levelled to accommodate bigger machines and to gain acreage. But these islands and fringes of brush not only shelter native wildlife, including weed-seed eaters and rodent-killing hawks, owls, and weasels, but also they anchor steep slopes. One Prince Edward Island potato farmer who removed his hedgerows in the sixties soon found himself trucking topsoil back uphill every fall. Finally he replaced his hedges. British farmers learned years ago that gullies are much harder to cure than prevent.

In New Brunswick's potato belt, bedrock is starting to poke through continuously cropped fields. Researchers found soil losses of 18 tonnes per hectare. Even minor sheet erosion adds up fast. The Atlantic Committee on Agricultural Engineering warns that a yearly loss of even 2 centimetres over a 20-hectare field translates to nearly forty truckloads of topsoil a year. As for nutrient loss, a Prince Edward Island study on potato land revealed a substantial loss of soil nutrients. As for gullies, they block access, alter drainage, and kill baby fish downstream with silt.

If corn is so bad, why hasn't there been more criticism? It so happens that you *can* grow corn year after year on the same acres and still get decent yields. Researchers have done just that on the Morrow Plots at the University of Illinois. After a hundred years they still get, depending on input, decent yields.

But Illinois ain't the Maritimes. Like other Corn Belt states, Illinois is mostly flat and treeless, with deep non-acidic soils. The Maritimes are mostly hilly with shallow acidic forest soils. Illinois gets little precipitation. We get up to 150 centimetres a year. Could the Illinois boys get similar yields here, and if so for how long? Maybe we'll find out the hard way.

Nature takes roughly five hundred years to build two and a half centimetres of living topsoil. Such soils teem with microscopic flora and fauna in exquisite balance. Raw chemicals and herbicides disrupt that balance. As soil chemistry shifts, less wholesome microorganisms take over. At last the soil becomes little more than a sterile growing medium. Robbed of cohesion and sod cover, it can't withstand the kind of freeze-thaw winters we've been getting.

If corn acreage continues to expand in Atlantic Canada, erosion will likely escalate until there's a public outcry. Let's hope plant breeders can develop and sell a less pernicious crop. Teosinte, a closely related perennial grass that grows wild in the Mexican state of Jalisco, looks promising. By crossing it with *Zea mays*, they may be able to develop a hardy perennial version better suited to our ecology.

If, further, they can implant a rodent-resistant gene, so much the better. Meanwhile, I expect more gnawing in the night.

Chipmunk Penance

In the late 1990s I began a series of watercolours on the theme of wildlife death, especially roadkill death. The catalyst was our tomcat's recent murder of a friendly local chipmunk. Festus had left it, uneaten, the way house cats will, outside our glass patio door as a food offering.

Of all wild Canadian mammals, the chipmunk is my favourite. They're cute, fun to watch, and, unlike woodchucks and tree squirrels, they don't try to move in with you. To atone for this one's needless death, the least I could do was preserve its image in paint. A gesture of penance, not only for the chipmunk but also for the millions of songbirds killed by unsupervised house cats in Canada every year.

Don't get me wrong. I've nothing against what US poet Mary Oliver in her poem "The Kingfisher" calls "a little dying," even my own. Without it, wild or tame or human, we'd have overrun the planet ages ago.

Thinking such thoughts, I began to sketch our sacrificial chipmunk. But because its fur was still matted and bloody from our cat's attentions, I decided to leave it to dry and paint it later—but forgot. Fortunately, the corpse was still there the next morning—but disembowelled now and eyeless. Too bad; I'd paint it anyhow. But as I began, the chipmunk's head slowly rose, swayed, then slowly descended.

What the...?!?

As I stared in disbelief, out from under the corpse's head came this robust insect robed in heraldic red and funereal black. The carrion beetle—for such it was, a *Necrophorus*—then began, ever so slowly, to circumnavigate the chipmunk's neck. Under, over, under, three times it did so.

Why? I thought. *Some bizarre invertebrate ritual?* Then it hit me; the insect was only doing what its kind was designed to do, namely bury wild corpses in the good earth. God's mini-undertaker, if you will. Amazingly strong for its size, a single pair can shift a dead rat to where they want it. But this one, strong as it was, couldn't do its job because our deck planks barred the way.

So now I owed Mother Nature *two* apologies? One for the chipmunk and one for the beetle? Okay, I'll draw the beetle too! Leaning close to do so, I saw another marvel. Parked on the beetle's back, precisely within its tangerine-red markings, nearly invisible though moving, were several red spider mites. They weren't eating their host—its leathery shell was too tough for that—they were simply doing cleanup while hitchhiking to their next meal.

Too much! Forget the apologies, the portraits! Lifting the little rodent by the tail, I flung it, beetle, hitchhikers, and all, into our artichoke patch. For an hour afterwards my skin crawled.

The only other animal still lifes I did that year were those of a bedraggled herring gull that washed up on our tidal flats and three roadkills: a woodchuck, a coyote, and a chickadee. The yellow swallowtail butterfly plastered to our car's grill I never got around to. Why go on about this? Because that little chipmunk opened a hidden world under my nose, one I hadn't really seen since childhood.

Nova Scotia's 2003 Floods

A tourist driving past our lush dike-lands shimmering in mid-summer heat might never suspect that only four months ago they were two metres under water. Not that March floods are rare around Nova Scotia's tide-churned Minas Basin. All it takes is a sudden prolonged thaw, a deep snowpack, and a couple days of torrential rain. What's rare is the combination. March 30–31, 2003, unlocked all three at once.

It began quietly enough. Here on the Shore Road, overnight the stream called Beaver Brook made a lake inside the dike. Meanwhile, 10 kilometres up the bay, Truro's Salmon and North Rivers did the same thing on a grander scale. Worse, the extreme tides of a waning moon played havoc with the aboiteaux, the Acadian hinged underwater gates, which bar seawater at high tide but let fresh water out at low. They simply couldn't handle the outflow. So when a section of dike gave way, the next high tide poured in. Basements flooded, foundations caved in, sofas floated, furnaces cut out. Parked vehicles played bumper car. In Truro, lumber piles came apart and rafted downstream. Floyde Johnson's Main Street garage burned because firefighters couldn't reach it in time — though they saved some cars from the safety of a front-end loader bucket.

By next day, 125 Truronians were homeless. Surrounding farms lay unfenced and strewn with logs, sticks, vegetation, plastics, even rocks. Truro's woes were multiplied province-wide as scores of roads washed out. With nineteen bridges gone, people holed up in shelters. Near Bridgewater an elderly couple drowned. It wasn't our worst deluge — in 1958 four people died, in 1956 over one hundred bridges went out—but it was bad enough.

Our Shore Road got off light by comparison. Two days without bills or daily papers isn't so bad. Three local farmers did suffer a glut of unsold milk. In fact Beth and I didn't even know we were cut off until Day Two, when an expected visitor called via cellphone to say the far end of our road was impassible.

Curious, we took the dog and hiked east on the old rail line to have a look. Here, let me confess that I love water in all its forms, fresh or salt, the look and sound and feel of it. Even as a toddler, they say, I was forever getting wet from wading. But what I saw that day was too much of a good thing. Our road was simply gone. Only wisps of drowned hedgerow marked the route.

My mind went back to the Valentine's Day flood of 1973, the time I canoed along that same hedgerow and over the railroad tracks and onto the Hendersons' back lawn. "Wanna go for a paddle?" I said when Marilyn answered my tap. "Sure," said she, not missing a beat. "I'll get my coat." We circled our new lake. Except for the roaring vortex at the dike's aboiteau, it was fun.

But this 2003 flood was grim. The only individual enjoying it that day was our Newfoundland dog. Rosie, a true water dog, scion of a breed that rescued mariners from sinking ships, thought floods were perfectly normal. She was right of course. After all, Beaver Brook had been inundating these flats at new moon and full moon for millennia. That's why they're here, that's why they're so fertile. The real anomaly was, and is, farming, first by Acadians in the 1690s, and then by New England Planters after the Expulsion of 1755.

Truro's history was no different until the early 1970s, when developers moved in. Ignoring the maxim that you never build on a floodplain—ditch it, dome it, seed it, yes; otherwise, leave it be. They gradually infilled its wetlands—natural sponges—then plastered them with high-rent strip malls and parking lots. After that, rain and meltwater had to find other routes to the sea. Ever since, even in normal years, and despite several costly control measures, "flood events" have been a headache hereabouts.

Well, floods happen. But let's not invite them. Much as I like to see Nature kick up its heels, I early learned to respect a flood's power. When I was ten, a flash flood in our Newfoundland village evicted us from our living quarters. That year for the first time we'd abandoned our drafty frame house for a traditional Newfoundland "winter tilt," aka log cabin. The winter had been wild and snowy, but our new home kept us snug as bears in their den.

The flood happened that March. The cabin, unlike our house, was on low ground. But since the nearest brook was half a kilometre away, Dad considered it safe. Two days of steady rain plus an upstream ice jam plus deep snowpack changed the equation. Around 2:00 a.m. we woke to loud splashing as he scooped me from my bunk, blankets and all, and carried me back, with Mom and my brother in tow, to the drafty house. Still...I missed that cozy cabin. A few days later I skated through its echoing rooms. But we never wintered there again.

A Calendar
of Roadside Flowers

Most of us spend far more time on four wheels than we'd like. Wheeling here and there, we *see* the passing landscape, but it's more a backdrop for our thoughts than the real thing. Oh, we'd love to ramble through Nature sometime like they do on TV, listenin' to the loons yodel, watchin' the trout jump...but there are deadlines, priorities, miles to go—to rephrase US poet Robert Frost—before we sleep.

But here's a thought: why not become a watcher of roadside wildflowers? From spring through fall, they grace our lesser rights-of-way—well, at least the ones we haven't landscaped—with colours and textures that shift and blend from week to week like northern lights. And because many of them bloom en masse, they're easy to spot while wheeling.

Not only that, each species blooms at nearly the same time each year. New England naturalist Henry David Thoreau could tell the calendar date within days by what flowers were in bloom. True, that was long before global warming hastened the process. Even so, the relative sequence will stay about the same. I find this comforting.

Here then is a calendar of our more visible East Coast roadside wildflowers, month by month. Of course, several kinds may have come and gone, depending. Never mind. Barring fire, flood, or whatever, they'll be back next year.

The soonest hereabouts is coltsfoot. By early March most years its dandelion-like, lemon-yellow flowers appear. The name comes from the hoofprint shape of its perennial leaves, which open a week or two behind the flowers. The Latin genus name *Tussilaga* refers to its value as a cough remedy.

Early May is serviceberry time. Several kinds, ranging from low shrubs to fair-sized trees, display fountains of white along forest edges then. Out West they call it saskatoon berry. Hereabouts, because its blossoming coincides with the upriver shad run, we mostly call it shadbush.

No calendar of spring flowers would be complete without those of forest trees. While conifers lack true flowers, broadleaf trees are bona fide flowering plants. They just don't flaunt it. Except for the dangling catkins of aspens, birches, and oaks, the flowers of most northern species are small and rudimentary. Among the more colourful tree blooms are those of red or swamp maple. Whole hillsides blush pink as its red buds on red twigs sprout red mini-leaves and red flowers. Since male trees carry wine-red blooms and female trees yellowish flowers, the overall effect shimmers like an Impressionist painting.

Meanwhile the fat green buds of red-berried elder, a tall shrub of forest edges and clearings, burst out in creamy sprays that linger for weeks. Another May treat, this time underfoot, is the tiny bluet, a four-petalled member of the tropical madder family. Within days it can transform a brown field to palest blue, as if the sky had fallen.

Mayflower is more modest. You won't see this queen of spring flowers — *Epigaea repens,* Nova Scotia's floral emblem — from your moving vehicle. It's too fond of shade. Besides, decades of plucking by admirers and sellers have made it scarcer than it was in the forest. Search instead along old fields or mossy paths through spruce-fir woods, looking for glossy oval trailing leaves (mayflower's official name is trailing arbutus). The fragrance of its pale pink bells is among Nature's finest.

See, already I've pried you out of the car. While you're out, why not hunt for these: spring beauty, bloodroot, trillium, lady's slipper orchids, and trout lily? They all hide in brook valleys or under sugar maple, beech, and yellow birch. And go early because they are all blooming before the trees leaf out so as to catch the full sun. To identify them you may need a field guide such as good bookstores sell.

One caution: don't pick or dig spring flowers. They're scarce, they seed sparsely, and they can take years to recover from disturbance. And unless one knows their special needs, transplanting them back home seldom succeeds. Admire. Sniff. And pass by.

No such restrictions or distinctions apply to dandelions. If dandelions were as rare as orchids we'd flock to see them. For in form and colour they're just as handsome as their larger cousin the chrysanthemum. Their prodigal abundance belies the fact that each flower lasts only a few days before turning into ghostly (some would say ghastly) grey globes that children so love to explode with a puff. Each globe contains hundreds of parachute-topped seeds able to ride the slightest breeze for kilometres downwind. "Dandelion" is pidgin French for *dent de lion* ("tooth of a lion"), referring to its leaf's jagged edge. For some reason my grandmother called them piss-a-beds and wrinkled her nose.

From the soft gold of dandelions we go to the glossy gold of field buttercups, which spangle damp meadows till fall. Both are accidental imports from pioneering days. The dandelion, besides making a great salad green (when young) and a respectable cup of coffee (from the roasted roots), also produces an excellent summer wine. And among herbalists it's a paragon of virtues. But buttercups are poisonous.

By late May, many woodland roadsides are awash with the delicate pink of wild rhododendron, an effect heightened by its unfurling jade-green leaves. A fortnight later comes the deeper pink of mountain laurel, an evergreen shrub common on burnt land. Farmers call it lambkill with good reason: the leaves are poisonous. Labrador tea, another evergreen shrub of the heather family, isn't; in fact the curled hair leaves make a good tea. Its sparse creamy white blossoms are out. On back roads through rich mixed woods, watch for the modest white umbrellas of the hobblebush, a *Viburnum* with big, wrinkled heart-shaped leaves. The name comes from its habit of rooting the lower branches, thus creating ropy loops which can trip horses and people.

By the end of June, the wild cherries have celebrated and gone, first the pin or fire cherry in old cutovers and burnt woods, then the chokecherry along hedgerows and forest edges. Both are native members of the rose family and produce clusters of small white blossoms. June hereabouts also sees two kinds of native mountain-ash (rowan) flower and fade, and the wild raisin. The latter's other name, witherod, derives from Old English *withe* via the Latin *vi(ere)* (to weave). Literally it means "weave-rod." So tough and pliable are the small stems, in Newfoundland they were plaited into circular loops to secure oars to a boat's rowing pins. By August its clustered pale pink berries do look like raisins. Bland tasting to us, they're prized by birds. June is also the month of wild sarsaparilla with its distinctive pale green sprays that develop into inky blue berries. The roots make a distinctive wine.

Which brings us to high summer. An intriguing July plant is Scotch broom, introduced and slowly spreading along Canada's east and west coasts. Dark and funereal all winter, it now decks itself in butter-yellow pea-flowers. (Broom used to be gathered for pharmaceuticals, but for what I don't know.) One good place to see it is on Nova Scotia's South Shore, between Shelburne and Birchtown along Highways 3 and 103.

Another striking exotic from the pea family is lupine. Long a favourite in East Coast gardens, this steeple-shaped West Coast plant now tints long stretches of eastern roadsides pink, purple, or blue, depending on soil acidity. A section along Highway 3 near Hebron in western Nova Scotia is called the Lupine Trail.

And then there's purple loosestrife. Pretty but problematical, this waist-high European invader is elbowing out native wetland plants and the creatures that depend on them. Look for its spire-like flowers in wet ditches and shallow ponds. The plant has no natural enemies here, so scientists are testing natural controls. Loosestrife looks good in dried flower arrangements, so pick all you want; just don't spread any seeds!

Two mid-season, white-blooming shrubs of forest edges are the blue-berried elder and high-bush cranberry, both native. This elder out-blooms its May-blooming sister, covering itself with exuberant creamy blossoms that suggest mock orange. The "cranberry" is in fact a *Viburnum*-like wild raisin. There's also a low-bush type. Their translucent red fruit makes one of the best jellies imaginable.

Midsummer also brings out those peculiar low, chalky white plants known as pearly everlasting or live-forever. A Newfoundland widow once showed me a bouquet her husband picked for her the year he died. Seventeen years later, its straw-coloured flowers still looked fresh. This time of year, you'll see the dusky gold of black-eyed Susan, the whites and lavenders of yarrow, and the pinks of wild rose. Wild roses are very fragrant—another reason to get out of the car! From late July to early August, native fireweed or willow herb puts on a pink extravaganza across miles of fire barrens and cutovers. Folklore tells us that six weeks of summer remain once its steeple-shaped pink blossoms begin to open.

Passing ponds and bog pools, watch now for the cup-shaped floating yellow flowers and floating oval leaves of the pond lily, and for its more elegant cousin the white water lily, a night-blooming cousin of the larger Nile lotus.

Another wetland plant of midsummer is the cattail. Its cigar-shaped green flowers are borne atop tall stems with sword-shaped leaves. The lower or female section of each flower turns into a fluffy cylinder that persists into winter, dispersing seed all the while. Queen Anne's lace, nodding its circular white flowers above the August hay, always puts me in mind of autumn. Another name is wild carrot; smell a fresh-cut root and you'll know why. Later the flowers curl into brown bird nests of coriander-like seed.

Mid-August to late September is goldenrod time, notably Canada goldenrod. We have over twenty other native species, each occupying a different eco-niche from woodlands to wetlands. For instance, you'll find seaside goldenrod at the high-water mark in salt marshes and along low muddy shores. Asters overlap the goldenrod season, their mauves and purples making a perfect colour foil. As frosts get sharper and autumn rains commence, they wither to rich tapestries of russet, tan, and grey, full of seeds that nourish thousands of southbound songbirds.

And there you have it. From springtime white to autumn gold, a fresh display nearly every fortnight, most of them visible from the comfort of your car. I've had to omit many species — notably wild strawberry — but this list should give you a blooming good start.

Tough Little Trees
of the Fringe

The last place I expected to meet a yellow birch that August afternoon was on the windy summit of Picket-on-a-Reef, a cusp of lichened granite jutting 533 metres above Bonne Bay in western Newfoundland. Yet there it was, many kilometres north of where it should be, anchored to an unstable talus slope at the treeline and overlooking a glacial rock-yard where only hardy Arctic cinquefoil flourished. Years later, that encounter still resonates in memory. For one thing, that little birch saved me from a broken leg, or worse. And it taught me something we never learned in forestry school—that forests are as mobile as clouds.

Conventional textbook dendrology (tree study) relied too much on tidy range maps, useful products, and "normal" dimensions to teach us about the little trees of the fringe. Now, whenever I think of that birch clinging to its mountain—or, for that matter, of Monterey pine bending to Pacific gales at Big Sur, of dwarf aspen gilding the High Sierra, or of a crabbed tamarack silhouetted against a Labrador sunset—I see the tough little outriders of forests to come. The great trees of the heartland I admire; the gnomic trees of the far hinterlands I love.

For weeks, Bill Whiffen and I had been working our way up Newfoundland island's 480-kilometre-long Great Northern Peninsula by pickup, canoe, and on foot. Our job was to collect data for the provincial government's Western Region before heading back to university.

At 49 degrees 25 minutes north latitude, Bonne Bay isn't exactly boreal. True, the Labrador Current can clog the nearby

Strait of Belle Isle with drift ice in June, and snow often lingers on shaded upper slopes here all summer. No wonder we hadn't seen a temperate tree species since leaving Bay of Islands some 300 kilometres south, weeks before. Picket-on-a-Reef wasn't really on our work agenda. Bill and I climbed it partly out of youthful curiosity, partly from Sunday boredom. The "reef" did indeed boast a surveyor's picket or stake, its red pennant long since weathered to a tattered pink rag. After a mug-up of tea with bread and jam we lounged in pale sunlight on a springy mat of crowberry that smelled of resin. North and east of us spread burly mountains, blue fjords, and the matchbox villages of Canada's future Gros Morne National Park. Westward stretched the flat-roofed, glacier-gouged Tablelands, 600-metre mountains of rust-brown peridotite, a geological rarity overthrust from the Earth's hot, deep interior.

While we gazed about, the sky clouded over. A gust of wind rattled the picket in its crevice. We took the hint and started down. As I descended the steeper west face, I turned for a last look at the Tablelands — and lost my footing.

A curious thing, the overstuffed brain of a keen university student fresh from Dendrology 101. While loose rock clattered down around me, it scanned the stunted tree I'd grabbed onto, noted its curly bronze bark and its fine-toothed, ovate leaves, and pronounced it *Betula lutea* (since changed to *alleghaniensis*), also called bronze, curly, or swamp birch; geographic range centred on Lake Ontario and reaching south to Alabama and west to Minnesota, with northern outliers on Anticosti Island and southern Newfoundland; full-grown trees reaching over 20 metres tall by almost a metre in diameter. By the time my boots found solid rock, I was taste-testing a twig for the telltale wintergreen: ID confirmed.

For many such heartland tree species, my part of Canada is the eastern rim of the world. In their post-glacial expansion, long before they confronted the ocean and quite apart from human interference, they faltered. Butternut and silver maple, accustomed to softer air and richer soils, dropped out in southwestern New Brunswick. Black cherry, its blossoms repeatedly nipped by untimely frost, got only as far as western Nova Scotia. Beech, sugar maple, and eastern hemlock colonized all three Maritime provinces but arrived too late to cross the newly flooded Cabot Strait into western Newfoundland. Red pine and white pine made it, so did red maple and yellow birch. Those four later spread across most of the island's southern half. But white elm and black ash managed only a toehold in the southwestern corner.

Except on good lowland sites, these temperate species seldom attain full stature there. Come October, Cape Breton Island's sugar maples glow as richly as New England's. But for commercial purposes they're "one-log" trees. Even so, it's the mingling of temperate and boreal species that has created the region's distinctive Acadian Forest, named after seventeenth-century settlers from western France.

When it comes to colonizing unfriendly territory, temperate interlopers are no match for their northern neighbours — especially black and white spruce, tamarack, and to a lesser extent balsam fir. Aggressive, opportunistic, and tenacious, they clothe our hilltops, bogs, and seashores. In doing so they've evolved a myriad of survival tactics. To escape untimely frost they flush late and close up shop early. To conserve energy they minimize flower and seed production. To temper winter gales and absorb solar warmth, they hug the ground. Above all, they exquisitely balance biomass production with nutrient availability. Living on the sub-boreal edge, they became Nature's bonsai trees.

But the cost is high. For example, black spruce and tamarack colonize acidic peat bogs that starve them of nitrogen and sometimes even oxygen. Often these dwarf trees seem scarcely alive. Many times I've counted one hundred or more annual rings on a three-centimetre cross-section. (Such wood is also very hard for ice storms to break.)

One summer, surveying coastal timber on the island's Bonavista Peninsula, we encountered so many such thickets that our tough army pants lost their knees. No wonder hares and voles, ever mindful of death from the sky, frequent these forests.

Among the harshest tree habitats is the North Atlantic coast. Fogs, gales, blizzards, ice storms, never mind salt poisoning, assail any that venture there. They may also suffer overdoses of seabird guano. Yet from Maine to Labrador, headlands and islands wear manes of pygmy white spruce and balsam fir. I've met seaside thickets so dense and wind-pruned you could clamber across them without falling through.

Sometimes even a forester can't identify these pygmy species. That happened to me on Nova Scotia's Scatarie Island. The evergreen's dark, leathery needles *looked* like balsam fir's, but with no cones in sight I couldn't be sure. Then, below the hedge I saw another forest — thrifty little balsam firs green as grass, symmetrical as Christmas trees. No matter how fierce the elements, DNA does not forget.

Still, what possible advantages can such places offer? The short answer seems to be freedom from multi-species competition and from temperate region pests and diseases. A longer answer involves the immense perspectives of arboreal time and climate change. Unlike individual trees, communal thickets are practically eternal. The conifer line stretches back to a time when dinosaurs were new, when the sun rose over an Atlantic Ocean not much wider than today's Gulf of California and set over a west devoid of Rockies. Broadleaf forests, more recent, witnessed the demise of those dinosaurs and the birth of modern birds, fish, and mammals, including us.

Is that why we sometimes feel awe in their presence? Like the mysterious arboreal Ents in *The Lord of the Rings*, they are friendly enough but almost from another world. To be even more shamelessly anthropomorphic, maybe those dwarf coastal conifers are waiting to re-green the Grand Banks, which melting glaciers drowned millennia ago. Sounds fanciful? Then what are we to make of ancient pine and beech stumps, which local fishermen sometimes find entangled in their nets, stumps with forest soil still clinging to their roots?

To me, colonizing the continental shelf is no more far-fetched than the stupendous feat of reforesting upper North America after the last Ice Age. Geologists tell us that that sixteen thousand or so years ago, the great Laurentide ice sheet reached as far south as Seattle, Missoula, Des Moines, Cincinnati, and Manhattan, including the continental shelf. Upper America was a white wilderness like today's Antarctica. By 8,000 BCE the ice had mostly melted. It left a sodden landscape, a continental gravel pit shimmering with uncountable new lakes, rumpled with strangely worn mountains, alive with tumbling rivers seeking new channels to rising seas. Southward stretched hundreds of miles of sparsely treed taiga flecked with herds of muskox and caribou. Future Canada was mostly muskeg underlain by permafrost. The temperate zone lay somewhere near the Gulf of Mexico.

Sometimes I imagine a time-lapse video of that epoch recorded from outer space. As the glaciers recede northward, a yellowish tide of lichens on bare rock follows, then a blue-green tide of mosses, sedges and rushes, ascending the alpine valleys, spilling around the newly created Great Lakes and finally overspreading the Hudson Bay Lowlands like ink on a blotter. Behind come ferns, grasses, and flowering plants. Spore by spore, seed by seed, shoot by shoot, they clothe the desolation. And finally, forests.

All these plants are still with us. Sphagnum moss is remarkable for its enormous thirst and for its ability to colonize shallow acidic ponds. And since in such bogs biomass production outstrips decomposition, undecayed material accumulates as peat. When the peat rises above the water table, shrubs like leatherleaf (*Chamaedaphne*) and bog laurel (*Kalmia*) seed in from the edges. Tamarack (larch) and black spruce follow. In time, the bog loses its central pond and becomes a forest. From the air, the swirling patterns of bog reclamation—moss-green, tan, tea-brown, indigo—resemble watered silk.

A few centuries from now, if warming trends continue, Labrador black spruce may well invade the shores of Baffin Island, and Georgia bald cypress may dip their knobby knees in Long Island Sound. But what if we get another global freeze? Then the oceans will dwindle and freeze as in past epochs and the ugly little trees of Mount Desert Island and Scatarie will have another chance at the continental shelf.

Did I say ugly? Did you say useless? The little trees of the fringe are often called such names. But their ugliness is only bark-deep. As for usefulness, though dwarfish they freshen our air and water, they soften the planet's bleak places, they warn us of climate upset. Above all, they helped reforest half a continent. And as a DNA bank they could prove invaluable.

Not bad for so-called useless.

Some years ago, a Hallmark greeting card survey revealed that America's favourite image is that of a blasted tree on a windy hilltop. That Lincolnesque icon of lonely strength speaks to us all. Yet it tells only half the story. The other half is that trees and forests are mercurial shape-shifters, tireless travellers marching to the slow drum of climatic change. Ancient as dinosaurs, modern as volcanic Mount St. Helens's new forest, they're forever poised to green the world anew.

Leaf Thief I

Every October, as the leaves begin to fall in earnest, I case our nearest town for loot. Not necessarily the wealthy streets, though often they yield better pickings, but the well-treed streets, the streets with maple, linden, ash, and poplar. Then, around Thanksgiving weekend, when folks are away or preoccupied with turkeys and family, I make my move. Two or three quick heists and the treasure is mine.

The treasure, you see, is bagged leaves, three or four dozen bags each fall. It's not exactly stealing; it's more like recycling, more like a public service, even a service to the planet. It began when I stopped manuring our veggie garden. I've nothing against manure as such. No genuine rural dweller really hates manure, or even the smell of it—well, maybe the smell of pig manure. I've used all kinds, especially cow manure.

It was the hitchhiking weed seeds made me give up the practice. Even well-cured cow manure, unless it's been properly composted, usually harbours the seeds of pigweed and couch grass. Certainly cow manure has its place. Its place is out on the fields. There the resulting weeds are generally manageable, unless of course they happen to be round-leaved mallow or jimson weed or such. And, except for the possible health hazards, the benefits in fertility and yields are generally worth it.

To be honest, I still manure our rhubarb and asparagus beds, our currant and gooseberry bushes, and I still put a shovelful under each pumpkin and squash hill. Anywhere, that is, where the accompanying weeds can be controlled. Just not wholesale on the vegetable garden. These days the only cow residue that goes on my garden proper is manure tea.

Let me say that I've nothing much against weeds either. Give me dandelion or pigweed greens over spinach or cabbage any time. Not only do most weeds pack more vitamins than conventional greens, their often deeper root systems recover leached nutrients. If weeds would behave themselves the way spinach or cabbage does, I'd even plant some. In fact, foolish as it sounds, I've just seeded an experimental bed with red-root pigweed (*Amaranthus retroflexus*), my favourite. The new leaves of this boisterous South American interloper come up so early and taste so good! However, my hopes of confining it to one bed are likely naive. Time will tell.

But to return to my pilfering. The garden was wrested in 1970 from a field of Queen Anne's lace, crab grass, eyebright, dandelion, yarrow, and hawkweed. Once plowed and tilled into submission, it proved surprisingly, almost alarmingly, fertile. That September our school bus driver stopped on her first trip to ask if it was all right to drive over my squash vines. "Go ahead," I said, "before they block the whole road."

Those meadow perennials were easily tamed—all but the crab grass. However, after five or six years yields began to fall off. That's when I started manuring, and that's when our weed problems really started. Suddenly we were plagued with dandelions, chickweed, pigweed, common mallow, purslane, groundsel, cadlock, sow thistle—all the common annuals whose seeds pass through a cow's innards unharmed. I became a hoe enthusiast.

My route to manure independence was to be long and arduous. I tried Ruth Stout's No-work Gardening Method. Stout's thick blanket of ordinary hay—"manure that hasn't gone through the cow"—was supposed to smother all weeds, jump-start the earthworms, fertilize the ground, and do away with tilling and spading.

She was more or less right—only now my work consisted of explaining to the world what I was doing, of picking thousands of slugs, and of trying to ripen tomatoes on cold, hay-laden ground. The only compliment came from our biggest local dairy farmer, who allowed he should be treating *his* fields the same way. I wasn't sure he meant it though.

Three years later, fed up, I took the conventional NPK chemical route. The raw fertilizer stung my scratched hands and burned my young plants, but it boosted yields and let me concentrate on the weeds. The trouble with fertilizer is lack of humus. Our post-harvest residues, mostly corn stalks and potato vines, were scanty anyway. Besides, so-called experts frowned on using it. Soon my earthworm count began dwindling.

Clearly, what I needed was a bulk supply of seed-free mulch. Marsh hay worked well, but there was never enough of it. Eelgrass from the seashore looked promising too. On one of our autumn beachcombing trips to the Northumberland Strait I brought home a sedan-load. It was wonderful stuff. But *Zostera marina*, a grass that shuns rough waters and rocky bottoms, doesn't grow along the Fundy shore where we live.

Then one August, touring the Kings Landing historical village in New Brunswick, I spied this patch of buckwheat. The sign said pioneers had planted buckwheat to break sod on cleared woodland to smother weeds. That got me into green manuring, using fall-sown annual rye grass to protect the soil over winter.

This worked well, though invariably I'd miss early-ripening buckwheat seeds, which would then become next spring's crop. Likewise a percentage of annual rye, though supposed to winter-kill, would green up next spring and go to seed that fall. So I ended up with two new weeds. Nice weeds, useful weeds, but weeds nonetheless. Like they say, a weed is any plant in the wrong place. Carrots in the lettuce are weeds unless you want them there.

Odd, isn't it, how easily we overlook the obvious? Each autumn Sunday, driving to church in town, we'd pass piles of bagged leaves stacked under the bare trees for municipal pick-up. Town folks want their lawns clean and green till Christmas, later if possible. Fallen leaves mess with that. And since the town now recycles those dead leaves to mulch its tulip beds, people no longer feel guilty about putting Nature's free fertilizer in the garbage.

Here was my bulk supply! But what would the property owners think? It turned out they all said yes. Some even offered me a rake and bags. The question of theft never came up. No, they saw me as helping to tidy their property, as easing the town's burden of collection.

It's odd, too, how one thing leads to another. Impatient for results, I immediately spread my leaves and started tilling. Not until the tiller coughed and quit did I realize we were out of gasoline. Before I could fetch more, the autumn gales scattered the remaining dry leaves around the county. For of course, people don't rake in wet weather, so bagged leaves come out tinder-dry unless the bag is torn. I tried leaving the bags open to get rained on, but this only made them heavier to handle.

Experience has since taught me to spread my leaves on a windless spring day with light rain. Soil organisms are pretty dormant in winter anyhow. But storing so many bulky bags all winter can be a problem too. Black and orange garbage bags don't exactly enhance a property in any season. In the end I stacked them against the house for insulation. The bags, jammed tight together, anchored with wooden pegs before the ground froze, and covered with snow-catcher evergreen boughs, they were almost invisible.

Next spring passersby saw me laying rows of multicoloured bags across the garden. I knifed them open as needed (very few are reusable, so I recycle them), and spread the contents ankle-deep in 3-metre swaths. Next, using parallel and then cross-ways passes with the tiller tines set progressively deeper, I soon had all the leaves chopped and buried. (With a smaller garden one could have raked and spaded them in.) Very little after-raking was needed.

You should have seen the mulch they made! Chestnut brown it was, rich and crumbly, fragrant as an autumn forest. Still, next summer would tell the tale. I was not to be disappointed. We hadn't seen such lush growth, such bountiful yields, for years. And the earthworm population rebounded. At the Woodslee Research Station in Ontario, Agriculture Canada reported one hundred and seventy worms per square metre of soil under a no-till cropping system. However, that number fell to twenty individuals per square metre after a single season under conventional tillage. When the field was left alone, the earthworm population required two or more years to rebound to its former numbers. Food for thought there. They say a teaspoon of healthy untilled soil may contain up to a million living organisms.

Goodbye tiller?

Leaf Thief II

Eyeing that fall's harvest, I wondered whether we could get by with even less garden. After our six kids had grown and flown, I had already reduced it from almost four hundred square metres to about two hundred and thirty by restoring lawn on two sides. Might we get by with just over half the original space? That way the other half could have all year to digest its added leaf mulch and green manure.

My souped-up half-garden, enriched by the previous infusions of leaves, did the work of two halves—almost. Actually, there was some accidental usage overlap between the halves, which upset somewhat my neat rotation plans. A couple more years should put that right, though I did have some concerns. Contaminating the soil with lawn chemicals was one. However, it seemed to me that harmful residues should be well diluted after travelling through the roots, trunk, and crown of trees, not to say passing through the digestive processes of soil bacteria and fungi.

Another concern was acidification. Most broadleaf trees have acidic foliage to start with, especially oak and maple. A steady diet of such acidic mulch could in time so impoverish my soil that only moss would grow. Fortunately poplar foliage is chemically "sweet," that is, alkaline. Which may be why beavers, porcupines, and even cattle are fond of aspen leaves, and why earthworms thrive in poplar mulch. British naturalist F. Fraser Darling called aspen a "calcium pump" and "the great ameliator." In general, broadleaf trees that turn red in autumn have acidic foliage, while those that turn yellow are alkaline or basic.

Ecology

It was a simple matter to change my liming schedule from every third year to every second, and adding it directly to the leaf mulch made it easier to remember. I also decided to seek out streets, like central Prince in Truro, that had mostly Carolina or Lombardy poplar.

My third concern was nasty surprises in the bags of leaves themselves, things like broken glass, dog turds, maybe even a live pet tarantula. However, in nearly a hundred bags the sharpest object I encountered was a spiky Douglas-fir cone. And the only garbage has been a couple of flattened pop cans and a Quaker Chewy Chocolate Chip Explosion wrapper. The most dangerous looking item was a hornet's nest—but it was empty.

Besides the obvious benefits—nil fertilizer, less tilling, more earthworms, better yields, a warmer house, meeting nice people, the sweet penance of recycling—there's been one unexpected bonus—tree seeds.

These stowaways never crossed my mind until I emptied the bags that spring. Yet I might have known. Tree seeds rain down on Canadian streets and lawns from June to October. And chilling bagged seeds over winter is a standard germination strategy for some. The stowaways, having lain snug against the house all winter, having been warmed by the April sun, were sprouting white roots and green cotyledons, eager to go.

There weren't many—only the ripped bags were damp enough—and my spring tilling accidentally got some of them. Even so, that summer my fallow strip was sprinkled with baby maples (Manitoba, Norway, planetree, sugar) and ash (white and green). God knows why—our property is already over-treed—but I tucked the stowaways into a new transplant bed. Already the oldest are chest-high. I can always donate. On the other hand, maybe next year a rare black walnut will show up, or a ginkgo, or even a magnolia. With stolen goods you never know.

Part Three
Wild Kin

The Lovely Duckling

Last summer, as happily married as most, I had an affair. "No fool like an old fool," they say. Like most affairs, it ended badly but was worth the pain. Let me tell you....

Our middle son, Matthew, teaches high school biology in Kingston, Ontario. From childhood he has loved animals. At last count he and his veterinarian partner, Heather Sims, hosted four dozen creatures on their four-hectare farm in nearby Seeleys Bay. These included two cockatiels, five cats, a goat, and a Newfoundland pony. And last June, a few weeks before Beth and I came to visit, they had added a wild duckling.

The duckling had arrived inside a greenish egg someone had rescued from a vandalized nest. Matt put it in his incubator with a clutch of hen eggs from the hatchery. Not one chick hatched, but on the appointed twenty-first day the greenish egg stirred, cracked, and released a mustard-coloured rag. The rag raised a wobbly head, opened a brown eye, got up on two leathery feet, flexed two stubby wings, opened and closed a rubbery beak, then waddled off. In an hour the duckling's coat had dried to a lovely ochre fuzz, marbled with chocolate brown. Nature, to camouflage the bird's bright eyes, had penned a black racing stripe along each cheek.

Species? Matt figured mallard or black duck. Boy or girl? Without adult plumage he couldn't tell. So he named it Dawn/Donnie. I'll call it Duck.

Since the 1930s, thanks to Austrian ethologist Konrad Lorenz, biologists have known that newborn geese and ducks will bond with the first moving thing they see: their mother, a dog, a sheep, whatever. Duck immediately imprinted on our son.

"Donnie heels better than any dog," said Matt.

When we arrived, the duckling was a fortnight old and already part of the menagerie. When Heather and Matt were away at work, the bird lived in a tall cardboard box behind closed doors in the house. Here, when not snoozing or eating chick starter, it spent hours cuddling its reflection in a mirror. A lonely life, but safe.

As for me, I'd arrived weary from finishing a long book, sore from recent surgery, and upset about losing my new $500 Pentax camera in Montréal. The moment Matt introduced us, however, my spirits lifted. Wild things do that for me. My father was the same. Dawn/Donnie/Duck was just the tonic I needed.

But five felines in the same house! It seemed a risky set-up. Back in Nova Scotia where Matt grew up, our cats routinely slaughtered any budgie, goldfish, gerbil, or pigeon the kids accidentally left unguarded. Yet, I needn't have worried. On this farm the lamb lay down with the lion and lived to tell the tale. Only Savannah, a relative newcomer feline, needed watching. One day I caught him stalking the bird. As for Bonnie the golden lab, she seemed to consider Duck just another playmate. Seemed.

Our first Monday dawned sunny, and since Beth and I had the run of the place, I decided to weed the strawberry patch. Dare I take the bird along? Would it follow me as it did Matt? Lifting it from its cardboard castle, I set it down and walked away. Duck came running, its flat feet pattering like raindrops on the hardwood floor. It struggled over the high outer doorstep, followed me to the tool shed, and followed me down the lane. Moving when I moved, stopping when I stopped, it also managed to stay inside my shadow. Already it knew about danger from the sky.

In the garden I went to work. Each time I pulled a plantain or pigweed, Duck rushed in to worry the soil with its beak. But when a great pink earthworm tumbled out, lashing furiously, my tiny helper back-pedalled in alarm. Not until I'd carved the monster into three pieces would it return and eat it. But the next three worms, being smaller, went down whole, wriggles, soil, and all.

For two hours straight, we weeded together in the warm spring sun. None of our kids had ever helped me weed that long. That evening Matt, hearing my worm story, said, "Donnie needs more protein." Next day he fetched home a sack of duck starter.

The time came to introduce this orphan bird to its natural habitat. Near the foot of the lawn, screened by willows and cattails, lay a tiny marsh complete with algae, pondweed, water lilies, dragonflies, water beetles, frogs, and mud. Arriving there with Duck in tow, I expected my companion to take one look and charge right in. Instead, it hesitated. No mother duck had ever taught it fear, no bullfrog or snapping turtle had ever menaced its young life; yet, now its genes cried *Beware.* Clearly Duck expected me to go first.

I removed my sandals, descended the concrete steps and waded into the muck. Bloodthirsty leeches crossed my mind but my grand-duck was watching so I hid that fear. Moments later the bird came tumbling down the steps and across the mud, printing moist triangles that slowly filled with water.

How must a debutante water bird feel, I mused, taking its first swim? As I watched, Duck stretched first one foot, then the other, paddled a little — *So that's what all that skin between my toes is for!* — tried a left pirouette, a right pirouette. Then, buoyant as a dry leaf, it swam straight to the first patch of pond algae it had ever seen and began to eat. The sound resembled a kitten's lapping of milk, only ten times faster.

After this outing, the mini-marsh became our daily destination. Still, the duckling never rushed ahead. Two whole days passed before, once there, it would enter without me. Even then it would stop feeding every few minutes to cock a nervous eye in my direction. And if I rose to go, it would clamber ashore and hide between my feet.

One afternoon as we headed back from the marsh, Duck suddenly sprinted ahead. Was it taking a shortcut through the hedge to outside? Recalling the busy highway beyond, I raced to head it off. Luckily it couldn't find an opening. I continued toward the house, coaxing it to come. After a while it rejoined me.

I liked to watch Duck feed. Skimming a beakful of algae or pondweed, it would tongue the water out through a comb-like fringe — new to me — along its beak, the way a baleen whale strains krill from seawater. One day while it was doing this, Bonnie startled us by bounding into the water between us with a great muddy splash. Until then the bird had shown no fear of the big Lab. Now in a blink it was gone, darting frog-like under water, surfacing two metres away to reconnoitre, diving again to shoot off in a new direction. So swift and erratic were these movements, I doubted that even a mink could have nabbed it. And now the wisdom of its marbled coat came home to me. Under water the ochre fuzz and chocolate stipples became sun-dappled muck.

That instinctive plunge taught Duck a new way to feed. Soon it was upending and grazing on the bottom the way puddle ducks had done for countless millennia. As if to celebrate, that evening in Matt's and Heather's swimming pool, it plunged a metre down through the turquoise water and surfaced under my chin.

If this fast-growing juvenile was so quick under water, how fast could it travel on land? Heading for the marsh next morning, I purposely began to jog. Right on cue, my tiny companion accelerated. Short legs pedalling furiously, skinny neck outstretched, snaky body waddling, it kept pace for maybe twenty metres, breasting the new-mown grass blades that bent under its low-slung belly and then rebounded in a silvery wake behind. Backlit by the sun, the bird was a little yellow tugboat in a choppy emerald sea.

Despite its snaky movements and scaly legs, Duck deemed itself a mammal. Else why didn't it join the six friendly bantam pullets, which had replaced Matt's failed hatch? It also ignored the noisy cockatiels, chumming around instead with the dog and even with the cats. Above all, it sought human company.

Especially humans who let it groom them. If I slouched in a lawn chair or lay on the floor, it would clamber up my nearest leg or arm and go to work. It would tweak my chest hair, gabble under my beard, nibble my eyelids, even explore my earholes. If I twitched or giggled it would pause and eye me reproachfully. And later it would bed down in the hollow of my chest, close first one eye, then the other, then both, and fall asleep. Never knew a hardwood floor could feel so soft.

Each day brought something new. One afternoon it began to pump its head up and down every few minutes like those toy wooden ducks that kids pull on a string—except this one pumped while standing still. Was it unkinking its neck? Scanning the world vertically? Was this where the phrase "to duck" originated?

Toward the end of our stay, Matt and I took our orphan boating on the Rideau Canal. Or rather, he took Duck kayaking while I took Bonnie canoeing. Setting his passenger before the cockpit, Matt paddled out from the dock. At first the bird seemed dazed. So much water and so little time! For perhaps twenty seconds it stood motionless like a captain on the bridge of a ship. Then it leaped. Soon it was a speck on Seeleys Bay. Matthew hastily turned, scooped it aboard on his paddle and set it behind the cockpit to see whether Herr Lorenz's heeling reflex would keep it there. It did stay put for perhaps two minutes, then dived after a whirligig beetle.

Meanwhile, I fretted. This water was too deep, the bottom too weedy and dark. Any minute I expected to see a snaggle of needle teeth amid a froth of bubbles where our bird had been. "Matt," I said, "this place looks pretty pikey."

"Yeah," said he, "there's pike, but we should be okay." Ever since boyhood Matt has had this admirable confidence that Nature would see things his way. Usually it does—which is another way of saying he sees things *Nature's* way.

In any case, I was too busy balancing the canoe to argue. Every time Bonnie spotted something interesting, which was often, she heaved her twenty-five kilograms around for a better look. To regain the dock without a ducking—there's another word—was a relief. Even better to be cruising home on four wheels over dry pavement with the bird asleep on my lap, and later to hear the leafy patter of its feet on solid wood again.

After that outing we decided Duck was ready for round-the-clock exposure to outdoor weather and fresh air. From spruce two-by-twos and chicken wire we built an open-bottomed pen with attached wading pool. This rig we placed on the grass (for food), under an apple tree (for shade), and near the hen coop (for company). Compared to its indoor cardboard shack, smelly wood chips, bare bulb, and cracked mirror, this was luxury. Or so we thought.

First Duck tried the tiny pool and seemed to like it. But when we made to leave, it dashed to and fro with loud peeps as if in distress. To this dependent juvenile, never before caged outdoors, our makeshift pen must have seemed a risky place just then. Still, by next day the duckling seemed content. Even so, at dusk we still took it indoors for safety.

Now began a different sort of vocalizing. Whenever we were near, indoors or out, Donnie peeped continually. The peeps were high in pitch but low in volume and came in pairs. They seemed to say, "Over here" and "I'm fine." Like tree frog notes, they carried surprisingly far and were hard to locate. In other words, a safe and effective way to maintain contact with the mother ship on the darkest night in the densest thicket.

On the second last day of our one-week visit, Duck began to rear up and flex its featherless stubs—one couldn't call them wings yet—several times an hour. It also began to waggle its rump importantly before and after voiding. The voiding followed too closely on the waggling to serve as a warning, but never mind. By now we'd come to accept an occasional watery green daub as a small price to pay for Duck's antics. And by now that rump was developing a pin-cushion of slate-blue quills that gave the bird a sort of adolescent flair.

Our orphan was definitely growing up. During our short stay it had nearly doubled in length. I bought a postcard depicting a full-grown mallard drake, intending to mail it to Matt after we returned home. At this rate we figured it would be ready to join autumn's southbound flocks. Matthew the foster parent accepted this; Matthew the biologist decided to band his baby. That way, should it meet a charge of BB shot over some Louisiana bayou, news of the kill might filter home. And if, next spring, the grown bird returned home, the metal leg-band would confirm its identity.

Observing Duck's headlong development, we marvelled that it already possessed, in the first fraction of its life, survival skills that we humans expend a fifth of ours to master. What takes us so long? Scientists cite our large capacity for language and thought, a capacity housed in a cranium so oversized that the human birth canal can barely accommodate it beyond nine months. Compared to other placental mammals, we're born prematurely. In contrast, a duck's reptilian pea-brain comes crammed with instinctual and learned responses in which language plays a minor role.

Our pleasant sojourn over, Beth and I headed home. A few days later, Matt telephoned in a choked voice to say there had been an accident. He'd invited his badminton team over for a school closing party. Someone had taken Duck out of its box. Badminton players are a nimble lot, but it was hard to keep track of a small and trusting bird down on the floor, and even harder for such a bird to navigate the herd of Reeboks and

Nikes shuffling to the music of human language and dance. One instant it was a darting miracle of electrified protoplasm, the next it lay dying.

It was a death for which Nature, with all its care for the species, had not prepared our individual bird. I wasn't too prepared myself. For weeks I seemed to hear its trusting patter behind me, for months I felt angry and cheated. Humans can be so stupid around Nature, I fumed, and here was a prime example! My mallard postcard lay unmailed. For Christmas, in solidarity, Matt carved and painted for me a beautiful mallard drake. But the ache lingered.

A year later, Matthew told me that a grade 10 student who'd been at the party confided that she had seen Bonnie bite the duckling. My son had no reason to doubt her word. For me the news brought some relief, for it meant that Duck's death had not been mindless after all but a nearly natural event. A jealous pet had simply reacted in the only way she knew. At least it made biological sense. Come to think of it, hadn't she warned us that day at the swamp when Duck had dived in panic?

Sometimes I still hear Duck's helpful gabble, still glimpse its mischievous brown eye in dark corners, still feel its cool and rubbery caress. As for my hurt, it has long since melted to a Duck-shaped warmth in the hollow of my heart.

Turtle Tale

I could have lost a finger, or worse. Not from a bench saw, nor from a carving knife. Just from curiosity and do-gooder meddling. It happened one June. We were heading east on Nova Scotia's old Highway 1 near Windsor when I spotted a big turtle poised to cross the pavement.

"It's gonna be killed," I said to my spouse, Beth, as we passed by. "The next truck will squash it for sure." I drove on in silence for a bit, thinking. Then I doubled back, turned, and parked a ways uphill from it. The turtle, as if listening for traffic, hadn't budged.

Walking down toward it, I'm thinking: *Which is it? Wood turtle? Nope, too big. Box turtle? No, tail's too long—and saw-toothed. Wait— don't snapping turtles have saw-toothed tails? If so, this'll be the first one I've seen outside of a book.* By now I'm close enough to make out the critter's dark, boldly embossed shell, its warty skin, its fierce reptilian eyes, its hooked eagle beak.

That beak gives me pause. That's when a quiet voice—not my wife's, she's still in the car—not the turtle's (though I can't be sure)—whispers, "Are you sure this is a good idea? Aren't snapping turtles bad-tempered? They say a big one can bite clear through a birch broomstick...and this is a big one. Why not take a good look and back off while you're still in one piece?"

But now I'm committed, and my wife is watching. I keep walking. This animal needs help. Not that the species is in any danger. I know that *Chelydra serpentina* thrives in wet habitats across southern Canada from the Rockies to the Atlantic and down into the Gulf States. Yet even a snapping turtle is no match for a big logging truck.

GARY SAUNDERS

"Well," the voice sighs, "make it quick. And expect a fight." At that moment the turtle pulls in its head, like a rattler about to strike. I take two long strides and pounce from behind, grabbing it hard amidships with both hands and yanking it off the ground at arm's length.

Hunh! Much heavier than I thought. But this is the easy part. "Hey Beth," I yell, playfully holding it aloft, feeling cocky, "Wanna see it up close?" She shakes her head firmly. That's when all hell breaks loose. Out comes the head, jaws agape, pink throat wide enough to swallow a kitten, neck much longer than I expected. The head lunges at my face, my hands. Each lunge has a recoil that nearly wrenches the heavy body from my grasp.

Meanwhile the turtle's hind feet swivel upward at an impossible angle and start to pry my fingers one by one from under its carapace. Finger by finger I recover my grip. Luckily the race is mobile fingers versus rigid claws. So the odds are on my side.

Okay, I think, *enough of this foolishness*! I check for road traffic both ways and start across. It isn't far. It just seems far, what with all this lunging, lurching, and finger-scrabbling. But as we reach the other side a strange thing happens. The beast goes limp as a wet dishrag.

Was it the sight of that gravel ditch sloping invitingly down to the river? The prospect of freedom? "No," laughed my son in Manitoba, when I told him about it a couple weeks later on the phone. "I've never picked one up, but the ones I see out here all seem to have the same bag of tricks, the same routine. They snap their jaws, hitch themselves round and round in a circle, blink their eyes alternately—that really freaks me out—and suddenly the fight goes out of them."

"Like a run-down battery," I said. "Being cold-blooded, maybe they use up their bit of solar energy and need to rest and recharge."

"Yeah, something like that."

It sure *felt* as heavy as a big battery while I stood there debating how to safely put it down. The ditch was deep, a metre at least, and steep-sided. Not much room down there for both of us. And me wearing sandals! *You'd best slide down sideways, set it down quick, and scramble out of there.*

It worked. By the time it turned to face me I was out of reach. Would have liked to linger and see its next moves, but we still had friends to visit and a long drive home ahead of us. As I got back in the car, still excited about the rescue, all my wife said was, "You probably separated her from her babies." I hoped not.

Two weeks later, on a fishing trip with a buddy, I recounted the adventure in detail. Unlike me, David is Nova Scotia–born and grew up knowing these reptiles first-hand. He filled me in.

"That was probably a female looking for a nest site," he said. "That ditch was likely just what she wanted. The minute she saw it, she forgot you." He went on to describe the egg-laying. "She plows backwards, scooping a hollow and raising a ridge. It could be sand, gravel, sawdust, or whatnot. After laying a few eggs, she covers them with her hind feet. She keeps doing this until all her eggs are laid."

"And leaves them for the sun to hatch?"

"Right."

That part I knew. Sea turtles do the same. So do alligators. So did the dinosaurs. Of course bears, raccoons, and crows find and rob many turtle nests during the four- to five-month-long incubation, but since there's up to thirty leathery eggs per clutch, enough survive. Primitive but practical.

Come October the surviving eggs hatch and the babies head for the nearest water, their natural year-round habitat. Once there, the tiny turtles eat greens and aquatic invertebrates until freeze-up sends them into hibernation in underwater mud or debris.

Almost fully aquatic, they grow slowly and can live for decades. Some reach lengths of up to 60 centimetres and can weigh up to 16 kilograms. Fully aquatic except while nesting, they'll eat most anything, living or dead: fish, ducklings, aquatic insects, and small mammals. People exaggerate their fierceness. But unless cornered or guarding eggs, most shun humans.

Driving home, I imagine coming back on a warm day next spring, locating her nest and observing the actual hatch: the gravel heaving as in a miniature earthquake, exposing one cracked egg after another, each releasing a wee turtle, until as many as twenty are milling around the nest. Getting their bearings, they instinctively make for the nearest water, trundling along like tiny tanks toward a river or pond they've never seen.

And if I hop-scotched ahead, say, and waited by that water for several days and nights, I might even see them arrive. Fewer now—given the hazards of the journey—I'd watch them plop in by twos and threes and dart off under water. Eventually, if I returned months later during a hard frost, I might even see some descend into the muddy bottom, there to sleep the winter away, confident of spring. One might even envy them that confidence.

So Excellent a Fish: Capelin

It is a night for love. Full moon, sandy beach, air spiced with kelp and salt, sea glittering like shook foil, flood tide fingering the driftwood line. Cool for June, but nice after weeks of rain and fog and ice. Waves slide up the strand, applaud softly, and retire with a sigh. Suddenly, a *frisson* of quicksilver sweeps the beach like wind over grass. Wave after wave deposits hundreds of wriggling fish, which the next wave washes away. The capelin have struck in!

Not long ago, from Labrador to Cape Breton, whole villages turned out for this annual spawning frenzy. Women hiked up skirts to scoop capelin by the basketful, men flung cast nets until their skiffs overflowed, kids and dogs got gloriously wet, gulls could hardly fly for gorging. For outport Newfoundlanders the "capelin scull" (school) meant many things: a taste of fresh fish after months of salt beef, fertilizer for the gardens, fuel for the sled dogs hauling next winter's stovewood.

Above all, it meant the cod were coming. *Mallotus villosus* is the northern cod's chief food. When the capelin head inshore to breed, cod follow—or used to. It was capelin that lured them inshore, and capelin that supplied the fresh bait to catch them with. It made a neat economic-ecologic loop and a crucial one, because without dependable fresh bait the summer trawl fishery could not begin. Back then Newfoundland had no bait storage depots, and cod traps were too costly for most fishers. Yes, come July, with luck, there'd be herring for bait and, after that, squid. But that was too little too late for the main fishery. For that, capelin was the key. Hence the excitement.

The 1992 cod moratorium changed all that. Today's week-days are Sunday-quiet once the seal and crab and lobster seasons are done. Oh, capelin still dance on the beaches in June or July (earlier along the Gulf of St. Lawrence), but few humans come to watch, let alone to harvest. Why bother, when the mart sells cello-packed capelin, when few garden anymore, and when outport dogs eat kibbles and canned horse instead?

However, capelin are still fished. Since the mid-70s the action has been offshore, where sonar-beeping purse seiners work the schools for overseas markets. That I knew. What I didn't know until Uncle Harry told me is that these markets take mainly female fish. It's the roe, the eggs, they're after, not even the flesh. Half the male capelin are still wasted.

Had the cod debacle taught us nothing? Were we overfishing capelin too? Clearly my facts needed updating. So much for romantic notions of beaches bright with green-and-silver bodies, of sod-capped Newfoundlanders twirling cast nets to feed their families.

As I telephoned the Department of Fisheries and Oceans (DFO), it occurred to me that they'd think me a crank, fussing over an insignificant minnow when they had more important fish to manage. The information DFO sent me eased my fears. Commercially, capelin *is* relatively insignificant. Yet ecologically it is the most important forage species in the Northwest Atlantic.

The level of capelin predation is astronomical. For instance, in the 1970s, when cod were up and whales and seals were down, cod consumed up to 3,000,000 tonnes a year. In addition whales took an estimated 400,000, plus harp seals 300,000, Greenland halibut ate 200,000—never mind salmon, plaice, and herring. In the Gulf of St. Lawrence alone the estimated overall con-sumption is a million tonnes a year. One compact car weighs about 1.5 tonnes. The average capelin might weigh 100 grams.

Seabirds feast on capelin too—250,000 tonnes a year by one estimate. Puffins, small birds, take 12,000 tonnes during breed-ing season alone. The nesting success of gannets and kittiwakes is known to rise and fall with *Mallotus* numbers. Small this fish may be, but insignificant it isn't. Like the plankton it feeds on, capelin is the linchpin of a whole North Atlantic ecosystem.

Ironically, this may have saved its skin. In 1979, DFO, aware of these facts and desperate to halt the cod's decline, curtailed both the foreign and domestic capelin harvest. In 1992, they closed the foreign capelin fishery altogether. Hindsight showed this to have been too late for the cod; yet, it may have saved the capelin.

As an added safeguard, DFO later pegged the total allowable capelin catch (TAC) at no more than 10 per cent of estimated biomass. (For 1999-2001, this works out to a conservative 50,545 tonnes a year — half Newfoundland's record 1990 catch, and roughly equal to Newfoundland's traditional harvest.)

To get a better fix on capelin biomass, DFO biologists probed *Mallotus*'s secret life. They learned that each female lays all her eggs at one go on a sandy beach between waves. That the eggs get sucked into the pebbly sand as deep as ten centimetres, where, if the temperature is right and the water clean, they will hatch in fifteen to twenty days. That most male capelin die of exhaustion and injuries from rolling in the surf while awaiting the females, littering (and fertilizing?) the newly seeded beaches with their bodies. That just before the next full moon and high tide, the capelin fry wriggle free to ride rapid surface currents seaward. That calm seas at this crucial time can entomb them.

Most of this information any cod fisher from Newfoundland, Iceland, or Europe already knew. Capelin are part of North Atlantic lore. The name itself comes from Old French *capelan* (Portuguese *capelinas*), meaning "chaplain," a reference perhaps to the male's twin cape-like mating ridges, elongated scales that likely help align him against the smaller female's flanks during spawning. (*Villosus* is Latin for "hairy.")

Some new facts have also come to light. Biologists now know that most capelin live for six or seven years and breed from ages

CAPELIN

three to four. That the capelin of Alaska, Japan, and Korea is also *M. villosus*, not a different species as once thought. That this pelagic (open ocean) species of Arctic and Subarctic waters, with its seasonal feeding and spawning patterns, is notoriously hard to track and tally. That, like its salmonid kin, it is temperature-sensitive. Should the ocean grow too cold or too warm, they're apt to skip town with no forwarding address. This happened in 1994, when capelin disappeared from northeast Newfoundland to show up months later on the Scotian Shelf. Abnormally cold water had driven them south; two years later they were back.

Given the difficulty of managing this species, it's unfortunate that DFO biologists are hampered by cutbacks. They must make do with scanty data from ships' logs, from on-board catch sampling, from occasional aerial surveys, and from talking with fishers. From such dribs and drabs, plus the usual surveys of predation, seabirds' stomachs, water and beach conditions, and the like, they must interpolate age and gender profiles, predict spawning success, and set quotas and seasons for the Banks and Gulf and Scotian Shelf. All that, and try to find markets for male capelin (cod farm feed looks promising). What they really need is an ongoing acoustic (sonar) survey like they had a few years ago.

One worrisome fact is that burgeoning harp seals now gobble at least 700,000 tonnes of capelin a year—almost twice what they used to—their share and the cod's too. What if the cod come back, only to find their cupboard bare? Reminds me of a Newfoundland riddle.

Townie: "What's a bayman's sandwich?"

Bayman (playing it safe): "Dunno."

Townie: "A capelin between two beach rocks!"

Truly, the excellent little capelin is between a rock and a hard place.

Gift from the Sky

Note: The dovekie is a small northern seabird of the auk family. The only previous recorded dovekie sighting in central Nova Scotia was about sixty years ago, when neighbour Jim Blackburn's dad found a live one in a nearby field.

It's not often your birthday present drops from the sky, but one recent November it happened to me. That afternoon my spouse had burst into the house, leaving the car door open and the engine running. "Come quick!" she said. "Something to show you." When Beth does that it never pays to dawdle. So I hopped in, we spun gravel, and there on the road shoulder near John's fire pond was her find, a small black-and-white something that might have been a kitten but wasn't.

"It's a bird," she said, "but what kind?"

"Bull-bird," I said without thinking. The word just popped into my head. Which surprised me, for that's what we called them in Newfoundland, but I hadn't seen one close-up since my childhood, and certainly never expected to meet one here in Nova Scotia dairy country.

"Bull-bird?" said my wife, pulling over, but not too close, so as not to spook it.

"Yeah," I said, trying to recall its textbook name. As we rolled to a stop I was already shucking my jacket and easing open the passenger door. My hope was to capture the creature before someone ran over it or it flew off. Then the official name came to me: dovekie, "*Plautus alle*, the little auk. Sort of a mini-penguin." As a rule Beth isn't keen on feathered critters, but I knew she liked penguins.

Edging toward the stout robin-sized bird now, I noted details: black tux, white vest, webbed toes? Yes. Conical bill, thick neck, stubby upturned tail, dovekie for sure. And it looked okay, huddled among the fallen maple leaves, making no move to fly. Dropping my jacket over it, I scooped it up. One brief flutter and it lay quiet as if exhausted.

"What a dear little bird!" cried Beth, peeping, disarmed. So dovekie—little dove—came home with us.

The trouble with adopting wild things, apart from maybe breaking the law, is the sudden responsibility. What to do with a tired and hungry critter from God knows where? My bird books weren't much help. They did explain that dovekies sometimes blow off course while migrating south to winter off our coasts. (A strong sou'wester *had* lashed the region the night before.) And that grounded dovekies find it very hard to get airborne again, preferring to launch themselves from vertical cliffs, ocean waves, even from icebergs. ("Ice bird" is its other common name.)

One thing was sure: the first priority was rest and food. Back home I mixed honey and brandy and eye-dropped it into the beak with a chaser of cod liver oil. The bird shook its head like an annoyed cat but most of the mixture went down.

Cats! I'd forgotten we had two! So our second priority must be security. We still had the kids' old bunny cage, but on second thought the bathtub seemed more logical. After all, cats hate water and dovekies love it. We'd just have to keep the door religiously shut between visits. So I half-filled the tub with cold water, stirred in some coarse salt as an afterthought—they say seabirds can drink sea water—and tipped her in. She landed sideways, but instantly righted herself to ride high as a cork.

My makeshift ocean seemed to raise her spirits. Suddenly her triangular black-and-pink feet came to life, swiftly propelling her the length of the tub and back. And then she spoke her first word: "Skreak!" Taking that to mean "More," I splashed her. The droplets rolled off like rain from a waxed car. Playfully I shoved her under. Instantly two pointed wings flicked out from her sides like switchblades and, in a blink, she shot to the tub's other end — underwater this time. No minnow could out-swim this bird!

Then she seemed to wilt. I used the lull to study her. From above she was decidedly boat-shaped, like a bluff-bowed Cape Islander. Her colour was more subtle than I'd thought, grading from glossy black above to dark umber brown along the cheeks and throat to milky white below. And she had oval white eyebrows.

Nature often uses dark patches to break the telltale outline of the eye. Wood frogs, shrikes, raccoons, and killer whales sport them year-round. Dovekies trade theirs in every fall for a white bib from chin to nape. Speaking of which, this bird had almost no neck. It was all head and shoulders, like a tiny bull. Of course, bull-bird!

Bull-birds don't breed in Canada, migrating instead to northwest Greenland each spring. Their Eurasian counterparts go to Spitsbergen, north of Norway, and to Siberian islands like Novaya Zemlya. There, on seaward-sloping cliffs, females squeeze into crevices and rock rubble to nest. Each lays a single egg, sky-blue with or without brown freckles. Nesting mothers coo "*Al-le*" to their fuzzy chicks — hence the Latin species name. The Icelander's *álka* (auk) may also echo this sound.

Through the long summer days, dovekies throng the cliffs and ice floes by the million. Arctic explorer Admiral Donald B. MacMillan, quoted in John Hay's *In Defense of Nature* (2007, 156), likened the sound of their massed choirs to a "great, pulsating, musical note which seems to fill all space."

When not pursuing minnows or marine worms under water, the birds skim plankton and small crustaceans from floating seaweed, which they eat as well. Parents regurgitate these tidbits into their offspring, who thank them by mewing like kittens. While dovekies don't breed in Canada, Greenland's colonies forage as far south as Baffin Bay and eastern Lancaster Sound in Canadian waters.

Small though ice birds are, their sheer numbers and ease of capture traditionally made them an important source of fresh meat and eggs for northern Inuit after the long, cold winter. Indeed, their arrival signalled the sun's return after the six-month Arctic night. Hunters scooped them from the air with long-handled nets and buried the surplus in the permafrost for later use. Women sewed the little skins into coats called *tingmiaq*. Eggs were gathered and stored.

Newfoundlanders also took a few dovekies while hunting the much larger murre and eider — but only if they could down several with one shot. Indeed, my first memory of hunting involves dovekies. My teenaged brother borrowed Dad's 12-gauge (with or without permission I'm not sure), and took me out in the boat (at age seven, a treat in itself) to try for a meal. As a raw east wind pelted us with wet snow, I wondered aloud whether so small a bird would venture out. "Perfect bull-bird weather," Calvin assured me.

Sure enough, we soon spotted small flocks of them sporting among the grey waves, their rapid wingbeats alternating with swallow-like glides. Calvin brought down three or four on his second try. We dip-netted them aboard. The sight of their immaculate feathers flecked with blood, of their dark eyes clouding in death didn't bother me. Fresh meat was scarce in our isolated village once the winter's venison was gone. Our sparse livestock — hens, dogs, horses, and sheep — were all working animals. Only the odd aging hen or lame sheep went into the pot. We got so tired of salt beef and Spam! Caribou and moose were plentiful, but since we lacked freezers nobody killed one until November. Small game like duck and rabbit and turr (murre) filled the gap. Bull-birds, like snipe, were almost too small, but just as tasty. And they helped train youngsters like me how to put meat on the table. It was survival.

Today dovekies are protected by law. That doesn't deter ravens and gyrfalcons, which pick them off year-round. Arctic foxes gobble both birds and eggs. The big glaucous or burgomaster gull preys on them relentlessly.

In fact, the dovekie is crucial to the Arctic ecosystem. New England nature writer John Hay, intrigued by these "pine-knots" frolicking in winter seas off Cape Cod, delved into this. His book *In Defense of Nature* (originally published in 1969) describes how in northwest Greenland dovekie guano, filtering down through bare rock rubble for centuries, nourishes lush moss meadows that not only brighten the drab landscape but also sustain ptarmigan and Arctic hare — plus their predators. Similar to our little smelt-like capelin, sustainer of whales, seals, a host of seabirds, and, until recently, schools of northern cod, this little auk carries a whole ecosystem on its teardrop-shaped back.

And now we Saunderses had one in our bathtub. For how long, we didn't know; a few days perhaps, followed by a Bay of Fundy release? Meanwhile, what about baths? It's true dovekies make dandy rubber duckies, but surely soap isn't good for them.

Nor does guano make good soap. Somehow we had to help this important bird on its journey.

Dovekie solved the problem for us. That afternoon we found her drifting, dead on the water, wings half-cocked as if for a final sprint. That buffeting sou'wester had done her in. Her five-thousand-kilometre odyssey was over.

The second big drawback about adopting wildlife is that you become attached. Luckily for us there hadn't been time. Or so I thought. In any case, some pen-and-ink drawings were in order. And it might be a good idea to take some photos for the grandchildren. And then bury her in the garden. With a flat rock on top to keep dogs out. Right.

Birthdays tend to be become low-key when you've made over sixty trips around the sun. A cake, a single candle (to avoid melt-down), a drop of wine, a meal with family or friends are celebration enough.

From now on, though, my Novembers will be brighter because of that boat-shaped auklet, that gift of a bird from home. Sadder too, for it will remind me of the flightless, man-trusting great auk, of how fishermen — from explorer John Cabot's time if not before — by herding them into boats for butchery, by indiscriminate egging, and by using them for fuel to heat iron pots to render out their comrades' oil, exterminated them from the planet. Last seen alive on Eldey Island, Iceland, June 3, 1844, the bird is now found only in dusty museum cases. Tiny Funk Island, off northeast Newfoundland, was once alive with them. Now all that's left is a brighter greensward where their mouldering bones fertilize the scanty turf.

Thank God dovekies are in no such danger. As you read this, millions are winging south willy-nilly along our shores, acrobats of the surf, glad to be alive in any weather. Sometimes it pays to be small.

God's Dead Dog &
Other Roadkills

Q: Why does a chicken cross the road?
A: To show the porcupine it can be done.

Cruising at 110 kilometres per hour, my mind on a Halifax medical appointment, I never got a good look at the tawny something lying dead beside the winter highway. Except to note that it seemed too small for a deer and too big for a fox...a dead dog perhaps? Anyhow, it was already behind me. But I clocked the distance to the next overpass, made a mental note to check it on the way home, and hurried on.

Three hours later, at dusk, on my second try, I found the roadkill. But now I was on the wrong side of four lanes of suppertime traffic. To cross a busy highway at dusk without becoming roadkill oneself is a nice exercise in timing, like skipping rope or singing alto. You pick a moment, walk to the median, pick another, and walk again. You never run; a stumble could be fatal. And you try to ignore the roar (how can cars be so quiet inside and so noisy outside?), the diesel stink, the wind-slam, the grit in the eyes, the naked car-less feeling. Highways are violent places.

The dead brown something turned out to be a young female coyote. Her toothy grin and yellow eye startled me. But this was no scraggly Disney stereotype coyote. Glossy and well fed, she looked more like a prize show dog. God's dog, I thought, recalling the title which mid-western Indigenous nations bestowed on this animal. So cunning was it, so smart, so *muy coyote*, they thought it would surely be the last animal alive on Earth. But this dog was definitely dead. Already the crows had been at work.

Why does a coyote cross the road? For any number of good reasons: to seek a mate, to escape danger, to rejoin its pack. Or to nurse a hidden pup, track a sick deer, investigate a smell, scout new territory. In fact, coyotes are inveterate right-of-way travellers. Unlike timber wolves, they prefer sunlit openings where mice and berries thrive. That's likely how this prairie native crossed half a continent in the 1940s and later, litter by litter, reached the Maritimes in the sixties and seventies, loping across the Canso Causeway onto Cape Breton Island soon after, even traversed ice floes to colonize Prince Edward Island and western Newfoundland in the 1980s.

Why, for that matter, does any wild creature cross a dangerous, noisy highway? Often because the highway blocks a traditional route. We forget that our trails overlie theirs, not vice versa. By fragmenting their habitat we force them into ours. For every winter coyote that bites the pavement, dozens of porcupines and deer also die. Porkies are saltoholics anyway. (They say if you're lost in the woods, follow one and it'll take you to the nearest highway.) Deer have a better excuse. In cold weather they must browse heaps of mostly hardwood twigs or starve.

Surprisingly, even snowshoe hares, which have been clocked at over forty kilometres an hour, get run over, especially during their eleven-year population peak. One December a dead bunny showed up in our town's downtown core. Jay-hopping the snowy streets in its white winter coat, I suppose it felt invisible. But it couldn't have picked a worse week. Harried Christmas shoppers ironed it flat as a pancake.

Come spring, the highway death toll escalates as hibernators waken, migrants arrive, and little ones try their legs. Groggy groundhogs blunder under eighteen-wheelers. Lovesick muskrats become squashed musquash. Juvenile raccoons, black bears, and skunks get hit. Rain-dancing frogs plaster the morning pavements. Birds aren't exempt. Warblers slam into windshields and grills. Pheasants sprint the wrong way. Grouse chicks march single file into oblivion. Even scavenging crows get smacked.

You'd think by now wildlife would be used to traffic. They would—if evolution weren't so slow. On Darwin's clock the automobile is barely minutes old. Karl Benz invented it only in 1885. And less than a century has passed since Henry Ford started mass-producing his Model T, the affordable, user-friendly car that sparked North America's love affair with the open road.

For the first few decades, traffic was sparse and slow. Rural roads were bone-rattling wagon tracks then, and tires were notoriously unreliable. That changed after the Second World War, when ready cash plus innovations like the bulldozer (offspring of the military tank), synthetic rubber, and paving machines put driving on the map. Today the fleetest highway interloper, however exquisitely tuned its senses, is hard put to evade the storm of two-tonne projectiles blazing with light.

So roadkills have become part of Canada's highway scene. Mostly we ignore them—unless we hit a skunk or something big. After all, no one *tries* to run over wildlife. And it's not as if wild animals lead risk-free lives. Those that survive sibling strife and predation face death by freezing, drowning, starving, parasites, and disease anyhow. Very few die of old age. If they did, every population would overrun its habitat. To maintain ecological balance, on average all offspring but two must die within their parents' lifetimes. That's the deal—for humans too.

Why then don't we see more wildlife corpses? First, we don't travel the woods enough, or know where and when to look. Second, Nature's sanitation crews are so efficient. Without those scavengers and decomposers the woods and fields would overflow with carcasses and excrement. Small victims are disposed of in days, big ones in months. Even bison and elk get processed in a year or two, bones and hide and all.

Our champion year-round scavengers are the resident birds: crows, ravens, magpies, jays, and gulls. (Why fly south when every highway is a meat market?) Foxes and coyotes help too. In summer, buzzards and bald eagles join the banquet. But insects and bacteria bear the brunt of cleanup. Even as wriggling maggots strip each carcass, carrion beetles in orange construction vests are tunnelling beneath. Bit by bit they lower it into the earth, dine on the choicest remaining cuts, and lay their eggs in the rest. Leftovers go to the soil's waiting hordes of worms, millipedes, mites, springtails, protozoa, bacteria, fungi.

Hair and bones take longer. Birds weave a lot of hair into nests. Rodents gnaw bones for the calcium and phosphorus, how voraciously I never realized until visiting Newfoundland's Brunette Island years ago. The island's recently introduced woodland caribou herd had prospered—but something was amiss. The ground was littered with cast-off antlers, some bleached driftwood-white. Brunette had no mice to recycle them. In time the already acidic soil would get sourer still, stunting future antlers.

Knowing Nature as we do, knowing that animals must die, why should we postmoderns mind a scattered roadkill? But many do. Is it because we glimpse our own demise out there? I prefer to think our genes recall the Pleistocene Ice Age, that white, harrowing time when animals such as these fed and clothed and sheltered us. Seen in that light, the modern highway—violent, polluting, habitat-gobbling, death-dealing for all its benefits—becomes a metaphor for our whole uneasy relationship with the Earth.

Oh, we can rationalize it. "Humans are part of Nature too, humans use tools, trucks and cars are tools, so it's okay. Cost of doin' business!" Well, no. Humans created the problem, humans should solve it. Aren't we *Homo sapiens*, the wise ones? I don't mean salvaging roadkills for the poor—though some jurisdictions do that and fresh venison *is* more wholesome than store-bought hamburger. A cheaper approach is the vehicle-mounted warning device. Canadian Tire sells a wind-activated, high-frequency, stick-on "deer whistle." Something similar, perhaps electronic, perhaps ultrasound, but targeted to a broader spectrum of species, might be the answer. A successful design would prevent countless collisions, save human lives, and make its inventor rich. Maybe we should launch a contest?

Lately I've found a better way. I draw and paint roadkills. Friends roll their eyes, but I figure I'm in good company. John James Audubon and Roger Tory Peterson shotgunned and stuffed thousands of birds in their day. My specimens come already dead. So far I've painted a hare, a groundhog, a chipmunk, and a chickadee. Their broken bodies teach me new ways of seeing. I never realized how golden a groundhog's belly fur is, how humanoid its little hands. My Christmas hare now lives in an art gallery. "No, I don't find it even remotely gruesome," one woman assured me. "I'm fascinated by the light you've caught."

Well, good for me. Good for her, too, for seeing the light. And good for you, for reading my dark tale. But if the three of us are ever hailed before a Canada Roadkill Tribunal with Judge Coyote on the bench, let's hope God's dog is having a good day.

Caribou Caper

Surely one of the most lonesome artificial sounds on Earth is the fading hum of a bush plane that's dropped you alone beside a remote Newfoundland lake without compass or matches and with dirty weather brewing. Straining to catch the plane's fading, wind-baffled note, I felt a surge of fear—and joy.

Fear, because in the excitement of our pontoon landing on a rocky, too-short lake, I'd left my backpack on the plane. Joy, because I was finally seeing Newfoundland's Buchans Plateau. As a forester and new Memorial University lecturer in the early sixties, I'd spent all winter tethered to a university classroom and lab, and badly needed a taste of real wilderness. But now, with the spring exams over, with my students' papers all marked, here I was with nothing to do but sketch calving caribou for two days. When the telephone call came from Heman Whalen, a technician with the province's Wildlife Division, I jumped at the chance.

Luckily my sketch pad and pens were safe in my parka pocket. But I'd still need shelter and food should the pilot fail to return with my crew-mates. *Best check out the wildlife cabin before the weather changes*, I thought. *But where is it?* Somewhere up that wooded slope, he'd said.

With any luck—if the bears hadn't trashed it—there might be some tinned bully beef or sardines, maybe some rabbit snare wire, maybe even some dry matches in a bottle. And should the worst happen, Howley was only a three-day hike away.

I scouted for caribou but saw none. Still, by now the pregnant does, intent on reaching these ancestral calving grounds, should be ghosting northward over well-worn tracks across tawny bogs and over rocky barrens, pausing only to quench their thirst or nibble the budding foliage of willow and dwarf birch. Once here, they would choose a sheltered droke of conifers, give birth, and linger a few days until their long-limbed calves could keep up. Then, off again to spend the summer in the area's many fertile stream valleys. Soon the landscape would be speckled with their slow-moving, ghostly white-and-grey shapes.

A century ago there would have been thousands. This we know because once the trans-island railway reached Port aux Basques in 1897, passengers were often forced to wait for hours, even days, while northbound "deer" crossed the track between Grand and Sandy Lakes, their crackling ankle joints sounding like an approaching brush fire as they headed for the Great Northern Peninsula.

All too soon, visiting "sportsmen" were slaughtering so many that St. John's enacted the colony's first game laws and marked off a sanctuary patrolled by wardens. In time the railroad slaughter stopped. But then lumber and pulpwood operations spawned by the railway began feeding their loggers fresh venison. The final insult was wildfires sparked by coal-burning locomotives. These fires, burning unchecked all summer and sometimes smouldering in deep turf all winter to restart come spring, destroyed the herds' staple foods, namely the slow-growing "reindeer moss" (*Cladonia* lichen) and maldow (old man's beard, or *Usnea* lichen).

Our expedition a century later had to make do with hundreds, not thousands. Our leader Heman was part of the government's ongoing caribou studies directed by head biologist Dr. Tom Bergerud, an American. Bergerud's current concern was mortality in newborn fawns. Trappers were reporting numerous lynx kills in the area. Some predation by lynx and bear was to be expected on a calving ground, including the odd sick adult, but an unnatural spike plus a fluke spring blizzard in these mountains could mean calf trouble. A lynx cull might be needed.

Also worrisome was a sudden drop in the local hare population. Though part of their normal boom-bust cycle, it meant that lynx, being chiefly hare eaters, followed that cycle a few years behind, which meant hungry cats. Heman's job was to size up the situation, collecting cat poop for signs of caribou hair, examining any fawn kills, checking live newborns for telltale wounds and general health.

When at last the Beaver float plane returned, it brought him, his assistant, and the rest of our gear including my pack. As they stepped out onto the nearest pontoon, a sleety rain began to fall. Quickly, so the plane could take off without delay, we hustled the rest of the gear ashore. With a deafening roar the Beaver was soon a speck in the eastern sky. For several minutes its widening wake lapped the shore. Then silence flooded back.

Fifteen minutes later, we had everything under cover, a good fire going in the tin stove, tea kettle on to boil, and beans and pork warming in the fry pan. My job was to document all this, and especially caribou, in pen-and-ink drawings for a future publication. Nice work if you could get it, and I had.

Next morning I woke at daylight to the rattle of sleet on the tarred roof. Padding to the east window I saw, beyond the trees, a barren snow-patched hillside sloping into grey clouds. Then one of the snow shapes moved, stood up, and began to graze, followed by others. Despite the wintry weather, they resembled contented cows in a balmy summer pasture.

That afternoon the sun came out, the sleet melted, the lake smiled, and the work began. It was odd work, even funny work, when I think about it now. To watch grown men leap from boggy tussock to boggy tussock, trying to outrun and out-guess a four-day-old fawn, was laughable. We whooped and hooted like kids on a playground. Only by teamwork did we catch any. As a group, wildlifers are a lot like youngsters anyhow. As youngsters they likely kept live snakes and worse in their bedrooms. And they never lose that love, putting up with privation and pain to practise it.

The caribou moms were funny too. Unlike the stags, which shed their racks in late fall, most does carry their smaller antlers well into spring. Still, those antlered mothers made no move to gore us. Instead they milled about uselessly, huffing and snorting, while the boys wrestled their offspring to the ground and tagged them, and then the does welcomed their young back, human scent and all.

Eventually, the guys caught and tagged about a dozen. For me that's all a blur now. What I do vividly recall, helped by my drawings, is the beauty of those boulder-grey creatures and the tender solicitude of the nursing does. That, and the onrushing Subarctic spring, which melted the icicles and snowbanks into rivulets, greened and tasselled the dormant alders and willows, transforming the austere landscape before our very eyes.

And now, in small groups and large groups, early and late, the caribou kept coming. And I kept sketching. When my pad overflowed I used Kraft wrapping paper. In the long twilights after supper, off duty, I roamed the plateau. On our last night, a full moon floodlit the plateau with theatrical brilliance. The dance of silvery light and indigo shadow on rock and snow was unforgettable.

The flight to Deer Lake (note the name) and the subsequent train ride to St. John's are blurry too. If my drawings appeared in the *Journal of Wildlife Management* as planned, I never saw them, nor do I much care. That was over fifty years ago. Back then I still thought the caribou would last forever. Now I'm not so sure. Overzealous sport hunting is no longer the problem. Nor are ATVs and snowmobiles, though they do disrupt ancestral migration routes and encourage poaching. A century ago, says Radclyffe Dugmore in his classic 1913 *Romance of the Newfoundland Caribou,* the mere scent of a human would panic a whole herd. Now half-tame caribou amble fearlessly past active lumber camps.

As for eastern coyotes — or *coywolves* to be precise, for most now carry wolf DNA — the jury is still out. Veteran outfitters say they kill for fun, leaving the meat. A Gros Morne Park tour guide said they've been known to haul a half-born fawn from its birthing mother — ghastly midwifery indeed. Some say our caribou numbers have dwindled since this new predator arrived on ice pans from Nova Scotia in the 1980s.

Time will tell. In a sense coyotes are only filling the niche left by the extinct Newfoundland wolf. If so, they're a poor substitute. Being smallish, averaging only thirty some kilograms, they kill clumsily, mangling and chewing until the caribou dies of shock, exhaustion, and blood loss. Real wolves weigh twice as much and kill cleanly with a bite to the windpipe or jugular. And they return to the kill until it's all gone. They also don't tolerate coyotes in their territory. Perhaps Newfoundland needs a few dozen wolf packs? But they'd likely concentrate on moose, which coyotes don't tackle.

No, the real threat now is wobbly weather. Already climate change is suspected in massive die-offs among some mainland herds. In normal winters, their leanest time, they easily dig through loose snow with their spade-like, keen-edged hooves — their Indigenous name means "shoveller" — one reason they migrate south each fall. But snow that's soaked in freezing rain soon turns to impenetrable ice, starving a famished herd. Lack of food also means fewer fawns come spring. True, caribou have starved in the past, but if such weather becomes the norm it could be fatal. No wild animal can adapt that fast.

Explaining all this to a youth group one day, I heard one of them exclaim, "What odds if they go? Hunters might care, but so what?"

"Well, son," I said, "it's like this. Without them your cup may still be full — but it's a pretty small cup!"

COVID-19 Moment

"After dinner, rest a while; after supper, walk a mile."
— Maritime Folk Saying

I like walking our Nova Scotia country roads. Summer and winter, spring and fall, if the weather's half decent, I'm out there tramping with a stout stick in case of mad dogs or bold coyotes. Getting started is sometimes hard, but always I return home refreshed.

Westward I can choose several kilometres of rolling fields backed by mixed wood forest with houses few and far between, including one ancient Acadian site and the supposed put-in point for Mi'kmaw canoeists heading to Prince Edward Island. Eastward, for a kilometre or two, I pass two homes, three dairy farms, a fire pond, and a diked marsh ending at Highway 236, the old Truro-Windsor route.

Mostly I go after supper, heeding the old folk maxim. Which from late fall to early spring, unless the moon is out, means walking in the dark. Truth to tell, night suits me better. For me, a landscape painter, daylight can be distracting. Night simplifies things, erases details, turns into silhouettes. Also, in summer especially, moist night air enhances scent and sound.

Speaking of sound, one windless May night I was trudging east, past the home of neighbours John and Sally Forbes, when I noticed a sound not heard since last spring, a high-pitched, distant trilling from our community pond.

Of course—spring peepers! The smallish pond, dug in the eighties as a water source for firefighting, mirror-calm that night under a sprinkle of stars, was hosting its first frog concert of the year!

In other words, the annual mating celebration of *Hyla crucifer* (Latin for the cross on its back), that thumb-sized, brownish-green tree frog, which most Maritimers have heard but few have ever seen. Recently emerged from hibernating in the pond's muddy bottom, the male peepers, eager to breed, had climbed the nearest willow or cattail, ballooned their throats and let go long trills audible for half a kilometre or more.

As I got closer, the din became deafening—part of their intention perhaps. Disorienting, really, as singer after singer cut in and out with rippling waves of harmony and dissonance. Sheer acoustic mayhem! Pretty soon I wanted to cover my ears and stumble out of there—or jump in the pond.

But I stayed, thinking, *What if I whacked my stick against that big sealed plastic pipe the local firefighters use?* Whacked, the pipe let out a resounding, hollow *boom*—and half the orchestra fell silent. My second whack silenced another section. Playing conductor now, I brought the choir to total silence. You could have heard a pebble drop. My poor eardrums tingled with relief.

Wondering how long this lull would last, I held my breath and counted. Three seconds in, off to my right, came a tentative "peep." Next, from the opposite shore, an answering "chirp." Then, from the pond's far end, over thirty metres away, two or three notes in unison. Scarcely had those faded when the whole orchestra exploded into full voice again.

Walking home that evening, I felt a new spring in my octogenarian step. COVID or no, those little cross-bearing amphibians had voted for Life and Love. So would I. So should we.

Catediquette

Last September my spouse, reading near the family room window in our renovated old farmhouse, sensed a movement on the deck outside. Intently watching her was a cat. Living next to a dairy barn as we do, we often see stray cats. But this one was a half-grown kitten, and a beauty at that—pure white with beige markings, a striped tail, and grey-gold eyes. Later we learned she was female.

What to do? Take her back to the barn, there to compete with several hungry adult felines for rats and mice? Instead, why not count ourselves lucky when thousands were seeking house pets to help counter COVID blues? So we adopted. Not indoors just yet, mind you; first she'd need house-training. Meanwhile we'd woo her with free meals on our roofed deck with slumber space below.

From the get-go she charmed us. Nervous at first, she'd flop belly up—the classic cat-dog submission signal—and *roll* toward us. And later, when we noticed her using a roof column as a scratching post, we strung fluffy baubles maypole style for her to play with. And did she ever, leaping and cavorting there several times a day.

But come October she'd need warmer housing. It so happened that years ago I'd built a mini-cabin for our last cat, Festus, a tom who, though a vet found no kidney or bladder problems, took to urinating outside his litter box—especially when I was away. In other words, marking territory. One of us had to go; hence, the cabin.

As a shelter it wasn't bad: shingled roof, gable window, cloth door flap to keep out the weather, floor cushion, walls and roof insulated with Styrofoam. Within a week kitty was taking her noon nap there.

Come dark, however, she'd meow to be let into the family room. Instead we lent her the sun porch, which has five big windows for fresh air and afternoon sun, ample space for feeding and play, and an old couch for sleeping. Also the French door to the adjoining kitchen would let her see and hear us. All she needed there was a litter box plus food and water dishes. Unlike Festus, "Miracle"—my wife's name for our new ward—used her litter box right away.

By Thanksgiving, with five family visitors and two pet dogs coming and going, we had to ease the house rules. Still, no way did I want her tainted footprints on our tables and counters— nor risk her leaping onto the hot wood stove overnight. Okay, she could come all the way inside if (a) someone carried her around; and (b) doors to the upstairs were kept shut. Just in case, I put a separate litter box in the downstairs hall closet and one upstairs.

These house rules our headstrong nine-year-old granddaughter reluctantly agreed to. If anything, it was my softer-hearted spouse who chafed under this regimen. Then one afternoon, while Herself napped upstairs, I invited "Ki-ki," as I called her, to tour the family room on foot.

Watching her explore was fascinating. Every nook, chair, and cupboard, even the woodbox and stove, had to be inspected. When she leapt onto the table I shouted, "No!" and put her firmly back down. Near the end, as a test, I flopped on the sofa and feigned sleep. Moments later she landed with a soft plop at my feet and started purring.

Even after exploring outdoors, Ki-ki still seemed glad to inhabit "her room." Which was good for another reason. By now, though smallish for her age (runt of a litter?), she was deemed sexually mature by our vet. Uh-oh. No more outdoor rambles until she's fixed, right?

Right. She now roams our downstairs. As further compensation, I took her, via the sun porch stairs, down cellar. There she found three boulder-lined walls enclosing an earthen floor that would absorb any little do-dos or piddles. If lonely, she could still hear us upstairs. Plus hunt the odd mouse. To ease her comings and goings I now leave the basement door ajar. Which is how things stand — for now.

Part Four
Invertebrata

Spider Love

Male spiders run great risks for sex. For some species it's a life-or-death game, with up to 30 per cent perishing in the attempt. Why? Nature's way of ensuring that proven genes spread no further than Her Highness? The female is much bigger—so it seems Nature is on her side.

One spring afternoon, laid up for six weeks from cancer surgery, with nothing to do but sleep, eat, read, and watch the grass grow, I witnessed, for my first time ever, two spiders mating. I'd recently graduated from deck chair to hammock, and slung as I was between a paper birch (east) and a tamarack (west), I had a good overhead view—or I would have missed the show.

In general I dislike hammocks. Even without surgery they're tricky to enter safely, and even trickier to exit. That day, very carefully, my stitches complaining, I'd managed to board without mishap and was settled on my back, giving me a perfect overhead view of both trees' lower limbs. Picture me then, swaying to the birch's gentle motion, gazing up into the sun-dappled foliage, when suddenly a movement among the sparse tamarack needles catches my eye. The mover is a small dark spider. Because it alternately sprints or freezes, I lose sight of it whenever it stops.

Then, higher up, another movement. And now I see the object of this sprinting. Backlit by blue sky, anchored by radiating silken spokes, dangles a taut spider web. And at its hub, motionless, each leg touching a spoke, dangles a dark shape three times the first spider's size.

Now the little male risks another sprint. No response. Well, of course. Spiders, though equipped with several pairs of eyes, can't see far, especially in sun and shadow. Instead she relies more on what those outstretched legs tell her, whether the visitor is friend or foe, dinner or no. Somewhere too I'd read how males of certain species employ music to safely woo egg-laden females.

A few more sallies and Romeo reaches his goal, a spoke leading to his love—and plucks it like a harp string!

"Honey, I'm here."

Instantly Juliet's telegraphic legs twitch. Someone below! Feels like prey! She stiffens, shakes the web violently to entangle the supposed prey before immobilizing it with a bite and sucking it dry. But this intruder is no buzzing fly. In fact the net now feels empty. And our hero, well aware that the radial spokes, unlike the webbing between, are non-stick travel lanes, bides his time.

Presently he re-plucks the line. Down she darts, meets him halfway. Brave little Romeo does not flinch. Again I wonder: why all this menacing foreplay? Also part of Nature's plan? Discerning female rejects cowardly genes?

Now I really want to see the outcome. And, thanks to cancer, I have all afternoon to do so. Romeo advances another decimetre. Plucks a third time. Juliet advances—less far this time. This minuet continues until they see each other plainly.

What happened next was too swift for me to follow. Googling the subject later, I learned that the female has a special abdominal pouch for male sperm packets. That their sexual congress is more like a FedEx delivery sans signature. None of your messy mammalian insertions here, no avian anal-to-anal smooching, no sticky amphibian shenanigans.

In an eyeblink it's all over. He darts to her side, shoots his package through the mail slot and swiftly retreats. She perhaps lunges—I can't see—but too late to bite. He, almost predestined to die in her embrace—don't laugh, it's been known to happen in humans too—has escaped with his life.

Can't vouch for this, but local gossip says Romeo was later seen in Truro's Engine Room being feted by his buddies.

Of Mayflies & Millennia

A spring morning, an alder-lined brook, and here comes a mayfly. Hatched last night and mated this morning, *Hexagenia bilineata* is on an urgent mission. She's laying eggs before dying of old age this afternoon or tomorrow.

Her nervous water-stitching speaks to me, white-haired angler that I am. Having just completed another trip around the sun, time and the lack of it are often on my mind.... I don't mean Time itself, that bugbear of philosophers and physicists, who devise pretzel-shaped universes to explain it. I mean Earth-time, sunrise-sunset time, the stuff of birthdays and anniversaries.

Not that Earth-time itself is without mystery. For instance, my mayfly. Why should her clock run down after a day or so, while mine is still ticking after thousands? What's the biological advantage of such a short stay?

What got me thinking along these lines was a recent visit to my dentist. Flipping through his *New Yorker* magazines, I saw a life insurance ad. It showed a barefoot businessman contemplating a totem of common fauna imprinted with their lifespans: butterfly 14 days, beetle 21 days, dragonfly 48 days, chipmunk 1.3 years, woodpecker 6 or 7 years — North American human male, 72 years. "That's life," said the adman — then made his pitch for a worry-free retirement.

That ad took me back to my first year in forestry school, to Dendrology 101, where I was surprised to learn that different trees have different lifespans — and wildly unequal ones at that. Wild cherry is senile at twenty-five, red alder and balsam fir fade at eighty years or so, but eastern hemlock can last six hundred years and Douglas-fir twice that.

Nor is it just a matter of size. A stunted black spruce in a peat bog can be a century old. Topping that are tiny white cedars over seven hundred years old clinging to the Niagara Escarpment's limestone cliffs. Most amazing of all, the oldest of Arizona's mountaintop bristlecone pines are pushing five thousand years, almost as old as Egyptian pyramids. As close to immortality as earthly organisms, other than redwoods, ever get.

Ah, immortality! Isn't that what we really want? To live forever, perhaps not as a tree rooted to one spot, but as a mobile sensate being, all but free of Time's constraints? Against that lovely vision, my mayfly's brief existence seems pitiful indeed. But is it really? Only if we focus on her moment in the sun. For she has a secret life. During the last twelve months she has prowled this stream bed as a fanged and gilled predator like a monster from a horror movie. Most insects lead such double lives. The stout brown June bugs thumping against our lighted windows every spring are fresh from a three-year apprenticeship as fat white larvae munching roots underground. In human terms that's like spending most of one's life in kindergarten.

Fortunately, I think, we back-boned critters—fish, frogs, salamanders, snakes, birds, mammals—lack a larval phase. Instead we go directly from egg to adult. This takes longer, but it gives more play to intelligence, allows more learning on the job, weakens the robotic grip of instinct.

Humans, it turns out, are the slowest learners of all. Born premature, like possums and kangaroos—so our outsized skulls can still squeeze through the narrow birth canal—we remain helpless for a year or two and juvenile for a decade or more after that. The problem is, we're hard-wired for language, and language takes long to master. Ask any serious poet. Perhaps that explains why we want not merely to survive and reproduce like other creatures, but to put off Death indefinitely and, if possible, cheat it in the end. Like the ancient Egyptians who pickled their kings and queens for posterity, we fiddle with resurrection technologies like deep-freezing and cloning.

From time to time (so to speak) it helps to muse on vaster chronologies. Under my workroom window sits a lichened boulder the size of a shopping cart. This hunk of whitish granite surfaced in my neighbour's field a few springs ago, brought there by glaciers and heaved up by annual frost action. Liking the look of it, I got John to dump it on our lawn instead of on his rock pile.

Rocks get around; rocks tell stories. Granite is rare in central Nova Scotia's sandstone belt, so this one likely rode the Wisconsinan ice sheet across the Fundy trough from northern New Brunswick some fifteen thousand years ago. Its crystalline complexion tells me it started life as red-hot molten magma. The coarseness of its crystals tells me that it cooled slowly, deep in the Earth's crust, not quickly, as in air or cold water. The last time magma oozed up hereabouts was when ancestral North America and Africa collided and built the Appalachians four hundred million years ago. Now *there's* longevity for you!

If such longevity is our goal, a rock has much to teach us. After all, our bones are mostly rock dust—calcium and phosphorus—gleaned from the produce of the soil, itself a mixture of minerals, humus, microbes, and water. When we "know something in our bones," maybe we're alluding to that link? The Christian burial service makes no bones about it: "Ashes to ashes, dust to dust."

Still, as Simon and Garfunkel sang in the sixties, a rock feels no pain. A shaman or Indigenous person might disagree, even insist that stones are spiritual entities. So might a devotee of crystals, arguing that they too can reproduce themselves, even "grow." Come to think of it, the frost ferns on our windows each winter *are* startlingly lifelike.

Depends on your point of view. A geologist would likely label my rock "quartz/feldspar/mica—glacial erratic." A metaphysicist would point out that at the sub-molecular level my rock and

I are virtually indistinguishable, it being mostly cold silica and oxygen, I being mostly warm carbon, hydrogen, and oxygen. If poetic by nature, she might call us both galaxies of electronically charged particles circling in stately minuet-like tiny solar systems.

Whew!

Pierre Teilhard de Chardin, that remarkable French priest who pioneered dinosaur research in the Gobi Desert between the world wars, pictured the Earth as layered with evolving consciousness like the rings of an onion. For the outermost layer he coined the term "noosphere," meaning the theatre of electronic and perhaps telepathic human communication, our global village overhead. In Pierre's model as outlined in *The Phenomenon of Man*, a stone is barely ticking over, a lichen is marginally aware, an ant is somewhat brighter, a sparrow brighter still, and *Homo sapiens* perhaps brightest of all. (Presumably today he'd include chimps, apes, and whales.) Fact or fallacy, it's a seductive idea.

At the other extreme of the immortality game is human cloning and other genetic tinkering. Without denying the tremendous value of xeroxing spare parts, beyond that lies a moral minefield. Who decides whom to clone? What about the long wait for the human clone to grow up and do the wonderful deeds expected of it? And how, in a rapidly changing world, do we also replicate the donor's entire environment and upbringing, without which any genetic gains would surely be diluted to uselessness. As Dr. Lewis Thomas has pointed out, to guarantee success we'd have to clone the donee's parents and kinfolk, the townspeople they grew up with, the classmates they studied with, heck, the whole town, the world. Worst of all, cloning bypasses sex. We'd all be identical clones. As long as life was single-celled, sex wasn't needed. Bacteria still don't need it. They just clone themselves every few hours and carry on. When things get uncomfortable, they cleverly encyst themselves (Lyme disease, syphilis), or entomb themselves (TB), to revive years or decades later. If travel is called for, they generate spores (e.g., anthrax).

Impressive as all this seems, they pay a heavy price. Unless and until a chance mutation shuffles the deck, all members of a species are identical. Precambrian bacteria look remarkably like today's. When a useful mutation comes along, their phenomenal reproductive ability swiftly incorporates it into the gene pool.

On the other hand, sexual creatures trade genetic material right and left. Even female aphids, which can breed without partners when it suits them, shop for sex now and then. Sex is life's genetic stock exchange. But the stocks don't come cheap. The price is individual death. We court and spark, then gutter out like candles in the cosmic wind. Yes, our genes do survive in our offspring, but only as a fading echo in the orchestra of our ancestors.

Someone, I think it was Joseph Wood Krutch, remarked that humans enjoy the odd distinction of being midway in size between Earth's smallest and largest creatures. Whether that's true of longevity I don't know, and Joe isn't around to ask. All I know is, the view from here is great. We humans now gaze into deep space, into deep time. We delve deep into matter; the atoms of Democritus (who defined them as *a-tom*, "un-cuttable") hold few secrets for us anymore. Thanks to books, plays, and films, we can explore the lives of people we've never met, and leave tokens of our own. We can even, through imagination, meditation, and prayer, transcend our physical limitations.

As I begin my latest circuit of the sun, I heed my body more. Older and wiser than my chattering cortex, it reminds me that Nature loves a circle—or rather a spiral—that life is short but love is long. As proof, there goes my mayfly, fragile yet imperishable, dimpling the dark water. At each dip she leaves a tiny circle, as if the sky were raining. It *is* raining—raining Life.

Potato Bug Waltz

When they cut out my cancerous prostate in the mid-1990s, the doctor ordered six weeks' rest and no lifting anything heavier than a dictionary. For an avid gardener with May in the offing and seeds in hand, it was a hard sentence. So while my spouse worked fork and shovel and rake, I did the heavy looking-on and dropped the seed. Typically male, some would say.

When the peas and onions came up I still couldn't swing a hoe, but hand-weeding was safe. Even so, time dragged for me. It was like the winter I was ten and housebound with an infected heel. Out my bedroom window I could see my friends skating on Grandpa Saunders's meadow, the meadow that flooded only once in a lifetime.

So, I hand-weeded. I also read those second-hand books I'd brought home two years ago. Caught up on my correspondence. Fiddled with the outline of a book I'd promised a publisher. For the first time in my life, I saw two spiders mating, start to finish. (The male managed to not get eaten.) I did my morning tai chi. I studied dawns and sunrises. Peered inside the private parts of flowers. Discovered that rhubarb is a member of the buckwheat family. Even studied the lichens on our shingled roof.

By midsummer my commonest haunt was the veggie garden — specifically the potato patch, squishing potato bugs, aka Colorado beetles (*Leptinotarsa decemlineata*— Latin for "thin-toed, ten-striped"), on sight. Then I quit squishing and studied their ways. By September I'd gotten to know them right well, even to admire them a little.

One has to marvel at their tenacity and tactics. Even after weeks of slaughter, I still found adult beetles feeding (sometimes two or three on the same plant), found beetles hiding on the stem or in the earth around the base, beetles ambling on the ground from plant to plant, beetles laying eggs on the undersides of leaves, and, in one case, a ménage à trois — or so I presumed.

Anyone who grows potatoes in these parts has met this pea-sized red defoliator. But while commercial growers deal with them by spraying insecticide from a tractor seat, we gardeners meet them one-on-one. Actually it's their smaller red-and-black, pear-shaped grubs that do the most damage. Hatching out from eggs laid on the emerging leaves by overwintering beetles, the blackish, pinhead-sized progeny make for the topmost leaves, the roof-top restaurant with the tenderest vittles if you will. Being cold-blooded daytime feeders, they need the sun's warmth to loosen their morning joints; the dark colouration helps with that.

Their timing is exquisite. As the topmost leaves unfold, they're waiting with knife and fork. As the plant expands, so do they. Their goal is to pupate into adults before every leaf is gone. As the grubs fatten, they become more visible to birds and to their chief predator, the ladybird beetle. So they move back downstairs to munch on larger, tougher leaves, while new grubs take their places upstairs. Soon the plant, half-stripped, hung with pulsing red larvae and skeins of bug shit, resembles a Charlie Brown Christmas tree. Meanwhile, below ground the spuds are few and stunted.

Just what is this pest? As its name implies, it's a western species. Since its main host is a South American import, what did this insect originally eat? The answer is nightshade (*Solanum*), a poisonous potato relative. It so happens that today's industrial potato, *S. tuberosum*, is a souped-up nightshade from the Peruvian and Bolivian Andes, an Incan staple millennia ago. (Tomato, eggplant, and tobacco are close cousins.)

As the potato spread — Spain had it from the conquistadores as early as 1573, then it reached the Netherlands and Switzerland, then England in the 1580s, and by 1719 Londonderry in New

Hampshire was growing plenty—so did this pest. It showed up in Ontario in 1870, and from there reached the Maritimes and eastern British Columbia by 1919. Today it's found country-wide except in Newfoundland and coastal British Columbia.

Being an import, the Colorado beetle has few natural enemies hereabouts. Their diet may help explain this, since all parts of the potato plant are poisonous, even the underground tubers if exposed to sunlight. (They turn a telltale green. Heat removes the toxins, but the tuber's ends should be removed before boiling anyway.) Proper hilling—covering with earth—prevents sunburn. And since the new tubers form above the planted chunk, hilling also lets them grow bigger. I once tried covering the cuttings with hay, but the hay rotted and let in too much light, resulting in small green spuds.

Normal potatoes are an excellent source of carbs, niacin, calcium, and vitamin C. In fact, with milk they make a perfect food. (Is that why I like scalloped potato so much?)

Sixteenth-century British housewives didn't know all this. They saw the new import as a nasty nightshade, unfit to eat. So when Sir Walter Raleigh introduced the plant to England in 1583, people treated it merely as a curiosity. Maybe it was Raleigh who started the rumour that potatoes would cure impotence. Rich men paid big money to try the Viagra of its day.

It took 250 years for its culinary wealth to be appreciated. By then it was a staple food on both sides of the Atlantic, especially in Ireland, whose cool, moist Andes-like climate was perfect. So much so, that when blight devastated Ireland's crops between 1845 and 1847, a million peasants starved and another million emigrated. Today North Americans consume on average 33 kilograms per annum, much of it in french fries and salted chips. Potatoes have become the world's fourth largest food and forage crop after wheat, rice, and corn.

Yet blight is still a threat. More than once the US would close its border to Prince Edward Island spuds because a single field showed signs of it. Agriculture Canada continues its vigilance at Newfoundland's Port aux Basques port-of-entry to prevent contaminated soil and golden nematodes (a tiny borer) from entering the mainland via North Sydney. On my second last trip they even confiscated some souvenir beach rocks I had in the car.

Next to blight, growers fear a beetle outbreak. The main options are insecticides or hand-picking. As a greenhorn gardener in the early 1970s, I opted for insecticides. It soon became clear that my bugs were immune. For years, I later learned, local seed potato growers had relied on chemicals like Paris green, nicotine sulphate, malathion, and Sevin. The weaker bugs had all been weeded out.

To my surprise, rotenone (aka pyrethrin) proved lethal. Seems the beetles had seldom or never been exposed to this natural pesticide. However, it was expensive, faded fast, and wasn't good for pets and wildlife. Reluctantly, I finally switched to hand-picking, with rotenone a last resort.

If our potato patch hadn't been smallish, one hundred metres of row at most, we couldn't have managed. Back then parenting and work and housekeeping kept us too busy. What we needed was one of those nineteenth-century, hand-pushed patented "Potato Destroyers" we'd seen at Nova Scotia's Ross Farm Museum. A water-filled tank on two wheels topped by a rotating wooden flail, it knocked the beetles and grubs off and drowned them below. That's when I turned to child labour. Neighbourhood kids and ours needed pocket money and we needed potatoes. Training was easy, and, because they enjoyed the hunting aspect, supervision was no problem. At a penny a beetle it was a bargain for me. At squishing the yellow egg masses they weren't so keen, so I handled that myself. This system worked well for a few summers. Then, suddenly—sunrise, sunset, where does the time go?—my workers grew up and found better jobs.

Sometimes my busy spouse pitched in. Meanwhile she was developing a big herb garden. Soon it was pick-my-own or quit

potatoes. So every summer, from June through August, twice
a day if the sun was shining, less if it was cool or rainy, I did
so, and still do. One good thing, the adult beetles are easy to
spot. Like most insects that taste bad, they wear bold colours,
in this case black stripes on yellow, which stand out against the
dark leaves, warning birds off. Even so, this insect makes use of
camouflage and playing dead. From my journal:

> When I touch them accidentally, or even shade them
> with my hand, they crouch lower. If I then poke them,
> they fold their legs and let go. A few latch onto a lower
> leaf and resume feeding, but most land in the furrow and
> roll to the bottom, where for a time they lie motionless
> among fallen yellow leaves, looking like a dusty pebble
> in the dappled green light, all but invisible.

Harder still to find are those that land belly up, their under-
carriage being chestnut brown like the dirt. So many land this
way that I suspect them of deliberately rolling over, like the
hog-nosed snake is said to do. But I've never caught one doing
so. More likely evolution, having made them bean-shaped, also
made them top-heavy. The first time it happened I blamed my
eyeglasses. They really do vanish.

One day I capsized a live adult onto my palm and observed it
through a 10X lens. For a long time the beetle struggled in vain,
working its legs like slow pistons. My hunch seemed as good
as proven. Then the bug surprised me. After trying repeatedly
to hitch to the skin of my palm with its needle-sharp twin
toes, it suddenly raised one wing cover, shot out a pink wing,
flipped over, refolded the wing, lowered the cover, and resumed
walking. The whole thing took less than a second. Oddly, even
then it didn't fly.

The wing itself was interesting. It was transparent, pinkish
red, and surprisingly long for so small an insect. As a reward
I let my guinea-beetle go. On purpose I placed it between a

healthy potato plant and a healthy bean plant about a metre away. The beetle, hungry from its exertions and from being interrupted at lunch, wavered only a moment before heading off. Fifteen minutes later it arrived at the bean plant, and, like Jack in the beanstalk fairy tale, commenced to climb. Alas, there was nothing to eat. It stood waving its antennae for a while, then made its slow way back down. In fairness, maybe the pervasive smell of potatoes confused it? I've had that happen myself, driving near chip joints on an empty stomach.

Then too there's the conical hole around each potato stem made by its motion in the slightest breeze. The falling insect, bounced inward by the foliage's natural spiral (which helps funnel rain to the roots), tumbles right down the chute! There, safe as a woodchuck in a rock pile, it waits for the gardener's footsteps to fade and climbs back up to eat some more.

While keeping emerging adults under control, I also look for eggs. One must, or it's game over. They appear almost as soon as the plants poke through, tiny clusters of five-millimetre–high yellowish cylinders. Glued to the undersides of leaves in stacks of a dozen or two, safe from birds, out of the rain, incubated by the warming earth, they hatch in ten days or so.

Trouble is, what birds can't easily see, neither can people. My best method was to walk the rows and, after nabbing the bugs, to sweep each spray of leaves upward with my open hand. Once an egg cluster is spotted, a sideways smear of the thumb is all it takes. If the mass is large, I remove and destroy the leaf. On the whole I was doing okay. I call it the potato bug waltz.

Eventually, I got tired of all the sticky brown goo on my fingers. Gloves wouldn't work, so I equipped a peanut butter jar with a funnel big enough to take two or three adult insects at once, and just tipped them in. To kill them I at first used kerosene, but soapy water worked just as well.

System or no, one day I was chagrined to discover fully one-third of my plants re-infested with newly hatched larvae. Within a week they morphed into masses of squirming hump-backed beet-red larvae, growing fast and chomping voraciously. Since they were too tiny to pick, I took to clapping the whole top of the plant, leaves and all, between my palms to crush them.

As the millennial summer waned, my technique improved. The rows greened up again. I let down my guard. It was a mistake. Three weeks later a new kind of potato beetle appeared, a smaller, paler version, noticeably softer between the fingers. The second generation had arrived. And because fall was coming, they were even hungrier than their parents.

A week or two and they'd be laying eggs. If I dawdled, they'd hatch a horde of overwintering insects for next year. I stepped up my patrols. By August my fingers were stained so brown people were asking if I'd taken up cigarette smoking — chain smoking at that. In the end I got a decent crop.

That summer of my recuperation was the last time I've been cozy with the Colorado potato beetle. As my health came back, I looked for shortcuts. A few years later, I tried genetically modified seed, i.e., potatoes spiked with the soil bacterium *B. thuringiensis kurstaki*. The BTK worked fine, but since the treated seed cost a third more and our co-op had only one kind ("Superior"), only a fourth of my patch got the royal treatment. Moreover, expecting miracles, I foolishly slacked off picking. The beetles cleaned up on the rest.

Until last fall, I'd found no better remedy for potato bugs than hand-picking plus rotenone, plus mulching, plus fall tilling and the usual crop rotation. Then I read some intriguing facts. First, potato bugs normally overwinter in the sod surrounding a garden, not in the garden itself, which means they must travel each spring to the new potato patch. Second, although they can fly, they prefer to walk. (Flying is hard work on an empty stomach.) Third, they shun slippery surfaces.

These facts have led me to surround my upcoming patch with a dry moat lined with black silage plastic. At the time of this writing (late June), it's too soon to assess this experiment. But, knowing my adversary, I don't expect much.

The Hornet Dilemma

One June day I was up a tall ladder, hat-less, eyeing a crack in my workshop wall when a small triangular face popped out. It was followed by a trim-waisted black-and-yellow body pulsing with nervous energy. Once, twice, this insect buzzed my bald head like a Star Wars interceptor, then landed, still twitching ominously, at my elbow.

Much as I admire hornets, they always rattle me. My hands tightened on the ladder rails. My lazy handyman thoughts gave way to primate fears of falling from my tree. I know hornets seldom sting unprovoked. I also know that of all the wasp tribe they are the most hot-tempered, and that, like their *Hymenoptera* kin the communal bees and ants, they often sting en masse.

Luckily this wasp didn't sting. Perhaps it was a male, which lacks the required ovipositor/hypodermic. So, more likely a female too busy to bother. Certainly she looked busy. To see why, I leaned closer. With her sideways jaws she was ripping up strands of weathered plank and kneading the grey fibres into a spitball, which she then airlifted into the crack. As she went in, another worker came out.

Then it dawned on me. Of course. They were making paper. For a nest. In my workplace loft! Part of me felt honoured that a queen wasp, sole survivor of a 1997 colony, had chosen me for her landlord. But another part didn't. No, a history of hornetries, some painful, some frustrating, some downright embarrassing, stood between us.

What to do? Ignore, for the sake of ecology, this ticking time bomb? Or simply caulk the crack, sealing her doom? Carefully, so as not to disturb my tenants, I climbed down to think it over. All afternoon my mind was on hornets. Most Canadians have

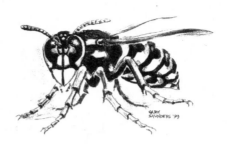

met *Vespula*, the genus to which our common yellow jackets (*V. maculifrons*) and bald-faced hornets (*V. maculata*) belong. Handsome, fearless creatures, nectar feeders, they often show up on sunny fall days to help people sip pop or eat ice cream.

My encounters with *Vespula* seem more personal than most. The earliest involved a wasp nest, which my cousin Frank and I found the summer we were nine and ten respectively, a nest we proposed to destroy with boiling water since no one would give us matches. The nest was a good five minutes' walk from home, yet no sooner had we emerged with the hot kettle than something nailed me between the eyes. We surmised that a sentry wasp, smelling murder, had shadowed us and waited. Extracting the sting was easy with Grandma Saunders's black mud cure. Curing my fear is taking longer.

A few years ago, watching three replica Viking long ships sail into Halifax Harbour and minding my own business, I got stung on the arm for standing too close to a trash barrel. There have been Septembers when hornets wouldn't even let me cover my firewood. One summer a hornet crawled up my pant leg during lunch with guests at my dad's fishing camp and...

But enough. Petty grievances aside, this insect, like the orchid and the octopus, represents a pinnacle of animal evolution. To look into its inscrutable face is like gazing across the gulf of evolutionary time. Insects were already ancient when conifers and dinosaurs appeared. They were the first to live on dry land, the first to fly, the first to see a flower. Hymenopterans invented farming, pottery, apartment living, air conditioning.

And of course paper. Yet we can't communicate with them. Biologically they're closer to lobsters than to us.

To me the hornet's jewelled eyes and improbable sideways jaws are both reassuring and discomfiting. Reassuring, because they prove that some of Nature's designs endure. Discomfiting, because they warn newcomers like us not to get too cocky. Later that night, flashlight in hand like a burglar, this primate crept up his ladder in padded slippers. Quickly, before Queen Vespula could rouse her warriors, he nailed a lath over the seam. This cowardly act bothered him until a couple of months ago, when he noticed a grey globe growing in the east gable of the family home, and he breathed a little easier in spite of himself.

Bumblebee Hotel

The queen bee sleeps. At least I hope she sleeps. If she doesn't I could get stung. For she's inside my patio woodbox where I store extra kindling. How did she get there? I invited her. Not knowingly — who wants a bee in their woodbox, let alone in their bonnet? Especially when she'll soon lay eggs and rear a buzzing brood? No, it was accidental. Unthinking, I'd bored six 3-centimetre ventilation holes along the box's base.

That's all it took. Next spring a scouting bumblebee queen, newly woken from her solo underground slumber — all her siblings having died or dispersed the previous autumn — checked it out. She'd already scouted our orchard, berry patch, two gardens, and the neighbouring fields to ensure ample nectar and pollen for her coming brood.

Normally, bumblebee queens nest in abandoned rodent nests, or they choose rock piles, grass tussocks, hollow logs, even old bird feeders. Why then would she choose an old woodbox given to me years ago? Likely because, apart from easy access, the box faces sun-ward, sits on a roofed deck, and is virtually rain-proof under its hinged tongue-and-groove lid.

Maternity site chosen, she wove a nest of fine grasses under the kindling. Then she secreted belly wax to fashion a honey pot to feed herself during egg-laying and mothering. Next she fashioned a waxen storage urn called a brood cell, which she half-filled with pollen. Onto this she then laid tiny eggs. Capping the cell with more wax, she brooded the eggs like a hen until they hatched. (*Bombidae* — their Latin family name — being larger than honeybees and furry, generate heat.) The hatched grubs spun cocoons, pupated, and emerged as juveniles, mainly workers two-thirds her size. The rest were future queens.

Come spring those workers, fanning out over the surrounding district, explored and mapped the best flower sites. From those, as spring unfolded, the workers harvested, in sequence, pollen from willow catkins, pollen from the flowers as they bloomed—coltsfoot, dandelion, shadbush, and mountain-ash—even the blossoms of red maple.

My first inkling of all this came one June morning on the patio as I did my warm-up stretches and tai chi. Hearing a hum, I turned to see a furry black-and-yellow bee tumble from the central hole. "Well, good morning!" said I, feeling complimented. Within weeks the other holes were busy every sunny day.

It was fascinating to watch close-up. Suddenly an outbound bee would appear, pause to orient itself, and hurtle away on propeller-like wings doing up to 130 beats per second, far faster than a honeybee's, so fast they were almost invisible. Physics says so bulky an insect with such small wings shouldn't be able to fly. Fly it does, and very well. Hairiness likely helps but high RPMs are key.

My box was busiest on windless days. Incoming flights, bulky with yellow pollen, sometimes jostled outbound traffic; generally, there were no jams and things went smoothly.

It helps that bumblebees are normally easygoing. I've had them come and go between my bare legs without mishap as I levelled a stone doorstep they were living under. Superior cold tolerance may account for this—a slower metabolism perhaps? Unlike the honeybee, introduced from Europe in the 1600s, they're a native insect fully adapted to East Coast weather. True, as honey producers they're so-so; as pollinators they excel.

Of course, if you grab or squeeze a bumblebee it may sting. Grandma Saunders got stung once. Unknown to her, the bee was in the rubber boot she was putting on and...Ouch! But the mistake was mutual and understandable. And Grandma didn't much mind, because by next morning her arthritis was gone!

No, bees are single-minded, doing a job both complex and urgent. Each type of flower offers only a brief harvesting window.

The blossom mix varies from week to week, forcing them to constantly update their flower maps. And of course most nectaries close up shop at night and before rain. Also there's competition from commercial hives, and from other native bees plus solitary species like mason and leafcutter types.

What the queen's hidden woodbox nest actually looked like I had no clear idea—and didn't care to peek. With the box so busy I avoided disturbing it. But after it fell silent that October I did peek. What I found was a fist-sized, pock-marked lump of yellowish wax with empty cells inside.

Never did I actually see Her Majesty. Down there in the semi-dark she led a pampered sultana life laying eggs, her every need met by nursery bees, while her outdoor crew collected and stored winter food. Such colonies can have several hundred adult bees, not counting larvae and pupae. And nothing is wasted. They even recycle empty pupal sacs into nectar jars.

The bonus for humankind and wildlife is superb pollination. By going from flower to flower, heavily dusted with living male pollen, tonguing nectar from each one, they fertilize fruit trees, berry bushes, cukes, squash, peppers, tomatoes, you name it. Further, bumblebees uniquely practise "buzz pollination"—microscopically shaking a flower till it releases its treasure. And, being so large and well furred, they can work in cooler weather and at higher altitudes than honeybees can.

Worldwide, with some four thousand species in North America alone, bumblebees make possible a third of our food, one of Nature's many essential services provided for free in perpetuity—if we're careful—without cost or fanfare.

Unfortunately bumblebees, like honeybees, are in trouble. According to *National Wildlife* magazine, four widespread continental species are already gone from parts of their former ranges, and a fifth may be extinct.

And by this summer my little bee hotel was vacant too. Did I do something wrong? Was it because I removed the empty honeycomb, which the queen and her brood left behind? Yes, the old queen had died; but where was her successor?

Whatever the cause, I'm now a landlord without tenants. To my surprise, doing my morning tai chi on the deck, I miss their morning company, their cheerful day-long industry. At first I blamed this year's massive crop of cattle corn north and west of us. Smart dairy farmers hereabouts rotate fodder crops: grass for a year or two, then corn, then alfalfa, then back to corn. Corn it was this year.

It seems counter intuitive, but corn (aka maize, anciently bred from Central American teosinte) is actually a grass. Grasses rely on wind, not flowers, to spread their fertilizing pollen. So, no nectar and no insects needed. Moreover, most farmers, before seeding corn, kill the previous year's weeds and wild-flowers with herbicides. So the field next door went from lush, flowering alfalfa (a legume) one year to instant food desert the next — though many deep-rooted dandelions survived. Worse, systemic pesticides like neonicotinoids can poison pollen and insects both.

Sure, my usual buckwheat cover crop helped the bees. So did our usual roadside parade of wild carrot, fireweed, golden-rod, and wild aster. But they alone couldn't bridge all the blossom-less or stormy days. There's another possibility. Last spring, to restore my garden's nitrogen, I sowed half of it to red clover — a bumblebee favourite. In fact, bumblebees are among the few insects able to reach the nectar in its tiny tubu-lar blossoms. By midsummer the clover was in full rosy bloom. Then, before it set seed and became a permanent weed, I tilled it under. And this year's cover crop is rye — another grass.

So maybe their sudden disappearance was my fault. There is *one* hopeful sign. On sunny September afternoons that year, our New England aster patch was alive with bumblebees harvesting late nectar. Three different bee species, no less! So by now, with frost in the air, there's a queen or two sleeping out there some-where. Just not in my hotel. Maybe next year.

Ticked!

" Gary, you've got a tick," said my long-time British Columbia
friend. He's visiting back East, and we've just returned from
a half-hour afternoon stroll along an abandoned railway line
nearby.

"I do? Where?"

"Above your right collarbone." He points. My bearded chin
is in the way, but the bathroom mirror confirms it, an adult deer
tick settling in for a blood meal. Already her head is buried in
me. The location being awkward for mirror work, I invite my
friend, an engineer by training, to do the honours. Fetching a
kitchen chair to the sun porch where the afternoon light is best,
I sit facing the window opposite him.

We both know the drill: using tweezers grab its head, not
the rear end, which can detach and leave infected mouth parts
embedded. Instead, grasp the front end as deeply as possible,
then pull slowly and firmly until the beast lets go. My friend
commenced.

In recent years this spider-like parasite, also called deer tick,
has become a real concern for anyone spending warm-weather
time in our outdoors. According to Dr. Vett Lloyd of Mount
Allison University's tick and Lyme disease research centre, Nova
Scotia's South Shore "is probably the worst place in Canada" for
this eight-legged arachnid. The province's Health and Wellness
department concurs. HWD now ranks over a dozen areas of the
province as high risk, double the number a few years ago.

Migrating birds — not bird dogs as once supposed — are the
major tick spreaders. And global warming is extending their
range northwards. Northeastern states like Maine and Vermont
used to be too cold for ticks to overwinter. Now the bugs not

only survive but breed earlier—and enjoy a longer season to do their mischief.

Once an adult female tick gets a full blood meal—mostly from mice or deer, including *their* diseases—she can lay anywhere from two thousand to five thousand eggs. By the time the hatchlings reach pinhead size—easy to miss during routine body checks—they're ready to boogie.

Even un-engorged adult ticks, not much bigger than an apple seed, are hard to spot. Fully engorged with blood, however, they're more the size of a small bean and unmistakable. Either way, the bite is painless—and doesn't always leave the telltale reddish ring.

At the time of writing there is no vaccine for Lyme. Prompt diagnosis plus antibiotics usually work—but not on a recently identified viral type. Worse, there's a new European strain of Lyme emerging, which standard testing doesn't pick up. The only sure protection, says Dr. Lloyd, is to catch them *before* they bite. "It's got to be like brushing your teeth," she says. "You do it before bed—and really you should be doing it every time you come indoors."

Lyme is a debilitating disease. Symptoms range from flu-like to lifelong maladies like severe headache, joint pain, facial palsy, heart palpitations, and nerve damage. Lyle Petersen, a director at America's Centers for Disease Control and Prevention, warns: "People really need to take this seriously."

Indeed.

No joking matter. But given my narrow escape, surely a guarded chuckle is okay? Like I said, we begin the extraction. A few minutes in, my friend—let's call him Doc—remarks, "Gary, do you still have that old Kephart woodcraft handbook I recommended? He has tips on this."

"I do. In my study upstairs." Doc detaches me and I fetch the thick little 1921 edition (22nd printing, 1965), and resume sitting. From page 255 he quotes: "To remove a tick without breaking off its head, drop oil on it, or clap a quid of moistened tobacco on it, or touch it with nicotine from a pipe, or stand naked in the dense smoke of a greenwood fire or use whisky externally, or hot water, or flame."

Patient re-attached, we try the whisky cure, Crown Royal Canadian rye to be exact. No response. Tobacco then? We're both non-smokers. At this my spouse, worried now, offers to borrow a cigarette from Farmer John next door.

"Wait," I say, "there might be some dottle in my old pipe I sometimes smoke on hikes. Lemme check my knapsack in the garage."

Again Doc un-tweezes Miz Tick and me. Returning with the briar, I find enough charred tobacco to make a nicotine paste, which Doc daubs on the beastie. All of her eight legs start to flail. Whoopee! But she still doesn't let go. After ten more min-utes of pulling, Doc leans close, squints hard at the tweezers' raised pup tent of skin, and mutters, "Maybe I should cut it."

Cut it?!? My long-time friend wants to cut me? Likely with an unsanitary pocket knife? Shaking my head, I say, "No-o," citing the risk. "Anyway, we're aren't giving the pulling method a fair shake," I say. "Each interruption lets the bug dig deeper."

Doc frowns. I press on: "It's sorta like team tug-o'-war, where any slack you give helps your opponent. No, believe me, the pulling method works. My 2016 tick took a good half-hour to let go. Taking a tiny chunk of me with it—but who cares?"

Doc's a reasonable guy, so he re-clamps and resumes. That's when I chuckled. Couldn't help myself.

"What's so funny?" says he.

"Well," I said, "what if my guest *likes* booze and tobacco with her blood meal? What if she's playing us for suckers?"

At this my wife, relieved, says, "I'll go make us a pizza for supper." Doc keeps up the tug-of-wills. I brace for the long haul. Fifteen minutes later, my parasite lets go. Should have got an antibiotic, but forgot. So far, so good. Knock on wood.

Part Five
Work & Play & Food

Down to Earth

a time to cast away stones,
and a time to gather stones together
— Ecclesiastes 3:5

The last thing I expected to see that spring day, hiking the woods and fields north of Truro in central Nova Scotia, was a patch of chives in purple bloom. *Chives?* I thought. *Out here?* Moments later I found a rectangular hollow lined with tumbled stones: a cellar. Highland Scots I guessed, early 1800s. Nova Scotia was a popular destination for refugee Scots back then. McCallum Settlement and McKenzie Settlement aren't far away.

A hole in the ground. Most pioneer homesteads began that way. Our old farmhouse straddles such a rock-lined hole. It was dug not by Scots, but by offspring of New England Planters who came here in 1761 to occupy Acadian lands taken in the exile. They dug such a hole to plant hope in, a reverse grave so to speak. Sobering thought.

Sobering—yet also comforting. For I like having raw earth and bare rocks under me. I was reminded of this during our February 2004 blizzard, the one that knocked out our power for thirty-six hours. I'd drawn off drinking water the night before, but to flush the toilet I needed one of the emergency pails of water I keep down cellar for that purpose (toilet water, you might say) and for washing.

The pails being in the earth-floored Old Part, where I go too seldom since we built the extension, I decided to revisit our foundations. Setting the pail aside and ducking cobwebs and low beams and furnace ductwork, I started my flashlight tour. These walls are barely 140 years old, yet they seem ancient. The

141

stones—mortar-less, uneven, and dusty—would not look out of place in a Roman dungeon. That's because they were placed hurriedly by farmers using whatever came to hand, catch-as-catch-can, between haying, turnip-hoeing, fencing, and the hundred other chores of nineteenth-century homesteading, with winter breathing down their necks.

Primitive though such a rock-lined hole seems, it was (and is) very practical. For one thing it buffered the upstairs cold in winter. Lowland frost in our latitudes rarely penetrates below one metre. Down there the temperature hovers near 10° C year-round. Ten degrees may feel chilly in mid-August, but in mid-February it's almost cozy.

However, winter warmth wasn't the old-timers' main reason for digging cellars. It was to store food. Lacking the luxury of a quick drive to the supermarket, they went "down cellar." It was all there, ready to hand: shelves of jam, pickles, wine, mother-of-vinegar; slabs of bacon and cheese; hanks of ham; barrels of apples; fragrant strings of onions; dried fruit; sausages and blood puddings; tubs of corned beef and pork. Root crops were mostly stored in a separate underground cellar; turnips smell bad come spring. Fresh beef and venison they hung on hooks in an airy next-door shed. Needing a Sunday roast, they sawed it from a rock-hard haunch. When mild weather thawed the outer layers, they ate steaks for a while. Security.

But the Saunderses aren't *that* secure, nor need to be. Yet there's a distinct sense of peace down here. Hearing a blizzard's muffled roar outside is only part of it. I never feel this in the new basement. On the contrary, its high cement walls and level cement floor seem to chide me: "You really should insulate," they whisper, "put up wallboard, lay a proper wood floor. Make us look respectable. Save on heat, too." Luckily, the Old Part is too low-ceilinged (or too high-floored) for easy renovating. Plus, it's damp. Without a major tile-drainage job, the new wallboard and flooring would be ruined in no time.

Anyhow, it would be a shame to cover those rocks. Our own private geology exhibit! Take the north wall for instance, the one with the outside hatch. Its topmost slabs are brownish sandstone and slate that originated as sand and clay sediments in some ancient lake or sea. Now they make a level base for the house's hand-hewn sills. The upper stones are smaller than the rest — not a bad idea if you're a short man lifting heavy rocks shoulder-high all day. (People really were shorter back then. If you don't believe this, walk up to a protective parapet of the Fortress of Louisbourg in Cape Breton and note how low they were.)

So the biggest, heaviest rocks sit at the bottom. Too heavy to heft, roundish boulders really, they were simply tipped into a prepared ditch and levered into line with crowbars and poles. And sheer brawn. Most consist of coarse-grained, whitish granite or diorite, glacial erratics brought here from kilometres away, from today's New Brunswick even. Dropped when the ice melted millennia ago, most were buried deep inside gravel domes and rolling drumlins. But the uppermost eventually got frost-heaved to the surface, menacing plowshares and drawing curses until each year's crop was hauled to a fence-line or, eventually, dynamited. And the best ended up in cellar walls.

Playing my flashlight beam around our walls, I look for other patterns. They're elusive, because all gaps are chinked with smaller stones. Overall the stonework resembles the rip-rapping that highway engineers use to bind steep slopes, except that most rip-rap stones are more angular, giving a tighter fit. I did notice how the workers laid, under the sloping hatch chute where firewood and harvest vegetables are tumbled in, two large horizontal stones, one slab above the other, for extra support.

Our stones range from football-sized to beach ball–sized. Their rounded corners suggest repeated grinding against other rocks, either in ocean surf or in a meltwater stream. The flat-sided ones got that way from being dragged over rough bedrock, like a block of cheese across a grater. The few angular stones were split by frost or by enormous pressure.

In this dim light, with all the dust, I find it hard to make out their real colours. Grey and tan predominate, but over there I see pinkish granite, and next to it some dark green coppery peridotite. All are foreign to this district, which is floored with rust-red sandstone, the same easily erodible formation that gives Minas and Cumberland Basins their pinkish water. Those greenish stones are metamorphic—altered by heat and/or pressure—and almost certainly came from the nearby Cobequid Hills across the bay, themselves the eroded roots of lofty mountains thrust up when ancestral Africa rammed the North American plate eons ago to form the Appalachian chain.

None of this geological stuff would have troubled the original workmen; they had too much to do. First of course they had to dig the hole. By their measurements, 5 feet deep it was to be—just enough for a shortish person to stand up—and 40 by 32 feet, allowing extra for the walls' thickness. In the old days that meant moving over 300 cubic yards of earth by hand. (We postmoderns, faced with excavating a basement for the extension that replaced the old porch, simply hired a backhoe. The operator managed it within a week. Watching him made me wonder how in the world those old-timers managed the main hole. Digging the nearby well I could picture, but...)

For it is and was dull, repetitive work. What did they talk about, argue about? The big topic of the mid-1860s was the American Civil War—uncomfortably close, really, and hard to stay out of when you had kinfolk involved. Then there was the impending union of Upper and Lower Canada. Mostly they talked small talk: the price of flour at the mill, a strange barn fire, so-and-so's fine filly.

Once the big foundation rocks were rolled in and aligned, it was a simple matter of laying stone on stone until the job was done. Well, not *that* simple. There was also endless sorting, matching, trading, and culling to do—and that outward tilt to maintain. Fingers got mashed, shins barked, knees knocked, backs put out (usually by young bucks showing off). It was a grand way to get hernias and hemorrhoids too.

With the topmost sill stones in place, the work would have shifted from amateur to professional. Pick and shovel and crowbar gave way to adze, auger, plane, chisel, folding rule, level, hammer, and saw. Heavy beams, horse-logged last winter and broad-axed on two sides—"toe the line, hew the mark, let the chips fall where they may"—became the rough-hewn wooden sills and joists. All were mortised and pegged together with whittled trunnels (tree-nails). Inch-thick hemlock planks, sawn last summer for under-floors, wall sheathing, and roof boards, were brought from the barn on padded shoulders and thrown down, sending thunderclaps across the fields, startling the cattle. A chorus of hammering broke out as handfuls of square iron nails were pounded home to make the squeak-free subfloor. In slanting light the boards showed the tooth marks of the local watermill's up-and-down saw.

Steadily the new house took shape. One week it would be walls and studs, complete with window and door holes. A few days later the upstairs subfloor was being laid, with a ladder sticking up through the stair hole. A few more days later it was rafters, then roof boards, then shingles. Splinters ran under fingernails, water blisters rose and broke, thumbs were whacked. Before the outer walls were boarded in, thin spruce laths were tacked across the outer studs and "rendered" with plaster to stop drafts and trap dead air—an early and effective form of insulation. Clapboard followed, plus pine soffits and fascia along the eaves, and pine-trimmed windows, doors, and corners.

Painters arrived and slapped on coats of primer and white paint outside—all lead-based, but no one knew the danger then. Inside walls went up. Bricklayers built up a twin-flue chimney, one side for the stove, the other for a wood furnace and parlour fireplace. Knotty pine floors were laid, windows and doors were fabricated and glazed on the spot. The inside ceiling and walls were plastered, completing the weather seal. And one fine day the whole thing was done. Whether the owners tacked a ceremonial pine to the roof-tree in true New England fashion I don't know. All I know is that for that one day, this old house was brand new. And that the dead Bishop Pippin apple tree down-slope, when I felled it and counted its annual rings, was 135 years old.

Sometime later, but long before our arrival, someone installed a concrete soft-water cistern fed by rainwater off the roof. The district's water was and is "hard" — rich in calcium and iron — which made it tough to get whites clean. A hand pump lifted this lovely soft water to the kitchen sink and washtub, easing the housewife's tasks considerably.

But this was small potatoes compared to the next improvement — a drilled well and electric water pump. These made possible an electric washer with clamp-on rubber wringer, hot and cold running water, a bathtub, and the wondrous flush toilet!

The cellar got complicated after that. Shiny copper lines and stout iron pipes branched off to all corners alongside the wood furnace's octopus of metal ductwork. Only one remnant of that era is still with us, a big cast iron pipe jutting from the south wall. It was probably cast by a mining company then active at Londonderry across the bay. A ghost town since 1913, in its heyday this important iron mining and smelting centre boasted five thousand people when our house was young. For decades, the company's four blast furnaces lit up the night sky. Several Maritime towns still use sewage mains supplied by it.

My underground thoughts are interrupted by a gurgle of waste water heading for the septic tank. Ahhh, the septic tank. What fun we've had together, me standing here, struggling to punch a hole through invading elm roots with a six-metre spruce pole, you trying to asphyxiate me with methane gas. Or me outside, pick-and-shovelling down through snow and muck, trying to locate your concrete lid for the cleanout guy, yet always missing it on my first try. *Aaarggh!* Let's not go there.

Back to my stones. Stones are mysterious. Mystics ascribe strange powers to them. Vibrating quartz crystals made early radios function. No less an authority than priest-anthropologist Teilhard de Chardin believed that stones possess a sort of pre-consciousness. I've often wished my stones could speak. What stories they could tell, tales of miners, diggers, builders, and renovators, not to mention the families who have lived here, ours included. On the other hand, would I want to revisit all the stupid things I've said?

Let's not go there either. Let's go outside. February's blizzard is long gone. The geese are back from South, the snipe are winnowing overhead, flowers are blooming. Underground is no place to be in springtime.

A Salmon for Supper

Some years ago I saw, outside a Nova Scotia fish shop, a sign saying "Fresh Salmon." Inside, a friendly aproned guy greeted me and began to recite his offerings: haddock, cod, flounder, sole. But I had a strong yen for salmon, and asked to see one. From the icebox he swung a small specimen onto the counter.

"Four pounds?" I said.

He flopped the salmon onto the scales. "Four and a quarter." Somehow the closeness of my guess tickled me. Some buried memory, some youthful memory had spoken.

"How much?"

"I'll give you that for $18.50."

"Is this the normal price for salmon now?" I asked, taken aback. "It's been a while."

"Well," he said," thumb-nailing a silvery scale off the counter, "it's a bit high due to the time of year. And this one came from a fish farm."

Later, driving home with my prize cradled in a newspaper full of ice cubes, I traced that buried memory back and back until I came to Uncle John Gillingham, salmon fisher of my Newfoundland childhood.

Uncle John was stepbrother to my father's mother and seemed incredibly old, at least seventy-five. I was maybe ten, so the year would have been around 1945. My father would have been upriver, guiding anglers to make a few dollars. "Son," my mother would say, "go see if Uncle John is in from his nets yet, for the tide is falling. If he is, you can get us a nice salmon for supper."

Out our gate and down to Grandpa's wharf I ran, whence I could see, eastward, the net stretched between peeled spruce poles from near shore to maybe a hundred metres into deeper water. Called the leader, it led the incoming salmon out to a triangular pound or trap at the outer end. You made a pound by folding two sections of the leader back on itself, leaving only a narrow vertical slit between. Floating corks, not poles, held those two sides up, while lead weights below kept them vertical in the tides. Beyond, securing the pound itself, were two rock-filled, homemade wooden anchors called killicks.

The incoming salmon, scenting their home river the Gander from several kilometres out to sea, would arrive some moonless night on a high tide. Trimming the shore where the current was weakest, they would blunder into the leader. Under water the leader's dark brown twine was all but invisible. To render it so Uncle John had steeped it in spruce cone tea, which also preserved it. Because its meshes were too small to snag them, they would turn outward and follow the net pole by pole until they saw the vertical gap.

Freedom! But once inside the trap few would escape; confused, they would mill around, get entangled and die. Thus Uncle John would catch a dozen or more each night. Sold, they would bring in enough dollars—no pension or Old Age Security back then—to feed his family through the summer. Come fall he would smoke a few dozen in a sort of tent to sell at a much higher price, keeping a few for family. I can taste them now—delicious!

A glance from the wharf told me he had just "hauled his net," lifting or dip-netting his catch one by one aboard. Now he was standing in his punt, pulling himself shoreward hand-over-hand along the leader, picking out the night's catch of flotsam—eelgrass, twigs, and driftwood—as he went. Then, still standing, he began to row ashore. He rowed facing forward, a little hunched, moving his elbows in wide slow arcs like a saddleback gull winging home.

I raced back and told my mom. She pressed a large silver coin into my palm. I fingered its ribbed edge and tried to read the twin inscriptions: "NEWFOUNDLAND, 50 CENTS, 1924" on one side and "GEORGIVS, V, DEI GRA. REX ET IND. IMP." on the other. According to my older brother Calvin, the words were Latin for "George V, by the grace of God, King & Emperor of India." Gripping the coin, feeling important, I hurried down the road to the Gillinghams' place. I knew how King George felt.

By now Uncle John is standing behind his large splitting table, tying the yellow oilskin apron around his lanky frame. Beside him on the table are a narrow knife and a dark grey whetstone hollowed from long use. In a wooden tub beside him lie eight plump salmon, bright from the sea. The table, though scrubbed, glistens dark with dried blood.

"What do 'e want, me zun?" the old man says, smiling down at me. All the Gillingham men are tall. His ancestors began fishing salmon here in the 1780s. Later they got a grant from Queen Victoria to do so. Like them he speaks the singsong dialect of England's West Country, the dialect of Thomas Hardy. They say *var* for fir, *linnet* for net (i.e., linen net), *athwart* for across, *duckish* for dusk, *doman* for woman. The words feel oddly comforting. Today our parents seldom use those old words anymore, and we youngsters almost never, except in jest. All we retain are the soft accents.

Waiting for my reply, my great-uncle plucks a flat black spidery thing from the largest fish's flank and grinds it under his thumb. "Sea louse," he says in disgust. "Bloodsuckers, they mostly falls off in fresh water."

"Sir, Mommy sent me to buy a small salmon," I say, flashing the coin.

"Oh aye," says he. "A five-pounder for your ma, then." He selects a suitable one, slides it onto the table, whets his blade on the smooth grey stone — two strokes this way, two strokes that — and deftly opens the snow-white belly from vent to crimson gills. Pulling out the guts, he flings them into the brook. "The eels eats they after dark," he says. Finishing, he deftly scoops dark blood from along the gutted salmon's spine.

Absorbed in the dance of hand and knife, I fail to notice what it is he so gently places in my palm. But as he finishes scraping the fish's scales I peek. It is the salmon's heart—still beating! Saucer-eyed I stare at this pale pink pulsing thing no bigger than a bean. The old man chuckles.

The salmon descaled and rinsed, he holds it out to me. We trade silver coin for silver fish, and I brace myself against its weight. A wet salmon is slippery; to drop it in the dirt would disgrace me in his eyes. Uncle John holds it out by the gills, but I fear their sharp edges. Instead I opt to carry it by the tail, the way all rivermen do. Gingerly cupping the heart in my left hand, I reach out my right, wrap my middle and index fingers round the small of the tail and clamp my thumb firmly behind.

Being too short to dangle the fish, I hoist it in front of me. Holding it so, elbow braced on hip, frowning with concentration, I parade up the road, past Dolf Gillingham's house, past Grampa Saunders's shop, past the ice house and wharf, past the cow meadow, to our gate at last. My arm aches, my fingers sting, but no matter. All I want is to show my mother the salmon's beating heart.

A fish out of water soon dies. A heart out of a fish out of water dies even sooner. When I open my hand for her, the thing lies still as a stone. For perhaps ten minutes I grieve over it, then something else takes my fancy and I forget.

Until, that is, decades later, when I bought that Nova Scotia salmon. I might have forgotten it too, but for the memory it triggered and the lesson it taught—that life and death, beauty and sadness, are inseparable.

Of Seals and Cod and Us

Walk early some weekday morning past my cousin Ross's service station on the Gander Bay road in northeast Newfoundland and you may hear hammering from the shed out back. That would be his dad, my Uncle Harold, building yet another riverboat. His mother's people began fishing salmon here in the late 1700s. He's lived here all his eighty-eight years, and there's little he doesn't know about the local wildlife. However, one recent summer he saw a new sight: harp seals cruising offshore. Harp seals, an ocean species, in the Gander River estuary, in summer? Very odd. And he wondered whether the cod crisis had something to do with it.

Well he might. Newfoundland's 1992 cod moratorium had been in force six years. Offshore there were still few fish, but in the bays cod seemed to be coming back. Maybe the seals knew this and were chasing them inshore? Maybe there were just too many seals?

Animal rights groups like the International Fund for Animal Welfare (IFAW) couldn't care less. Their emotional ads target alleged cruelty and insist that even the limited hunt be halted. But the Canadian Sealers Association wants the hunt expanded. Who's right, and what's to be done?

No one denies that the seal hunt has been inhumane. And it's true that human greed did more to destroy the cod than ever seals did. Cod aren't even a big part of a seal's diet—perhaps 15 per cent at most. For an adult harp seal that works out to a mere 7 kilograms or less a week. Many pet dogs eat more protein than that. But it's not that simple. We need to ask how many seals are at the banquet, and what they eat besides cod. Several decades ago, when cod were still plentiful and seals scarcer, seals reputedly took more commercial fish than all the Gulf of St. Lawrence and Grand Banks vessels combined.

In 1994, federal scientists estimated the Gulf and Front herds at 4.8 million harp seals, increasing annually by 5 per cent, or 750,000 pups a year. The 1997 estimate, minus a harvest of 270,000 adult seals, was 5.8 million. The Canadian Sealers Association maintained that if we add hooded seals and the four other common species, a 1998 figure of 8 million was not far-fetched.

Why so many seals? They weren't always so plentiful. As recently as the 1940s, St. John's merchants like the Bowrings and Crosbys were fretting over dwindling catches. Originally the industry was land-based and small. Men strung great hempen nets between headlands and islands in December (hence "seal fishery"), and caught the southbound harp seals by winching the nets up and down on a lookout's signal. The resulting income, coming as it did in the off-season, made it possible to overwinter in an ice-bound northern outport after the fishing season closed. Many northern outports owe their very existence to sealing.

Then in the late 1700s, someone discovered the vast whelping grounds off northern Newfoundland — "The Front" — and sealing moved from a mid-winter subsistence enterprise to a major springtime industry. Sturdy fishing schooners were sheathed below in tough greenheart wood and copper, fitted with ladders ("side sticks"), extra bunks, and water tanks, crewed with hardy fishers, and sent "to the ice." In 1832, an exceptional year, this matchstick fleet fetched home 744,000 pelts.

The coming of steam and steel around 1860 enabled vessels to punch their way to the main herds, and half a million pelts a season became common. Captain Abraham Kean alone fetched home over a million pelts during his long career. The herds got a respite during the latter years of the Second World War, when Hitler's prowling U-boats kept the ships in harbour. By 1947, the hunt was going full steam ahead again. Norwegians, Brits, and others competed with Newfoundland and other Canadian vessels. For the first time, radio-equipped spotter planes scouted the way.

It couldn't last. Newfoundlanders themselves began to demand strict quotas. Dr. John M. Olds, head of Notre Dame Bay Memorial Hospital and fleet surgeon in 1947 and 1948, warned in a report to the Newfoundland Fisheries Board: "At the rate they're going, not a seal will be left in ten years." He also protested the killing of whitecoats and the inexcusable waste of good meat.

Although politicians were slow to listen, the groundswell of protest grew. By the 1970s, thanks to the media savvy of Brian Davies and the help of French film star Brigitte Bardot and others, it had become an international issue, sparking first a boycott of all Canadian seal products and finally a total ban on the hunt itself.

Was the ban too much of a good thing? It is a biological truth that, other things being equal, mammals under heavy predation produce more and healthier young. Nova Scotia's small game biologist Neil Van Nostrand proved this in the 1960s by experimentally trapping long-protected beaver in western Nova Scotia's Tobeatic Sanctuary. Is it possible the seals, suddenly released from decades of hunting pressure, rebounded like a coiled spring?

And might this seal resurgence, coinciding as it did with unprecedented pressure on cod stocks by domestic fleets and foreign factory ships, have contributed to the cod's demise? For even if each seal eats an average of only two kilograms of cod a week, that's over one hundred kilograms a year. For the whole herd it must add up to around half a million tonnes a year. Moreover, even if seals never touch cod, they compete with the cod for capelin, herring, and squid, its principal prey species.

So, of course, do we. During the cod's catastrophic decline, Ottawa allowed unparalleled harvesting of capelin and herring for overseas markets. I never realized how vast an appetite this fed until one afternoon in 1984. I was visiting my mother's younger brother, Harry Layman, at his home overlooking St. John's Harbour, when a huge deep-laden tanker appeared below us, gliding seaward through the Narrows.

"That," fumed Uncle Harry, "is full of capelin for Japan. How many Newfoundland beaches do you suppose they stripped to fill a vessel that big? A damned good many! And d'you know the worst of it?" He lit a fresh cigarette and took a long drag. "The worst is that the buyers will take only spawning females. The males must be dumped!" We watched the tanker for a while. Then Harry, son of a Fogo cooper who fed his family by building fish barrels for the Labrador cod trade, stubbed his half-smoked cigarette in disgust.

Later, back in Nova Scotia, I saw news clips showing bulldozers burying truckloads of fresh herring, rejected by buyers for the same reason.

We may have put yet another nail into the cod's coffin. A friend of mine who installs sonar gear on longliners believes undersea oil exploration may hurt codfish and that they've hushed it up. Petroleum geologists, in order to locate and map subterranean gas and oil deposits, routinely set off underwater explosions and record the echoes. Because fish, in order to navigate, locate prey, and find mates, depend on input from delicate sensors along their lateral lines, he feels sure that explosion process is harmful. Indeed, while testing newly installed sonar equipment at full volume, he has seen groundfish rise to the surface and circle aimlessly. He maintains that if sonar beeps can stun fish, then undersea blasting can kill them. He may be right. As a teen I once fired a .22 bullet into a school of brook trout and was startled to see several turn belly up, stunned but not dead.

Even if he's wrong, how could any fish, even one that lays some three hundred thousand eggs a year, withstand the pressures cod have endured? And, once depleted, how tiny an upset would it take to seal its doom? Perhaps only a few degrees rise in water temperature, a shift in water chemistry, a little more pollution, a die-off of plankton could bring it on?

So blaming seals for it all is like blaming the cute raccoons that pilfer our garden corn or the graceful coyote that lopes into the dawn with a newborn lamb in her jaws. Yet suppose those raccoons increased a million-fold, stripping fields of cattle corn, driving up the price of beef, milk, and cheese. Or suppose coyotes multiplied until sheep-farming became impossible, until no small mammal could be left outdoors unguarded? Bleeding hearts or no, the public would demand strict controls and bounty hunters would be cheered.

The difference with seals is that their depredations are far out to sea, out of sight and out of mind. Most of us never see a seal except in a zoo or wildlife park. To watch these splendid carnivores performing in captivity is one thing, to see them at work in the wild is another. My father once witnessed a seal feeding frenzy at a federal salmon-counting station on the Gander River. As hundreds of salmon milled around, waiting to get through the gate, a pack of harbour seals arrived. First they glutted themselves, then they went slashing right and left through the schools, tossing salmon heads and tails in the air like beach balls, until the river ran red. An artificial situation, true—but instructive. My father itched for a shotgun.

One can perhaps understand such anger. And perhaps we can pardon out-of-work fishers and sealers for feeling that seals are sea-going coyotes, and for objecting to IFAW's slick anti-sealing ads. They reject the notion that seals, because, unlike cows and hogs, they live "wild and free," are therefore sacrosanct. Canadian Standards Association (CSA) spokespersons rightly point out that humans have already altered the seal's world irrevocably, just as we have altered the bison's and giraffe's, that if we hadn't ruined the cod stocks and decimated the seals' natural predators in the first place, seals mightn't pose a threat.

But we did, and they do. Like it or no, we have a duty. How can the moratorium and 200-mile limit succeed when hordes of hungry seals skim off every small gain? How can we let millions of seals fatten on scarce protein while half the world starves? For here we have on our doorstep a cornucopia of high-grade protein, oils, and pharmaceuticals (e.g., natural insulin), not to mention leather, furs, and fertilizer. This horn of plenty flows continually without pesticides, herbicides, growth enhancers, antibiotics, gene tinkering, soil erosion, pond eutrophication, or wildlife habitat destruction. Tapping its wealth entails no more cruelty than a well-placed bullet or a sharp blow to the head—standard techniques in any well-run abattoir. It entails none of the inhumanities of muddy feedlots and fetid poultry barns, nothing as unwholesome as mad cow disease, no subtle cruelties like denying a barn-shackled dairy cow the feel of spring rain on her back.

No, the hunt must be expanded, not reduced. Our herds are in no danger of extinction. Even the IFAW doesn't claim that. Indeed, a population so bloated is courting starvation and disease—Nature's cure for overpopulation—a remedy that would leave us without either cod *or* seals.

Nonetheless, sealers needn't kill whitecoats. Nature already prunes them hard. Even before their mothers abandon them at three months to breed, untold thousands are minced by storm-churned ice pans. Thousands more are gobbled by polar bears, sharks, and killer whales on the long journey north. Others starve or succumb to parasites or disease.

Instead, hunters should concentrate on adult harps and hoods and maybe greys. (As for harbour seals, which eat mainly coarse fish like sculpins and eels, let them remain a tourist attraction.) And from now on, sealers should bring back the whole animal, not just the flippers. To discard good red meat may be convenient but it is inexcusable. Nothing whatever should be wasted. Seal meat has been proven to be very high in protein and iron and very low in "bad fat." Seal-based salami, pepperoni, sausage, and tinned meat have easily passed market tests. Seal oil capsules are on some drugstore shelves and selling well. Although Ottawa said it would withdraw funds for seal R&D, market research demonstrated that the industry holds great promise beyond its traditional trade in hides and oil.

If tinned seal meat takes off, the planet will have a new protein source, one which Indigenous Peoples and New-foundlanders have enjoyed for centuries. Conceivably, idle longliners could be refitted and silent fish plants could hum again. Apart from creating desperately needed jobs and taking thousands off the tax rolls, an expanded sealing industry would gradually prune the herds back to healthy levels. And maybe, just maybe, it would save the cod, capelin, herring, and squid for our children's children.

Oatmeal Shenanigans

❝Eat your porridge or you'll be late for school!" How many outport children have heard that admonition on cold winter mornings? Half awake at the kitchen table, sky still dark outside, ready for school more or less, but still shivery from your warm bed. Someone—mom, grandma, an older sister, maybe dad, has spooned hot oatmeal porridge from a saucepan into your bowl. Thick grey glutinous stuff. Not at all appetizing.

Yet.

"Pass the brown sugar, please?" In with the sugar. "And the butter?" In with the butter (or margarine). "Milk?" In with the milk. Now, spoon in hand, you poke at the goop. Slowly the hill of sugar subsides into a pale syrup over which the butter melts, floats, and spreads. Pressing your spoon into this, you flood it with the milk. Suddenly, archipelagos of gold and white appear, a dreamlike world.

"Gary, stop playing with your food! And don't spoil your appetite by eating just the sugar!" You stir it once, twice. The islands disappear, you pout a little, then settle in. Actually, it's not bad. Anyway, I always ate it first. Only then would my appetite for the rest, toast or egg or whatever, kick in. Moments later, as I dressed for outdoors, my stomach would feel warm and full. That bowl of porridge would carry me through long division, the Battle of Hastings, and the geography of the Amazon, all the way to lunch.

Such winter mornings made me a porridge eater for life. Oh, there have been flirtations with Cream of Wheat, puffed rice, and the like. Corn Flakes too, because back then the Corn Flakes carton featured a ship model you could cut out and assemble. And some had a coupon you could send away for a free jet plane ring. (The spring-loaded plane launched but wouldn't fly.) And later there were relapses involving our own kids' breakfast fads, their chocolate-coated this and honey-coated that. But oatmeal porridge always wooed me back, especially in winter.

It wasn't just the subtle bread-like flavour — if anything oatmeal's bland — but what I could put *into* it. That's the great thing about bland foods — they invite experimentation. With porridge that could include more daring adulterations. Let me tell you some of mine.

But first let's look at the grain itself. Compared to wheat, rye, barley, and rice, most of which predate the Egyptian pyramids, cultivated oats, *Avena sativa,* were a relative latecomer. Oats didn't become popular until European farmers started using horses as draft animals some two thousand years ago. This aggressive wild grass proved ideal for horse fodder. It thrived on poor soils and, being frost-hardy, could be grown farther north. And pound for pound it contained more protein. Thus, farmers could graze their idle ponies on cheap hay, switching to high-octane oats for jobs demanding more horsepower, or for foaling. "Feeling her oats" is thus no idle phrase. Dairy cows were also fed oats to give more milk.

Some years ago, roughly 50 million tonnes of oats were grown worldwide annually, mostly in the former USSR. Of that, only 5 per cent or so goes for human food, usually as breakfast cereal. In Canada our average annual per capita intake has dropped from 1.53 kilograms in 1976 to 0.81 kilograms in 2001. Our grandparents ate far more, especially if they came from Scotland. Scots loved their oatmeal almost as much as their malt whisky, and their oatcakes are still legendary. (I ate some with a real Scotsman in the Highlands so I know.) Oatmeal was also used for quenching thirst. Haying in hot weather, our neighbour Carman and other old-timers would add some to their water jugs because it soothed their dust-caked throats and tongue membranes. Skin specialists still swear by it.

Well, times change, customs shift, even eating and drinking habits evolve. Wholesome commonplace things become quaint and comical. Centuries ago, the English made jokes about the Scots' love of oatmeal. Dr. Samuel Johnson (1709-1784), author of England's first real dictionary, penned this definition: "OATS—A grain which in England is generally given to horses, but in Scotland supports the people." The English writer Sydney Smith (1771-1845) called Scotland "that knuckle-end of England—the land of Calvin, oatcakes, and sulphur."

Never mind, Sam and Syd. The Saunders' household still does its best to boost that 5 per cent. Though our kids have grown, oat bran muffins and oatcakes still disappear pretty fast. Some oatmeal even goes into bread recipes. One daughter eats it to avoid wheat gluten. We drink gallons of oat straw tea, a most soothing beverage. The bird feeder claims a fair bit too. My shaving cream allegedly contains oat oil. But by far the most goes into porridge. Actually, oatmeal is a misnomer. Technically "meal" means crushed grain, a substance slightly coarser than flour, more like the stuff in those little packets of pre-cooked instant oats served in B&B breakfasts. Real rolled oats consist of hulled and steamed kernels (groats) that have been squeezed flat between steel rollers and dried.

"Porridge" itself is an interesting word. Derived from "pottage" (i.e., something made in a pot), it arrived via Middle English *porrey* and Latin *porrata*, a broth of leeks. From the same word comes "porringer," a special bowl for that cereal. As a child I had my own porringer, a heavy white china thing with a wide flat rim, untippable. It had the alphabet printed in block letters around the rim and a barnyard scene painted on the bottom inside. Did that dish make me a writer on rural themes? Could be.

As I said, it wasn't the porridge alone that captivated me. My experiments in adulteration began with "rounders" in pre-Confederation Newfoundland. Rounders are young cod taken as by-catch (i.e., accidentally with the main catch). Being too small to lay flat, they were pickled and sun-cured in-the-round. Pre-soaked in hot water and drained, they made a nourishing protein snack—and were delicious shredded into hot porridge. My father showed me how.

Later, in college Upalong, I experimented with other supplements. Spices, for one. To me, cinnamon was no good in porridge and ginger was not much better, though candied ginger root was nice. But nutmeg! A few flakes grated onto porridge improved the flavour wonderfully. One taste of that piney flavour and I knew why Western navies fought to control its Asian sources. This relative of mace was literally worth its weight in gold. Long since introduced and grown throughout the tropics, it's now cheaply available everywhere. However, nutmeg contains the poisonous hallucinogen myristicin, which they say addles the brain. Being already half-addled, I try not to use too much. Liquor is quicker anyway.

Speaking of liquor, an elderly neighbour gives me a bottle of whisky whenever I do some little thing for him. The trouble is, a 26-ouncer normally does me a year. "Bob, if you must give me something make it Belgian dark chocolate." But Bob likes his malt so the whisky keeps coming. You can only store or give away so much whisky. When I heard that alcohol is good for the arteries, I tried some in my porridge. Not bad! The alcohol evaporated, but the smoky oak-wood flavour stayed.

That was my only health-driven adulteration. For oatmeal isn't lacking in health benefits. Fibre, for example. Regularity, as health writers so delicately phrase it, becomes more important as we age. They recommend half a cup a day, any kind. However, chewing straight wheat bran is like gnawing shredded tree bark. Sprinkling it on hot oatmeal helps—but why, when oatmeal itself has fibre enough? Whichever, be sure to drink lots of water. "If you don't," a nurse once told me, "it turns to concrete!"

The great thing about bland fare like porridge is how well it blends with other food. Later, to save time on busy mornings and to entice our kids, I premixed my oatmeal with blueberries, raisins, peanuts, pitted prunes, dates, and for a time, chocolate chips. (Not so good.)

Hereabouts is as good a place as any to confess my weirdest oatmeal adulteration. When my youngest heard about the garlic she cried, "Dad, how can you eat *that* in your porridge? Yecch!" Shocked by her revulsion, I replied, "Well my love, garlic is *good* for people, the more the better! We eat it in salads and stir-fry, why not in porridge? Just think of me as a space alien with outlandish dietary habits."

But she was right. Garlic really *does* spoil the taste. And one *can* take food experiments too far. For instance, my experiment with dulse, a seaweed. Though a neat organic way to get my dietary iodine, sea salt, manganese, and gold, it failed for the same reason. Heated, the stuff just turned rubbery. And afterwards the kitchen stank like low tide at Grand Pré.

Failures aside, I'm proud of one time-saver. No dishwashing chore is more disgusting than a cold porridge pot caked with grey goop or carbonized oatmeal. That's likely why so few people bother with oatmeal anymore. Ideally one should either soak it overnight or slow-cook it in a double boiler like our grandparents did with coarse oatmeal. "Quick" oatmeal hadn't been invented, and the wood stove was on all night anyway. We postmoderns can't in good conscience run the electricity or gas all night for that. Even firewood is too expensive for that these days. It so happens that my smallest stainless steel bowl exactly fits the lid of the sizable kettle we keep on the wood stove for winter humidity. Seeing this I thought, *Why use a pot at all? Why not cook it right in the kettle?* Voila! — a double boiler.

Recent changes to my less-work power breakfast have been minor and health-driven. Instead of boxed bran (often high in sugar), I add fresh-ground organic flax seed or chia before cooking. I also add a tablespoon of soya flakes (for the lecithin). The cancer-fighting properties of certain small fruits have led me to top the cooked cereal with a handful of frozen blueberries or homegrown black currants. They chill the cereal, but cooking them would destroy valuable nutrients. Finally, instead of butter or margarine, I use cold-pressed virgin olive oil.

For sweetening — I gave up brown sugar years ago — I add a dollop of organic blackstrap molasses. Blackstrap is ordinary molasses without the sugar. Pours slow in cold weather and stains your oatmeal dark brown, but what odds? A bit bitter too, but loaded with iron. That's why old-time doctors prescribed it for anemia. My uncle Aubrey, recovering from TB circa 1947, took a daily dose — and gave me my first taste. Ever since, I've liked the name. Sounds like something out of *Treasure Island*.

Part Surgeon, Part Seamstress: A Fly-Tying Memoir

One March some years ago, I took in the Atlantic Sports and RV Show, and there, behind the muscular speedboats and knobby-tired ATVs and gleaming trailers, lay a little artificial fly-casting pool. The winter had been long. I hankered for the sight of open fresh water, any open fresh water. I stood for some time and stared at this pool, fascinated by its ripples and reflections. They conjured up the kiss of a well-placed line across a curling riffle, the quicksilver flash of a salmon's rise, the swirl and suck of tail and fin as it struck, the cicada song of the reel as it bolted. And it brought to mind one long-ago winter in Toronto when I tied two hundred moose-hair flies.

The flies weren't all for me. As an art student with a wife and infant son, I couldn't afford even a fishing licence that year. No, the flies were for my father and his brother Don to sell at Saunders's Camps on the Gander River in northeast Newfoundland. When my father launched the business in 1948, he'd fully intended to make and sell his own salmon lures. He did buy the wherewithal—only to discover that the dexterity and patience required to fasten slippery feathers onto little hooks were not in him. So at age fifteen I inherited a fly-tying kit and a hobby.

In pre-Confederation Newfoundland most angling supplies came by mail from Hardy's of Great Britain or from a St. John's agent. And though that venerable house in Great Britain stocked just about anything an angler might need, to my knowledge they stocked no moose-hair flies. Back then maybe no one else did.

The credit for introducing the moose fly to the Gander usually goes to Sandy Parsons, a local guide and outfitter. My older brother Calvin, himself an outfitter later, recalls seeing it fished near O'Leary's cabin on First Pond Bar around 1945. Of course the fly was said to be deadly—what new fly isn't?—but in fact it *was* very effective under the right conditions of water and weather.

Parsons, it seems, never marketed his pattern. Over the years, various local guides played variations on it, yet no standard local design evolved. British or American clientele who'd heard of the fly couldn't buy one locally. Fifteen years later, this was still true. My father, frustrated by this, asked me to design one. "Something respectable, something an angler would buy. I'll pay you two dollars apiece for all you can turn out—and I'll supply the moose hair." (Dad and Uncle Don also ran hunting camps.)

It was a deal, and for me a welcome one—though Dad couldn't have made much on it. You could buy fancier flies for less in most tackle shops. It was, I see now, his discreet way of putting some bread on my table.

For here was his younger son, a recent University of New Brunswick forestry graduate, newly married, with a better-paying job than he himself had ever had, chucking it to become...an artist. To this veteran of the Hungry Thirties, my enrolling at the Ontario College of Art in Toronto must have seemed a ticket to the soup kitchen. And with a baby on the way!

Saunders's Camps were doing fairly well by then. But the season was short, and after paying for the summer's food and gas and oil, plus the cook's and guides' wages, not to mention a new fridge or roof, there was little cash to spare. In any case I never asked.

The kit would need refurbishing. Fortunately, my mother had stored it during my college years. The cement was hard as a rock, and I was out of hooks. I got off a prepaid order to the

States and arranged for Dad to mail it and the little suitcase-kit to Toronto as soon as Beth and I had found an address. Meanwhile I'd design his Respectable Pattern.

The suitcase and supplies arrived in good order. Dad was always a great packer. It came swathed in heavy brown paper, lashed four ways with unbreakable cod line and secured with his trademark woodsman knots. It reminded me of the ten-day survival kits he packed for fly-in caribou hunters. I saved the cod line.

In December the second parcel arrived. It contained a stiff slab of salted moose hide bristling with wild brown hair. For days afterwards, our small apartment smelled like a hunting camp. But our landlady never complained. By January I was in production—and our first son had arrived. Such a task in such a setting demanded a methodical approach. Each afternoon, after my long trek up Spadina Road (to save the fifty-cent trolley fare) and west on Bloor to Howland Avenue, I'd climb the two flights of stairs, greet my spouse, and play with Danny if he was awake. Quickly then, before my resolve faded, I'd clamp vise to table and tie three or four flies before supper. After a week or two of this, it became as natural as brushing teeth—and about as challenging. It was just a way of making grocery money.

My workplace was pleasant enough. We rented from the Roms, a middle-aged Hungarian couple who had fled the Soviet tanks that overran Budapest in 1956. Their three-storey brown brick house had seen better days, but it was clean and warm and dry. Morning sunshine poured through the tall east windows of our bed-sitting room, spilling across the blond oak floor and Danny's crib. Our kitchen down the hall opened onto a tiny balcony overlooking a strip of pale lawn with two flower beds, a Van Gogh fruit tree, and a clothesline. Every fine Monday, lines of washing blossomed between the grey board fences. On a west wind we could hear the rumble of Bathurst Street traffic day and night. At night the sound was distant and restful, like the muted roar of distant rapids. Here, dreaming of another river, I drew and painted and studied—and tied twenty or thirty flies a week.

The origins of dressing a hook to look like an insect to fool a fish are lost in the fogs of time. Today fly-tying is a major hobby and a minor industry, even though a good fly-tyer must be part seamstress, part surgeon, part artist, part model builder—and an angler in spirit if not in deed. For me, half the magic was in the materials. Even my small kit boasted some fancy stuff. I never opened that scuffed imitation leather case smelling faintly of acetone and naphtha without a small kick of delight.

I liked the surgical glitter of its stainless steel vise, scissors, and clamps; the wicked precision of its barbed black hooks; the Persian richness of its spools of silk and skeins of lustrous floss and chenille. There was elegance in the delicately barred hackles of guinea fowl and eider, gaiety in the dyed feathers of assorted barnyard fowl. There was something Christmassy about the glittering coils of tinsel, the metallic sheen of teal specula, and peacock feather eyes. Even the spiky moose hair was pleasant to the touch.

And the corked vials of red, yellow, and blue cement had a painterly look. All this wealth I got by mail, not from Hardy's now but from Herter's Incorporated of Waseca, Minnesota. Herter's always put a moth ball in any order for feathers or furs, hence the naphtha smell.

Wealth or no, that winter I stuck to my severe regimen of moose hair, black wool, dark hen hackle, and a bit of tinsel. My only extravagances were two epaulettes of jungle cock and a golden pheasant tippet for the tail.

Anyone who has tied an artificial fly knows the routine. There's a soothing rhythm to it, like practising guitar scales after a hard day or, I imagine, suturing a patient after a difficult operation. It demands attention, but not overmuch. Clamp hook in vise, uncap waterproof cement, dip bodkin tip, replace cap, smear hook shank, secure first thread.

My moose-hair lure went like this: Snip some fine tinsel, secure end, wind thread and tinsel forward a few turns, tie off, add cement, position and fasten the tail, add another drop of cement; fasten wool and tinsel, spiral first wool and then tinsel, forward, tie off, tiny dollop of cement; choose and trim a hackle, fasten small end, coil it round itself till the filaments splay out like legs, tie off, dollop of cement.

I built these lures at speed, mindful of my fast-drying cement and the need to clear the table. To rest my eyes, I'd leaf through my book of coloured fly patterns, patterns I'd forgone that winter, beauties like Blue Charm, Thunder & Lightning, Royal Coachman, Jock Scott, and Dusty Miller. Magical names, water jewels, icons of the angler's art. Silk purses compared to my humble pattern.

Anyhow, tying the classic patterns took more time and money than I had. I knew a few of the tricks though. Thus, to render lifelike insect legs, fasten the hackle farther back and wind body material and hackle forward together. To mimic a woolly caterpillar, thicken the body with chenille. To create a multicoloured wing, marry the feathers.

Marry the feathers? That's right — stroke the different colours between thumb and forefinger until they mesh. They mesh because the filaments are edged with microscopic barbules or hooks that zipper to each other like Velcro. (A preening bird does this with its beak.) However, fly-tyers go the bird one better, blending filaments from several different feathers, even from different birds. The trick is to match the filaments. Feathers have a right and left side. Right-hand filaments won't marry left-hand filaments and vice versa. They unzip on the first cast.

Eyes rested, I'd snip a tuft of moose hair (not too little, lest the fly look skimpy; not too much, lest it float), and discard any broken or split hairs. The good ones were dropped tip-first into an empty .30-30 rifle cartridge, which was tapped until the tips lined up. Then the butt ends were cut to length and neatly snugged down—not forgetting the shoulder epaulettes. It only remained to finish the head.

No granny knot would do; it had to be a whip finish. Lacking a whip finishing tool, and unable to master the cat's-cradle finger method, I managed with a bodkin. One final dollop of cement and the fly was set aside to dry. Knuckle sore eyeballs, clamp another hook in the vise, start again.

In essence my moose hair was a slightly gussied up Black Dose. In designing it I followed a proven local formula: "Drab + Sparse = Irresistible." It wasn't just the high cost of fancier materials. Our salmon were consulted too. Like most fish, salmon see colour. However, for some reason Gander River fish favoured sombre-hued flies. It might have been the peaty water.

In any case, I'd been raised to mistrust fancy flies that were designed more to catch anglers than fish. One day a Gander River guide, seeing his sport about to put on a Silver Doctor, politely asked to examine it. Casually he took out a great pocket knife and, frowning through a haze of cigarette smoke and mosquitoes, pruned the fly severely. Just as casually, he handed it back to the sputtering client with a murmured "Now try 'un, Skipper." The sputtering stopped when the fish struck.

I recall too that, except for trout, all the old-time Gander guides swore by low-water hooks, sizes 6 and 8. The small sizes made sense, since our fish were mostly smallish called grilse. But I wonder about the low-water hooks. Their turned-up eye was supposed to keep a fly from diving, but perhaps this preference was a Hardy holdover, like the two-handed split bamboo rods used in Grandpa's day?

All our early patterns were "fished wet" until the late forties, when renowned angler-writer Lee Wulff discovered the Gander. His White Wulff was probably the first dry fly to tickle our pools. Elam and Reg and the other guides were curious, of course. Yet, like self-respecting angling guides everywhere, they took their own sweet time conceding that, yes, maybe, under certain conditions of light and water, a floating fly *might* do better—provided it was plain. (Embracing The Bug would take them even longer.)

In its time and place, my Moose Hair was popular. For a time I cornered the local market. Then came various jobs and helping to raise a family, so my kit went back into storage. Years later, a daughter who liked to fish expressed an interest, so I taught her the basics. It was good to watch her nimble seamstress fingers ply my youthful trade, to see the kit restocked. One day I said, "Gillian love, it's yours to keep." When she left for university around 1994, I kept it in a closet for her.

Until lately. Researching this essay, I wondered if my fingers still knew how to tie a fly. Opening the dusty suitcase, I felt the same old kick, sniffed the same memories. One of them involved my late mother. One day she took a newly completed US order to the post office for me. As a hobby, fly-tying was still unusual in Newfoundland. The mail clerk, reading the foreign address, asked what was in the parcel.

"Flies," replied Mom absent-mindedly, rummaging for change in her purse.

"*Live* flies?" said he, shaking the package near his ear.

"No-o," she said, still fishing.

"*Dead* flies then?" he said, raising his eyebrows.

"Oh my, no!" she exclaimed, coming into focus. No, they were artificial lures her son had made, because, you see, her family operated a fishing lodge on the Gander River, where the limit was eight salmon a day and you could fish great spots like Joe Batts Brook and Fourth Pond Bar and the Sunshine Pool, so why didn't he come down sometime and try his luck? They had a good chat, and she found a new customer.

Dike-Land Rambles

One spring, after my aforementioned cancer surgery, unable to garden seriously or to split wood, I did a lot of walking, either alone or with our dog Sidney. From my journal:

> *Late May, 1995:* Into our corkscrew creeks the pinkish
> Fundy tide rises at the full moon's command, flooding
> the greening *Spartina* grasses. Backlit by a sinking
> coppery sun, their wiry black reflections cross-stitch
> the wet mud. My white retriever—spaniel Sidney half-
> wades, half-swims the rising creek, snapping right and
> left at minnows that flick their tails and escape. Sid
> comes ashore, shakes himself vigorously, a brown
> dog now.

With peeper season past and my garden weeded, Sid and I turn north down a tractor road to the dike-lands half a kilometre away. Farther than we usually roam, but my body complains less now. Our favourite destination is a treed marshy hollow just inside the dike. Here a brooklet, entering the aboiteau which runs under the dike, has made a shallow, reedy pond.

May month here is resurrection time. Now that the male tree frogs (aka spring peepers) are done serenading and their females are busy laying eggs, several kinds of aquatic insects are hatching. One by one they emerge from the dark sun-warmed muck, shed their pupal sheaths, swim to the surface, take their first breath of undiluted air, unfold their wings, rest, then flit off to explore this new world.

The shallow pool, sheltered by tall aspens and fringed with chokecherry just now blooming, is already patrolled by ancient dragonflies. These Maritime dragonflies differ from the big bluish ones I know from Newfoundland, which my Dorsetshire-rooted Grandma Saunders called "horse-stingers" — "horse" being Old English for big — as in *horse*chestnut or *horse*radish — and "stinger" referring to the thin, ten-centimetre-long blue-dappled body.

Instead, these Fundy dragonflies are brownish and smaller with stubby, dark-banded wings. But they hunt the same way, alternately darting right and left between short glides, scooping small flies into the open cage of their dangling legs and up into their jaws. (They remind me of a time, timber cruising on Newfoundland's Avalon Peninsula, when such a horse-stinger alighted on my lapel with a still-buzzing "stout" [moose fly] in its sideways jaws. Bite by bite, starting at the fly's green-eyed head as I watched, it crunched its way from thorax to tail, letting the wings fall free. Moose flies have a painful bite, so I was grateful. Ignoring my thanks, the dragonfly rattled its four wings and was soon hawking high and low for another meal.) Here and there, on tall cattails and rushes, I saw others parked vertically, heads up like linemen on power poles. Their primitive wings, being unfoldable, stayed open.

It was during that walkabout spring that, thanks to cancer, I first studied mayflies, one of the planet's earliest winged creatures. Barely a third as long as the dragonflies, often sky-blue, they're hard to spot until they flit across a ray of sunlight. What they live on I don't know. Tiny midges? Nectar? So much to learn.

A week later Sid and I explored the dikes beyond. First built in the seventeenth century by Acadian emigrants from north-west France's Normandy and Brittany, they fell into disrepair after the 1755 Expulsion. Much later they were repaired and even expanded — for the lush hay they produced. By the 1960s, fully 80 per cent of Maritime wetlands, salt and fresh, were thus so enclosed and drained. A great loss for waterfowl — just ask Ducks Unlimited — but a great boon for farmers.

The original dikes, several metres wide, sodded over, steep-sided to seaward and sloping gently to landward, then stood a metre or so above the highest tides. Now, with rising sea levels and fiercer storms, dikes in sensitive areas (e.g., around Truro) are not only being raised but also armoured with broken rock.

Outside our dikes the commonest plant was and is the afore-mentioned remarkably salt-tolerant *Spartina* grass, forming a virtual prairie clear out to the Salmon River's winding, silty channel. Partly flooded twice daily during the waxing and waning moon, wholly submerged twice monthly at full moon and new moon, the marsh makes nutritious coarse hay—once rain and snow have rinsed away the salt.

Also common in salt marshes are the rosettes of a triangular-stemmed springtime delicacy locally called goose-tongue or marsh greens. To me they taste like fiddlehead ferns. Next come clumps of seaside goldenrod. Inside and upon the dike itself we find the usual fringe of chokecherry, alder, and willow, grading into mountain-ash, white birch, and aspen.

Shading my eyes against the westering sun over our Salmon River estuary, pondering the Acadian Expulsion, that *Grande dérangement*, I envisage, silhouetted against the mud flats, their conical stacks of scythed marsh hay heaped on tent-like French *staddles*, safe above the swirling tides. I also imagine groups of Acadians venturing at low tide onto the sun-dried outer mud flats with horse carts and homemade wooden shovels, loading the rich mud to fertilize their garden plots. To keep the smallish horses from sinking in the soft mud, their hooves are fitted with wide wooden shoes. During dike construction the Acadians also, to prevent the river from undermining the dikes and spoiling their hard-won fields, interwove cartloads of evergreen boughs ballasted with rocks.

The incoming New England Planters and Londonderry Irish who replaced those peaceful folk here in 1761, ignorant of dike-building, preferred to clear woodland. A generation or two later they would learn to their cost that rocky forest soil, especially under conifers, is acidic and soon runs out unless routinely limed and fertilized. Before the advent of commercial fertilizers this meant animal manure. Indigenous farmers farther south, lacking cattle, routinely fertilized their corn and squash plots with fish offal, inter-planting beans to capture nitrogen. Some Newfoundlanders still use fish offal to boost their potatoes, cabbage, and turnips in such soil.

Thus my dog and I, rambling within and without the dikes at low tide, spent many happy hours exploring, breathing the salt-tanged air, smelling the silty muck. Along the high-water mark, especially after gales, we found interesting surprises: tumbled driftwood, lost fish-weir poles, old wharf timbers damaged by giant Fundy tides or ice pans. Or we found uprooted trees, even the odd highway sign, all salt-bleached and interwoven with dead brown eelgrass. Gleaming like stars among the grass lay hundreds of chalk-white baby clam shells, the soft parts eaten I suppose by gulls and other critters. Occasionally we'd find the purplish, four-pointed, empty egg cases of northern skates, a cousin of the giant tropical manta ray fish and, more distantly, of the shark.

One day we found a large dead herring gull, not a mark on its snow-white feathers, its leathery webbed feet still bent in the act of swimming, its hooked yellow beak half open, its upturned amber eye, lifelike in death, glaring accusingly heavenward.

Gardening Lite

L ate one May, having been laid up for weeks by my cancer surgery, I felt it was time to forego deck chair and hammock and get down in the dirt. Or so said my spirit. My body wasn't so sure. True, my morning workouts now included tentative roll-ups and push-ups again. I'd also upped my rainy-day patio walks. Pacing our U-shaped deck from south-side porch to north-side bay window gave me twenty-five metres one-way. So twenty round trips made roughly a kilometre, a safe walk sans ankle-twisting potholes and loose rocks, and a third of it roofed over. And, as my long-time spouse put it, why live in the country and not grow one's own veggies? Still, when we bought the place in 1969, gardening was the last thing on my mind. In fact, when she asked where it would be, I'm said to have replied, "What garden?"

Hard to believe now, for gardening, heavy or light, soon became a big part of my life here. And as a teen, at my mother's urging, I did grow some carrots one summer. For she was born on rocky Fogo Island in northeast Newfoundland, where every bit of rock-free ground was treasured. They even fenced off plots inland among the rocks and bogs, fertilizing them with seaweed and fish offal. Compared to that, our Nova Scotia property was the Garden of Eden.

So, reluctantly at first, my green thumb re-blossomed. Still, starting a garden means spading, which means lifting. And since for our already sizable family we wanted a spacious plot, I hired a guy to till a level space roughly twenty by thirty-five metres down by the gravel road. By June the following year we were in business. Across the road lay the Forbes's south cow pasture greening up.

The plot's only flaw was that, being downhill, it collected cold night air. Chilled air being denser, it would pool there—hence "frost pocket." Many's the time on frosty evenings I've rushed out with bed sheets to cover tender tomato and squash plants. Or, failing that, rushed out at dawn to save them by sprinkling ice water. After several frost episodes we switched such tender crops to Beth's uphill plot.

Why I stuck with my downhill plot was its natural fertility. Long ago, before the road was built in the 1940s, a seasonal brook flowed through my space. Every spring and fall for millennia, swollen by silty meltwater, the brook had widened to a shallow pond and dropped an annual layer of silt. Thus fertilized, the site became a rich alluvial flat. Moreover, for fifteen years it had lain fallow, untilled and ungrazed, a rough pasture knee-deep in yarrow, aster, daisy, tansy, goldenrod, and eyebright.

So now, a year later, I wanted to garden early but couldn't without flouting doctor's orders. The thing is, gardening, like time and tide, cannot wait. And (I reasoned) shouldn't walking on uneven garden ground benefit one's pelvic cradle violated by prostate surgery? The gentle rocking motion promote healing? So why, I asked my wife, shouldn't moderate seeding and weeding do the same? Gardening Lite, if you will? She was skeptical.

But digging after major surgery is dicey. We should have thought of that three weeks ago when, awaiting surgery in Halifax, we'd filled out our spring seed order. For we knew that come May, the warming sun would steam away the muddy snowbanks and dissolve Fundy's dank morning mists. When that happened, we'd be checking our mailbox for the familiar Veseys package promising lush this and that: early lettuce and spinach, crisp peas and carrots, succulent zucchini and winter squash. From her garden would come tarragon and comfrey along with, to quote Simon and Garfunkel's 1966 traditional ballad, "parsley, sage, rosemary, and thyme."

Thus tempted, awaiting that package, by early May I was thinking, *Surely I can hobble down there today, dibble some holes, and drop some seeds in? And later manage some weeding and bug-picking?*

Herself wouldn't hear of it. And, truth to tell, though my urine had lost its bloody tinge, my body still wasn't up to it. The problem wasn't my dozen abdominal staples — they'd recently been removed — it was the risk of bursting internal stitches before they dissolved. That could land me back in hospital. (I would soon land there anyway.)

Regardless, by mid-May, on the sly at first, I began seeding the early greens, the radish, carrots, and beets. I was like that tippler in the Russian parable, who, forced to choose between church and tavern, said, "The church is near, but the road is icy; the tavern is far — but I'll be careful!" Carefully then, kneeling like an old person and using a hand trowel instead of a digging fork, I began. But that wouldn't work for potatoes, without which no garden seems complete. Hadn't my Newfoundland ancestors always said, "Feller's got nar pratie, he's got nothin'"?

Still, potatoes need furrows, in my case sixteen-metre furrows, seven or eight of them, all to be covered with earth once the eyed tubers were cut and set. And later, as the tubers developed, they'd need hilling — more covering — once or twice so the tubers wouldn't sunburn and taste bitter. "Still," whispered my better angel, "best not push it. For now, just prepare the cuttings and get help for the rest; maybe one of the girls will be home."

In the end, my good wife took pity and did both.

Chaga Saga

What are the odds of finding something said to grow on only one in forty thousand birches?

Pretty low, as my neighbour Fred and I learned last winter after searching his woodlot for half a day in vain. Embarrassing for him too, since his young grandson had found some without hardly trying.

But that's the nature of chaga, a parasitic fungus (*Inonotus obliquus*) of birch trees. North Americans are just discovering what Siberian and Chinese peasants have used for centuries to boost and balance their immune systems while promoting overall health. We're also learning that not only is it a potent antioxidant, far surpassing blueberries and the like, this woody fungus is also rich in minerals, flavonoids, phenols, and the superoxide dismutase.

When my hiking friend Ron Kelly told me about this mushroom in 2015, I was keen to see it for myself for two reasons: as a forester, I should have known about it already, and because last Christmas I'd been laid up for a week with some mysterious bug that left me completely exhausted. Maybe chaga could have prevented it.

So when Fred showed me his grandson's chunky find — it looked to me like charred and peeling rubber — I wanted to see the mushroom in the wild. Especially after he gave me a small bag of the ground-up, ginger-brown powder to take home.

"How do I prepare it?" I said.

"Just steep — don't boil — a teaspoonful for five minutes," he said. "Tastes like old socks smell, but sweetened with maple syrup or honey it's not bad."

Well, at least now I knew what to look for. In late April, I'm trouting in northern Nova Scotia with Dave, another hiking buddy. And I'm keeping my eyes peeled for chaga. Pretty soon it's time to boil our noon kettle — half the reason for those hikes. While he's collecting dry kindling, I scout the area for birchbark to start it with.

Nearby, overhanging the stream, is this stout birch. And it happens to be a paper birch, not the yellowish, curly-barked kind that yields very little. Even so, this one lacks the loose papery sheets I'm after. And skinning the inner bark could kill the tree. About to pass it by, I see, on the side of the tree facing the river, a dark, half-metre-long overgrown vertical scar made by high-water ice floes gnawing the wood.

Could that be…?! I peer closer. It is!

Long story shortened, with my axe I chipped and pried off several chunks — too many, really. For I've since learned that these growths take decades to form. Besides, one should leave some for others. On the other hand, over time chaga can girdle and kill a tree. Anyhow, I brought my prize home and ground some in our Lehman's hand mill.

The fish I caught that day are long gone, but I'm still enjoying (and sharing) our chaga tea. Like I say, what are the odds…? About the same, I'd say, as someone finding and returning to me, weeks later, a favourite old woods hat I'd lost that day while taking a cliffy river-bend shortcut. I figure some bushes yanked it out of my jacket pocket. The finder was David, on a repeat angling trip. Had he not done so I'd still have been happy. As it is, I feel triply blessed — for the chaga, for the hat, for such friends.

Cold Room Capers

all be safely gathered in,
Ere the winter storms begin.
  "Come, Ye Thankful People," Hymn, H. Alford, 1810-1871

The August night that lightning set fire to our cellar, suddenly we had a crowd down there. Most were firemen making sure the fire was really out, and the rest were the firemen's girlfriends I guess. As they were leaving around midnight, a teenaged girl asked me what was in the little room behind the furnace.

"Hunh?" I said. Because just then the only thing on my mind was whether, when the power was switched back on, a second electrical fire would toast us in our sleep. "The one with the Frigidaire door," she added, pointing.

"Oh that?" I said. "Vegetables. It's a cold room."

"Oh," she said, and left with the rest.

Back then our volunteer brigade was new. Today's likely wouldn't tolerate camp followers. Yet the girl meant no harm. Another time, I'd have been happy to answer her questions: like how the room's two high vents delivered cold outside air to the floor while removing stale air. How the thickly insulated outer walls and ceiling buffered the nearby oil furnace's heat, while its bare rock walls chilled the contents during mild weather. How I'd rescued the room's fridge door from the town dump.

Even if she had merely suspected me of hiding something in there—a moonshine set-up?—I still might have won a convert to low-tech self-reliance. She might have been surprised to learn that this dinky structure, built in the mid-1970s, my first cold room, was linked to major world events at the time. OPEC's 1973 oil embargo had just driven fuel prices sky-high, scaring the industrialized world into recession. The Cold War was still hot enough for fallout shelters to be on people's minds. Above all, the environmental movement was then brand new.

Maybe it's just as well she missed the lecture. By now, my survivalist zeal was fading anyway. Oil was again dirt-cheap. East–West tensions were easing; soon it would be Business As Usual. Moreover, my storage system was ailing. Mildew was invading from the earthen floor. Soap and vinegar could fix that, but our garden was outgrowing the space anyway. Already I was storing the overflow under the north wall's firewood hatch. This meant leaving the hatch lid ajar all winter, which wasted furnace oil, chilled the bathroom tiles overhead, and could freeze nearby water pipes.

Ailing though the room was, it taught me something about potato thermodynamics. For whenever the first snows came late on frozen ground, the potatoes kept much longer. Why? Because the insulating snow kept the nearby stone wall frosty. Yet they never froze. Potatoes are pretty hardy for a South American species. Dad once took a load eight kilometres by horse and sleigh in sub-zero weather with only a blanket over them. "Won't they freeze?" said Mom. "Not while they're in motion," he said. "The jiggling keeps them warm." And it did. On the other hand, when our Nova Scotia snow came early, burying hatch and all before the ground froze, holding in the warmth, pretty soon the spuds, figuring spring had come, began to sprout. Supermarket spuds don't do that because growers treated them with growth inhibitors. And what about those pre-harvest herbicide sprays big growers use to zap the tops? Another reason to grow one's own if possible.

And what I needed right now was more storage space. The girl's question had simply revived the issue. We had a garden, we grew potatoes, and hungry kids needed more than greens to grow on. Wasn't it Napoleon who said an army travels on its stomach? I'd just have to build a new cold room.

But where?

One night that winter, down cellar, on my knees again, not praying but culling spoiled vegetables, I had an idea. Two, actually. One idea was to enlarge the cold room by tunnelling out under the lawn. (But what if the house settled or the lawn caved in?) The other idea was to convert our concrete soft-water tank. We never used it anyway, not since I'd diverted rainwater into it during a downpour and found it leaked. (The only beneficiary of that experiment was a spotted salamander who tumbled in and spent the summer snatching mosquitoes from a floating pine chip until her world went dry.)

Dry or no, first I'd have to cut a door through eighteen centimetres of flinty old concrete. Back then you could rent a jackhammer for twenty-five dollars a weekend. But never having used one, I feared the racket, the dust, the risk to eye-ear-nose-throat-teeth-lungs-toes. I quietly dropped both ideas. Definitely one of my better moments.

Okay, I'd compromise. Cold Room Number Two would be underground, but separate from the house. Technically that would make it a root cellar. Root cellars had been part of my childhood. In pre-Confederation Newfoundland almost every village had them; some still do. Low, sod-roofed structures they are, their double wooden walls stogged with dry seaweed or sawdust. With their grassy domes, stubby vent pipes, and small doors, they look like hobbit homes.

I could see my Maritime version now. I even pictured goats (to go with the chickens we then had), on the roof. Even though my parents' root cellar wasn't sodded, two of our goats frolicked up there anyway. And when their sharp hooves punched through, Dad had to mend and re-tar.

The best root cellar I ever saw belonged to Mom's sister Fanny and her husband Jabe out on rocky Fogo Island. Their house backed onto a steep cliff featuring a roomy cave. Fitted with a thick wooden door, the cave proved ideal. Nothing ever froze in there. Aunt Fanny would take her basket, step across the yard and vanish into the solid rock like Ali Baba in his cave.

G. SAUNDERS

Lacking a cave, I'd have to dig. To stiffen my resolve I dismantled Cold Room Number One (CR#1), saving only the shelves, fridge door, and pink insulation. From Garden Way Publishing of upstate New York I ordered Bulletin A-76, *Build Your Own Underground Root Cellar* by Phyllis Hobson. She recommended locating the cellar on one's highest ground (for drainage), and close to the house (for minimal snow shovelling). Our ridge top seemed ideal. Its reddish sandy loam made for easy digging. By September the roof was sodded, vent pipe installed, inner (fridge) door hung, steps in place. All it lacked was a storm door. The thing looked almost authentic. I could hardly wait to stock it.

Surely humans are hard-wired for caves. After all, it was caves and fire that got our northern ancestors through the last Ice Age. Why else would people flock to the Cro-Magnon sites in France and Spain, to Kentucky's Carlsbad Caverns? Toddlers still delight in dark cupboards and broom closets; ours certainly did. Later they created "Monster" games wherein willing adults (mostly me) ambushed them noisily from darkened upstairs rooms. Sometimes I scared myself. Or fell asleep, waiting under a bed, when they failed to find me.

When CR#2 was finished I tested my cave theory on guests. Men invariably liked the idea. This was years before pop psychologist John Gray published *Men Are from Mars, Women Are from Venus.* Gray claims we males need a "cave"—alias workshop, hunting camp, den, study—to retreat to when baffled, riled, or sad. (Women just grab the nearest phone.) One day I took our pastor down there. I thought, pastors deal with birth, death, and eternity every day; if anyone needs a cave, surely he does. Sitting in the dim cool silence, he sighed and said, "I could use one of these. Do you rent?"

It was not to be. That fall, with no rain to speak of, the water table rose and rose until my floor was nearly half a metre under. I was dumbfounded. "Water tables are funny things," said neighbour John consolingly. "Remember the old McCurdy barn that used to stand right over there? It had a root cellar. They say some years Raymond had to bob for his cattle turnips."

Grimly I knocked down my handiwork, shovelled the dirt back in, and put my lovely fridge door in the fall cleanup. Of course that year we had a bumper crop. Worse, Y2K was looming. And because the world's computer clocks had never been programmed beyond CE 1999, experts were predicting economic chaos, blackouts, and even nuclear mishaps. Canadians, already rattled by the Great Ice Storm of 1998, hunkered down with candles and battery radios while hired geeks scrambled to save the planet. No time to be without a cold room/bomb shelter.

That New Year's Eve, fed up at last with withered produce, I embarked on CR#3. Why New Year's Eve? Fact is, I had nothing better to do. Somehow that year we'd neglected to invite friends over, and being averse to kissing half-soused strangers at anonymous parties, we found ourselves at home, glumly watching the festivities on TV. Presently I retreated to the basement.

Actually, I'd been researching indoor cold rooms. As luck would have it, that month Happy Harry's Affordable Building Centre in town had a special on 3/8-inch good-one-side plywood. Also, I had two-by-fours left from a summer renovation. And just in case, I'd picked up more pink insulation, a couple of long hinges and a box each of No. 10 and 12 Robertson flathead screws. I even had a spot in mind—the northwest (coldest) corner of our new extension. It was half-blocked by a post anyway.

Eyeballing the corner that night, I felt sure it would work. While the concrete floor was too dry for root crops (CR#1 had an earth floor), at least mildew wouldn't be a problem. The eight-foot ceiling offered ample shelf space. The two exposed concrete walls would hold the cold. There was an electrical outlet nearby for a light and maybe a fan. Best of all, the transom window—small, high up, shielded from rain and snow by the patio deck—would ventilate well. Unlike outdoor cellars, which are naturally cold and need only a small vent pipe, indoor rooms in heated spaces must be able to gulp frosty air in spring and fall, our trickiest storage seasons.

For a carpentry-challenged writer type, the job went surprisingly well. I credit my new cordless drill from Santa. Until now, on principle, all my screw-driving was hand-done. For bigger jobs I just used nails. However, anyone who's nailed full-sized sheets of plywood overhead, solo, knows how wrong-headed that was. One-armed paper hanging is easier. Fixing mistakes is also easier with screws. And for late-night work the cordless is nice and quiet.

By 1:00 a.m., as Ottawa commenced celebrating, I had the insulated ceiling up and the wall studs in place. By 2:00 a.m., as Winnipeg chimed in, I'd sheathed the two outer walls and placed the shelf racks. When I crawled into bed around 3:45, only the insulated door remained to do. Within days our produce was snug inside, potatoes and all. With room to spare.

For me the whole exercise was wonderfully therapeutic. For my spouse and visiting daughter it was, well, less so. The holiday season is stressful enough without Don Quixote banging around down cellar. Still, I felt forgiven when bottled jams and pickles began appearing on the new shelves that summer and fall.

And our produce got a new lease on life. The buttercup squash and Funny Face pumpkins kept well into March. The Yukon Golds, Netted Gems, and Pontiac potatoes lasted well into April. The big Always Tender beets, bagged in peat, stayed sweet into June. Carrots we freeze young—root maggot problems. (Apples we keep elsewhere, because they emit ethanol, which they say causes veggies to sprout.)

Happiest of all were the onions, of which we grow lots. Recently their traditional winter space along the sun porch beams had grown too cold, several braids having frozen. The culprit was our new airtight stove, whose higher output was overriding the upstairs furnace thermostat. Now the onions coasted right into chive season.

Yet CR#3 is pretty basic. No thermostat, no automated window, no fan. Temperature control is *my* job. Fall and spring, unless it's balmy outside, the window stays wide open all night, varmint-proofed with an old fridge rack. On most winter days an opening two or three fingers wide keeps everything just above freezing. During cold snaps and gales the window stays tight shut. Colder still, I leave a 40-watt bulb on. Bitter cold, the door stays ajar. Too Antarctic altogether, I pray for a south wind. Last winter was so severe, so prolonged, I had to insulate the window itself.

I like playing human thermostat. It keeps me attuned to the inner and outer weather. It's like managing a greenhouse, only in reverse. (Have I told you about the mini-greenhouse I built from discarded steel awning frames? How it withstood Hurricane Juan in 2003 and, during the Blizzard of 2004, shouldered a mountain of hard-packed snow without collapsing? No? Another time?)

Funny, how one thing leads to another. One of my rural delights had been to dodge down cellar in the dead of winter, unwrap a Bishop's Pippin and bite into it. The privilege of doing this again inspired me to build a real apple-picking ladder. Compared to those rattly, sharp-cornered, bruising aluminum extension jobs, this boat-shaped beauty is a joy to use. Now all I need for picking perfect Pippins is one of those long handles with a bag on top.

But every silver lining has its cloud. Building that ladder meant sacrificing a straight 18-foot red spruce pole I had lovingly selected and sap-peeled and planed and stored some years back. It was to have been the mast of a saltwater craft my older brother and I had bought in hopes of someday sailing together. Now for sure this mast, sawn in two for ladder rails, will never loft a spread of canvas over Notre Dame Bay. Instead, it keeps an aging apple-picker from falling out of his tree.

SUMMER
STOVE WITH ROSES

GG
July 20/17

Part Six
Householding

This Old House: Honeymoon & After

Last fall, winterizing our century-plus farmhouse yet again, I wondered for the hundredth time was I a damned fool back in 1969 to buy it. The upkeep takes so much time, money, and energy now. New bay window this year. New roof and drip boards — another year. New eavestroughs before that, and so on. Scraping and repainting alone is a major chore if you don't like vinyl siding and can't afford a professional painter. Yet, this old house is full of memories. And it has taught me plenty. To sell it now would feel like a betrayal.

Assuming other rural householders might feel the same way, I proposed a householder series to *Rural Delivery* editor Dirk van Loon, himself a farmhouse dweller. "Make it seasonal and you're on," said he.

My wife and I both have rural roots. Gardening, keeping animals, berry-picking, wood stoves, all that. We even got married in a country church. Still, until moving to Nova Scotia in 1965, we'd always lived in towns, renting. And since in 1964 my new forestry job was in the town of Truro, and as yet we had no car, not even a driver's licence, it made sense to keep renting. We ended up buying a car and renting a place ten kilometres out in dairy country.

I found the place through Hazel, who worked down the hall in the same building as me and lived out there. The farmer who Hazel steered me toward offered a vacant farmhouse for — wait for it — twenty dollars a month. "Outdoor toilet," he explained delicately as my jaw dropped. "For now. And we store cattle turnips in the cellar." We didn't mind. With three kids by now, we'd use the extra cash to pay off our new car loan. As it turned out we were keeping the place warm in hopes their middle son returned from Yukon Territory to help run the farm.

There was another reason we moved to the country: Hazel's high regard for the older Forbes couple we'd be renting from. Indeed, we felt an instant liking for Carman, the witty, soft-spoken farmer who was to become our landlord, and likewise for his spouse, Vi (short for Viola). A third reason was that neither Beth nor I wanted our children to grow up thinking milk came from a carton, water from a tap, and meat only from a grocery store. We also wanted them to feel the seasons change, to see the stars dance in smog-free skies, to learn Nature's linkages.

Soon the house and its sheltering barn became like old friends. And we enjoyed the surrounding sugar maples, the skating pond down the hill, the Dominion Atlantic train that thundered by twice a day, the engineer exchanging waves with our eldest boy Danny, then five or six. Carman and Vi's four offspring having all grown up and left, they doted on our three youngsters like grandparents. For instance Carman, grinding the cows' morning turnips in "our" basement, would get four-year-old Matt to sing for him. And Carman and I had great chats. "How come," said Beth one night when I returned late, "it always takes you two hours to pay the rent? It's only a three-minute walk."

"Oh," I said, "we were talking astronomy. Astronomy and Longfellow's *Song of Hiawatha*." Buying a sack of potatoes took even longer. One night I brought back a puppy inside my jacket, a brownish Airedale-boxer their daughter had adopted but wasn't allowed to keep in her tiny Halifax apartment. After that we got barn kittens for our kids. And then came a baby girl, and a baby boy.

That old house gave us four good years. Then in the winter of 1968-69 came news that middle son John was coming home after all. While we shared his parents' joy, for us it was house-hunting time again. Half-heartedly we scanned the suburban listings. But by now we had no wish to rent a CMHC bungalow with plywood floors, a postcard lawn, and low tolerance for small kids, let alone pets. Nor did we relish raising children next door to a big new mall. Besides, Danny and Janice were already enrolled at the local school, and we knew and liked the principal and the teachers.

In short, we had put down roots. A few frustrating weeks later, Carman discreetly suggested a two-storey farmhouse he owned just down the road. He'd bought it and its half-acre plot years before, but assured us that although the house needed paint and had been vacant for years except for summer visits from its previous occupants, it was structurally sound. We asked some questions, had a look, walked the rooms. Inside, daylight showed through two corners, the ceiling plaster was cracked, and the kitchen floor sagged under a massive chrome-plated cook stove. The place was over a hundred years old and showed it. Outside, the stone foundation had gaps, there were bird nests in the eaves, and the furnace chimney had lost some bricks.

But the roof was level, the shingles tight, the remaining foundation intact. And the well was said to be good. Except for the attached summer kitchen with its headless chimney and its leaning privy, everything was fixable. "How much?" The price Carman named was more than fair. The lot alone was worth more. We talked to the bank again and took the plunge.

The plunge was the easy part. Ahead of me lay a very steep learning curve. My parents, faced with our Newfoundland village's chronic lack of teachers and medical help in winter, kept us on the move, renting town apartments here and there. Renters seldom need to fix things, so I didn't learn much householding except how to replace a light bulb. In the one Toronto high school I attended that offered shop, I took art. At university I studied forestry.

Like they say, we grow too soon old and too late smart. So here I was, catapulted into householding. Oh, I could hammer a nail straight, saw a board true, age a tree accurately. But fixing a water pump, mortaring a chimney, shingling a roof daunted me. Against a plugged toilet, forestry and fine art are next to useless. "An ass-hold around the housette," my long-suffering wife once called me. Ouch.

Since then I've learned a lot. I'm still learning. In this, owning an old home is a lot like life. In fact, a farmhouse is a lot like a person. It has a cellar (the subconscious), an attic (the spiritual realm), and it has...but enough of that.

Oh, but it felt good, walking together that April day around our own property, a decade of renting finally behind us! Soon, likely through Carman, we located a contractor known for fixing up old houses. The first thing Russell did was jack up the works, level it, replace the bad sills, and cement the loose fieldstones back in. (Seems the previous owner, Raymond McCurdy, had a team of horses that "liked to kick." At first he let them punish his woodpile. But they kept knocking it down, so one day he gave them a corner of the house to practise on!)

With the foundation in order and new posts and joists in place, Russell and his nephew Leland tackled the upstairs. To a carpentry-challenged person like me, this was an education to watch. Each day, coming home from work, I'd see progress. Chimney re-mortared with new flashings. Rotten eaves and drip boards replaced. Old wood furnace and pipes yanked out. (Its cast iron "pig" became a dandy garbage burner.) New oil furnace and ductwork put in. Rotten bathroom floor ripped up and replaced. ("Old Raymond must have sloshed his bath water a lot," joked the carpenters.) New tub, new sink, new toilet. Cracked plaster drywalled. Whole place rewired. All I did, besides paying the bills, was get the old Duro water pump refurbished and the well flushed out until the water tested (and tasted) clean.

Finally, the last wagonload of scrap lumber was towed away. As soon as the plaster dust settled we'd be in business. That is, once the carpenters left. Why were they still puttering? They were good men, slow and meticulous, not like me — but our landlord needed his home back! I'd paid each bill on time, dropped broad hints. One morning they found us camped in sleeping bags and blankets on the floor. It was Beth's idea and it worked. No hard feelings, boys, but get lost! We moved in soon after.

But now, a dilemma. Outside, spring beckoned. Indoors, everything looked raw and unfinished. Beth naturally wanted to make it livable as soon as possible. So did I, but I also wanted to plant trees. "An apple tree takes four or five years to bear fruit, so the sooner..." "Your apples can wait, love," said she. "Those walls need paint and that horrid red Muresco has to come off the ceiling." In the end we compromised. She scraped the ceiling and I painted the walls. And planted apples and plums and pears on the sly.

We're still compromising, still renovating. Some days it seems we've accomplished a lot. Other days we seem to be falling behind. Yet for all the frustrations, this old house has given us contentment, even joy. We still scan the classifieds sometimes, but we always end up staying.

Getting to Know You, Old House

Most of us know our houses inside-out — not so well outside-in. The best way to know the outside of a house, especially an old one, is to paint it. I've painted ours, oh, two-and-a-half times since we stopped hiring professionals over ten years ago, and it's been an education. I've discovered things professionals seldom report: rotten corners, split clapboards, sprung nails, cracked caulking. I've solved the mystery of the mysterious rattle that announces southeast gales (loose downspout). I've learned a new respect for old-time craftsmanship. I've even picked up some architectural jargon.

However, half the learning has been in the scraping. For you don't just up and paint a house. First the old paint has to come off. "'Tain't the work that takes the time," says the old-timer, "'tis the gettin' ready." So true.

Hand-scraping paint off old clapboard *is* a royal pain. Like so many of life's chores, the satisfaction only comes after the fact. If ever I switch to vinyl siding, scraping paint will be the reason. There must be a better way. I've tried a wire brush on my cordless drill, but it hops around too much. I've considered chemical paint-removers, but they're either too dear or too dangerous or both. Scratch, sharpen scraper, grin-and-bear-it seems the only way.

Scraping is also hard on the wrists. Years ago, my right one stiffened and grew a worrisome lump. After it went away, I asked my doctor about it. "Bible cyst," he said.

"*Bible* cyst?"

"Country doctors used to whack 'em flat; a small Bible was ideal." Right.

Once I get squared away, though, house painting is almost fun. Unlike indoor painting, it's a summertime sport. You get to smell the breeze, hear the birds, take a tan. With a two-storey house like ours you get a higher perspective on the neighbourhood, which always helps. There's also enough risk to make it interesting. Like rock-climbing with something to show for it.

But I never paint the whole house at one go. Not that our place is big. The Old Part is only about 7 by 10 metres, and the one-storey extension barely half that. Call it laziness, call it misguided male logic, but a wall or two a summer suits me fine. Actually, my piecemeal approach is practical. Exterior paints age at different rates depending on how much sun they get. This is obvious with a north/south orientation like ours, less so with a catty-corner house. First our south wall peels, then the west (all that afternoon sun), then the east wall (shadowed after about 10:00 a.m.), and finally the north wall (no sun except morning and evening in spring and fall).

So, like a beaver felling a popple, I just track that sequence. The math gets complex, but my clapboards know when. It does mean repainting somewhere every summer — but lots of country chores are like that.

Systematic as all this sounds, some painterly things still puzzle me. For instance, should a person paint and scrape as they go, or scrape everything first? Most professionals do the latter — but then they don't have my distractions and temptations. If I did that, in our climate, I'd be painting wet wood half the time. So I scrape as I go.

Another question concerns types of paint. For years I was a thoroughly oil-based man. After all, generations of East Coast fishers protected everything from dories to schooners with oil paint. Before the age of fibreglass, repainting wooden boats was a springtime rite. Come June, outport air was perfumed with linseed oil and turpentine. On every second beach you'd see men with paint rags in their arse pockets, slapping it on.

And they had a system. First thing after scraping they'd brush on a primer coat of white lead (no fear of nerve damage back then) cut with turpentine to make it really soak in. Next came a thicker coat, sanded rough, and then the oil-rich outer coat that dried to a hard, glossy finish. Finally, below the boat's waterline, they brushed on red lead to repel ship-worms.

I figured if oil paint can withstand salt water, seaweed, cod slime, salmon guts, squid juice, rope burns, wharf thumpings, and grapnel scrapes, surely it can protect a tree-sheltered farmhouse for a few years? So when we finally got a house of our own (this), I naturally chose oils over the other alternative, "rubber-based."

In doing so I ignored a few things. Those fishermen used *marine* paint, a tougher variety. Also, they painted their boats almost yearly, outside *and* in, so the wood stayed pretty dry. Old clapboard gets painted only on the outside, and is usually dampish from windblown rain underneath. Apart from rain and fog and normal household moisture, it may also have to cope with earthen cellar floors, eavestrough overflow from leaf buildup, and condensation from uninsulated pipes and water pumps.

Linseed oil is wonderful stuff, but it has two faults. Chemically it cures to a rigid film that can't accommodate the natural swelling and shrinking of wood. And it can't handle internal moisture. (By trapping moisture, oil paints can actually hasten rot.) Two, three years and your paint starts to peel — unless scraped off first.

It was the perennial scraping that finally led me, reluctantly, to become a water-based man. Reluctantly, because those early latex, vinyl, and resin paints were no great shakes either. Sure they were simpler to clean up after, didn't stink (but still gave off unhealthy fumes), could be applied in damp weather, and were less flammable. However, one thundershower could undo a whole day's work, and twenty minutes' neglect could ruin an expensive brush. Where they excelled was in the ability to expand and contract with heat and cold in sync with the wood. And, thanks to microscopic surface shedding, they kept their brightness.

Those advantages undermined my oil-or-nothing bias. It was more nostalgia than science anyhow. Those pipe-puffing childhood fishermen of mine weren't just painting boats. They were swapping yarns, recounting family history, telling jokes, sharing male lore, singing ballads, passing (but never to me) the rum bottle. All of this I inhaled with the smell of paint. And my bias — infatuation — only deepened when I became a teenaged landscape painter in oils. Even today, one piney whiff of turpentine lifts my spirits.

Bias aside, I came to see a more serious problem with water-based paints. They wouldn't stick to oil. "Thou shalt not put water paint over oil paint," said the commandment. (Oil over water was okay, since oil floats on water.) Switching to latex would mean scraping the whole house first. But then the paint-makers proclaimed a new commandment: "Prepare thy surface with trisodium phosphate/sodium carbonate, and all shall be well." A big job, yet far easier than scraping. So last summer I started to convert.

It wasn't that simple. Residual oil in the bare wood yellowed my white latex priming coat and threatened to stain the final coat. Fortunately the makers of oil-based paints had also been busy. Besides solving (almost) the odour problem, they now offered hybrid emulsions that stuck like glue. My dealer produced a resin-based primer, fortified with silicates of magnesium, sodium, potassium, and aluminum, which he claimed would both hide the stain and stay put.

So far — knock on clapboard — it has.

But surely putting oil over latex over oil is tempting fate? If so, I pin my hope on technology. (Don't we all?) I dream of a superpaint, something non-toxic (all those metal silicates can't be so good either), odour-free, affordable, fireproof, enviro-friendly, that sticks to anything, cures fast, won't ruin brushes, needs only one coat, stays bright, and lasts a lifetime.

Wait a minute. Our forebears mostly did without. In old albums the houses are usually weathered grey. (They never cut their lawns, either.) The settlers did have whitewash for special occasions, the same watery stuff Mark Twain's Tom Sawyer got his buddies to put on Aunt Polly's fence. A typical recipe called for half a bushel of lime, a peck (one-quarter bushel) of pre-dissolved salt, three pounds of ground rice, and a pound of "clean glue." They simmered this "in a small kettle inside a big kettle," added five gallons of hot water, and let it stand a few days. The recipe guaranteed "a brilliant white if put on right hott."

Guaranteed or no, whitewash soon wore off. ("Whitewash job" still implies a hasty cover-up.) It worked better in a sunny climate, not in our humid East. Half the charm of those dazzling Spanish hillside towns is whitewash.

The pioneers' first real outdoor paint was oxblood. Made of buttermilk and bulls' blood — truly organic, a drinkable paint! — it suited our climate. This rust-brown pigment served countless farmsteads well until oil paints appeared in the nineteenth century. Soon, oil-and-red-ochre graced fishing premises from Nantucket to Nain, while houses sported yellow ochre. As late as the 1960s, before the damned pastel revolution, I sketched a village lane in northeast Newfoundland where every building was done in red or yellow ochre. Trimmed in white, set off by white picket fences and ornate gates, they looked at once homey and elegant, like a hobbit village from *Lord of the Rings.*

Unlike today's paints, those old-time pigments were cheap and locally available. Limestone and iron oxide could be quarried and dug locally, as place names like Nova Scotia's Lime-kiln Brook and Ochre Pit Hill attest. Glue could be had by boiling animal hooves and hides. Blood flowed freely in the November slaughterings. Cod livers, seal fat, and whale blubber supplied the oil. Talk about smelly.

Compared to whitewash and oxblood, oil paints were quite durable, especially on the rough-sawn wood that was the norm before mechanical planers became common. Rough wood offers more "tooth," like wool to Velcro. Given a choice, I'd use unplaned any day.

In fact, I did just that during renovations to my Newfoundland place last summer. To adapt this 1880s fisherman's house for landscape painting, I raised the kitchen roof, steepened the pitch, and added large windows. And instead of sheathing the new gable in 1970s Colorlok siding — assuming we could find enough — we used unplaned clapboard. To protect the wood and save time, I simply brushed on white latex primer tinted to match the weathered Colorlok's yellow ochre. It looks so good I may finish the rest of the house that way.

Meanwhile, back in Nova Scotia, my west wall is calling.

No high ladder work here, just the one-storey extension's gable and wall with its five double-hung wooden windows, and, above that, the old two-storey gable. The latter peak is high, but reachable by stepladder from the extension roof. It entails considerable trim-work too: wide window caps, heads and jambs, fluted corner posts, and eighteen-inch moulding.

Apparently these features identify the Classic Revival style of 1820-60. Until reading in a book of it, I never knew our house *had* a style. It was a fad imported from the young American republic, where architects fancied its clean Grecian lines and columns. Painted pure white to resemble marble, it also made an anti-colonial statement against imperial Britain. Some US builders took this to ridiculous extremes, but here in these monarchist Maritimes the style was muted. Even so, my wraparound eaves or *returns* are wide enough to serve a four-course meal on.

Next year's project, the east wall, is more challenging, twenty-four feet of sheer clapboard from lawn to peak with no roof to stand on. Scaffolding would be safer, but hardly worthwhile for one wall. So far I've suffered only a stiff neck and mild panic from leaning backward. Last time, to reach the apex, I duct-taped the brush to a pole and stick-handled the paint on. One good thing about gables is that each clapboard is shorter than the one below.

One bad thing, that time, was hornets. They kept whizzing past my left ear like .22 bullets, roughly one a second. I froze, pole in hand. Suddenly the lawn seemed a long way down. Then I noticed hornets returning with mouthfuls of grey fluff. So they were making a nest. In our attic. And using the house for building material. I wasn't surprised. A few summers earlier, preparing for a home wedding reception, we had blasted a fat, humming nest out of the selfsame gable with a garden hose. Gingerly, glad that hornets have short lives and shorter memories, I swabbed the remaining bald spots, and, quiet as a burglar, climbed down.

Such adventures make my day. House painting goes so slow. This year's should go faster, though, thanks to a suggestion my Newfoundland neighbour made last summer. Hardy, a professional house painter before he turned commercial crab fisherman, remarked that he and his buddies routinely painted three bungalows a day in Gander.

"Three? How?"

"Rollers," he said. Although I'd used the short-haired type for years indoors, I was skeptical. "Shag rollers," he added. "They hold more paint."

Next day, the weather being sunny, I bought two of these deep-piled cylinders plus a screw-top handle and a tray. After supper I was tentatively swabbing my sunset wall when Hardy came by in his blue pickup.

"Well?" he said, leaning out the cab window.

"It's certainly fast," I said, "but Hardy, what about the under-seams? They'll still need brushing, so where's the gain?"

"Roll them too," said he. "Just use more paint." He dodged over, dunked the roller, and deftly swiped it sideways along a seam. The paint covered it beautifully. As he climbed back into the cab, I playfully lunged at his new truck with the wet roller. He whooped, spun gravel, and was gone. By dusk I'd finished not only that side but also the whole front wall.

Window Talk

Along about now, as our hemisphere tilts toward winter, away from the sun, I feel our old house has too much glass. For it's window maintenance time again, and wooden storm windows, especially old ones like ours, are high-maintenance. And the job should be done, I remind myself, while the weather's still warm, not when my fingers are scrammed with cold and my putty is stiff like frozen butter.

My window apprenticeship began soon after we bought the place in the late sixties. All summer we had tradesmen underfoot, but in October, on my own now, I started thinking storm windows. I found them down cellar. Big old cobwebby things they were, thirsty for paint, hungry for putty; but they'd save us buying new ones. And they matched the house.

The art of puttying, like several other handyman skills, found me wanting. Didn't even own a putty knife. My late father puttied neatly with a discarded table knife. Okay, I'd do the same. But his knife was wide-bladed, round-nosed, and limber, while mine was narrow, pointy, lopsided, and stiff. So I went to town and got the proper tool. Caulking with a gun never entered my mind, though I've used them a lot since. It's faster, but no more durable.

Face it, wooden windows take time no matter how you do it. One thing leads to another. Rule One: A little dab won't do. Don't be like those government road crews who never really fix your road. Rule Two: Think like a dentist; get to the root of the problem.

You start innocently enough, picking here and poking there, when suddenly a whole strip of old caulking lets go, exposing bare wood. And because bare wood sucks the good out of putty or caulking, it must be primed. Back to town you go for oil-based primer paint—and a new brush, since the one you have is stiffer than you thought.

Still, two hours should do it. But what with prising old putty out and waiting for the wood to dry and trying to avoid priming the glass and letting the paint dry and scraping paint off the glass and going back to town for new glass to replace the pane you cracked, not to mention buying "glazier's points" to replace the original metal triangles that fell in the grass. What with all that, your two hours can easily swell to half a day.

My own early window work took more like a week. For this old house has eleven big windows—twenty-two, counting storms. Ample windows too, each with twelve generous *lights* (I looked that up), 9 by 12 inches upstairs and 10 by 14 inches down, 264 panes in all!

But of course it's not the glass that takes the time, it's the weatherproofing of all those thin wooden frames, all those *muntins* (looked that up too). How many inches, I wondered one day, would a beetle have to walk to trace their combined perimeters? I did the math and came up with 13,824—nearly a quarter of a mile. And that wasn't counting our four small horizontal vinyl slider windows—utility room, bathroom, kitchen, dormer—nor the five large two-light sash windows in the sun porch. True, those are pretty low-maintenance: replace the odd vinyl strip, touch up the paint, that's about it. Yet sun-baked vinyl will crack over time, and screens pop out of their splines.

Our only truly trouble-free windows are the two new vertical aluminum storms installed in the west gable in the mid-1970s. Except for ice damage to their rubberized bottom slider grooves and a malfunctioning sash, they're almost as good as new. Modern windows seem designed to be replaced.

So I guess old wooden windows aren't so bad. The workmanship alone—all those grooved and mortised muntins and sashes, each handmade using only saw, mortise chisel, auger, and rabbet plane, plus the drain boards top and bottom, and the bevelled moulding all around — is admirable. A pro picture framer could do no better. After all, wooden windows are really multiple outdoor frames for panes of glass instead of pictures, all assembled without nails (which would rust) and glue (which would dissolve). Moreover, raise-able sash windows, unlike storm windows, must slide smoothly over each other without rattling in dry weather or jamming in damp.

As an amateur picture framer I can only marvel. Still, those craftsmen have one advantage, namely old-growth white pine. If a wooden window is not to "go out of true" (i.e., warp) the wood needs to be knot-free and even-grained. If it's also durable, easily worked, and holds paint well, so much the better. Old forest–grown white pine excels in those traits, and was plentiful when this house was built. No fake "verola pine" for them.

Workmanship aside, windows and window glass are fascinating in themselves. The Neolithic original was likely the smoke hole in a shelter made of skin or bark. Later, small openings were cut in walls of mud or wood. How small is suggested by two ancient Anglo-Saxon words for window, namely *eagþyrl* and *eagduru*. The first meant "eye-drill" (peep-hole), the second "eye-door" (shutter). Our "window" comes from Middle English *windoge*, meaning "wind-eye," akin to Icelandic *vindauga* (*vindr* + *auga*). (Grandma Saunders always said "winder" for "window"; perhaps she had Viking blood?)

Such small windows made for gloomy interiors. This didn't bother nomadic hunter-gatherers much, but as agriculture wooed people into villages, windows got bigger — and being glass-less, let in more weather. Rush mats solved the problem in summer; in cold weather, translucent animal skins were commonly stretched across the openings.

Window glass took centuries to appear. Strange, since glass is essentially melted sand, which is mostly silica, Earth's most abundant surface material. Moreover, Nature produces glassy material like obsidian and amethyst all the time — not to mention ice. Inuit igloos had ice skylights long before our ancestors had window glass. In fact the Egyptians discovered glass over five thousand years ago. They made it by heating pure sand with soda and lime in ceramic pots over charcoal fires. At first they used it for glazing wooden beads and pottery. Some fifteen hundred years later, they invented glassware — goblets and such. But their hot dry climate needed no window glass.

For this the world had to wait until the Phoenicians invented glass-blowing around 50 BCE. Being great sea traders, they were soon hawking glassware — including crude sheet glass — around the Mediterranean. From there the Romans, the first to use window glass, spread the idea throughout the Middle East and Europe. Even so, it was slow to catch on. Early glass, besides being fragile and expensive, was thick, lumpy, and brownish with dissolved iron. It took medieval glass-makers another millennium of tinkering with additives like lead and manganese to create workable, thin, reasonably clear sheet glass. By framing coloured glass in lead they gave us the likes of Chartres and Coventry Cathedrals, Gothic masterpieces of light and colour. And London glass-makers gave us lead "crystal."

Fat lot of good it did the peasants. Their hovels were still so gloomy they could hardly tell day from night. Even the wealthy had nothing better to read or sew by than the dim light of mica or marble. So the first true window glass seemed a miracle. Sunlight on the kitchen board! Draft-free light in the dead of winter!

Miracle or no, it was still costly. As late as 1900, sheet glass was still being hand-blown at great risk to life and lung, often by child labour. Glass-blowers produced either a bottle-like cylinder or a circular "gob" up to a yard wide with a central bull's eye now prized by collectors. Gobs could be cooled and cut right away, but cylinders had to be reheated, split, and flattened before cutting. Meanwhile optical glass-makers were perfecting and polishing lenses. But flat glass still had far to go.

All that changed with the invention of plate glass less than one hundred years ago. The new technology entailed pulling a large film of liquid glass of the desired thickness directly from the "melt." After being cooled and polished it could be cut to any size. Speedy as this was, machine-polishing was costly. In the 1950s, England's Pilkington Glass Company bypassed this step by floating the melt on molten metal to produce a mirror-smooth finish, a process still used.

When we bought our farmhouse, it had only two window types: large vertical double-hung and small un-openable horizontal. Our only major change in the Old Part was to replace one window with a patio door. So the original exterior still looks much as it did in 1900. A few summers ago, we hosted a tour of people who had grown up in the house. "Oh," said one, staring out a window that had been replaced, "it's gone." Another, relieved, cried, "The hall is still the same!" Overall I think they approved. For they found no eyebrow dormer windows, no ribbon (side-by-side) windows, no pivot (centre-swivel) windows. There were no awning (camper-trailer type) windows, no fanlight windows, no clerestory windows. The only casement window (side-swinging with inner crank) was in my studio over the garage, where I put it to help flush out paint vapours. They didn't even find a louvred (metal or plastic slats) gable window for ventilation. Our old house ventilates itself.

They did find a new bay window. But that was in the New Part and so didn't count. And we did have a picture window, that 1960s cultural import from sunny California, but it too was in my studio. I'd bought the monster for ten dollars at a local construction site. Manhandling it into its hole on the second floor took my husky friends Sandy and Reg a full hour (and a case of beer). It still gives a good north light, ideal for a painter.

And it faces the salt water. Many older picture windows in Atlantic Canada don't. My guess is that veteran coastal dwellers have seen too much of the ocean's moods to invite it into their living rooms. They'd rather contemplate something friendly, like a nice flower garden.

Big windows are great—until they need replacing. Our three-pane bay window began to fail in the early nineties. I know because I checked the warranty date and it said 1973, the year we built the New Part. The first sign of trouble was condensation in the centre pane's left bottom corner. But because the wetness showed only in cold weather and hardly then, I let it go. Big mistake.

Over time, unknown to us, that moisture rotted the untreated wood. Eventually, the moisture froze, expanded, and cracked the glass. And because (a) the crack didn't leak, (b) the warranty had expired, (c) new bay windows were expensive, and (d) the two side panels were okay, again I procrastinated.

Until, that is, a local home improvement firm sent a flyer offering replacement windows for 20 per cent off—installed. I signed up, but after four frustrating months with no follow-up despite reminders, I cancelled and reclaimed our deposit. About then Eldest Daughter and her husband arrived from Washington State on a ten-day visit. And they brought our only grandkids, two girls and a boy, all under nine. Grandparental bliss!

However, my handyman son-in-law soon hankered for a useful chore. Noticing the cracked window, he kindly offered to replace the bad wood if I'd order the glass. At first I demurred, figuring home repairs just now would spoil our fun. But his offer was too good, too timely, to refuse. So I measured the three panes and went shopping for lumber, screws, and caulking. Soon our kitchen had a plastic-sheeted, eight-foot-wide hole in its north wall. Unfortunately, my glass shipment was delayed once, twice. By the time it arrived, our visitors had departed. However, just in case, before they left we put the old panes back in, loosely screwed and without caulking. Double work—but at least the bad wood was gone. By now the big middle pane had several cracks. September is hurricane season in these parts. Would a big blow spray our kitchen with broken glass?

Hurricane Juan arrived a couple weeks later. As usual it came from the southwest, sparing our north-facing wall. Soon afterwards my new panes arrived. Faced with installing them myself, I felt some trepidation. Such pristine, beautiful, heavy sheets deserved abler workmen than me. Too proud to ask our neighbours for help, I waited for a windless afternoon. Then the weather turned cold. "Use only above 5 degrees Celsius" said the label on my tube of caulking. I covered the outside with my painter's throw-sheet and kept a heater going all night inside. The next day it rained. I tacked the plastic back up. By suppertime the next day, working alone, I had the two side panes up, levelled, screwed tight, and caulked. By nightfall of day two, heart in my mouth, I'd wrestled the four-by-four-foot central pane into position. And it fit! By ten o'clock that night it too was installed, and I was refinishing the inside pine trim.

That was my third solo window installation, and I hope my last. At least it wasn't a clerestory window, high up under some cathedral's eaves to light an inner passage blocked by a nearby tower. I've enough glass to tend as it is. Not that I don't enjoy it—once a year. My favourite time is a sunny fall afternoon with the crickets in full chorus and the late apples nearly ripe. Spider webs can be a problem then, so I keep a broom handy. Hornet nests can be a hazard too, but a garden hose fixes those. I also like the putty smell of linseed oil, and clay's cool, earthy feel. Above all I relish the prospect of November ice pellets rattling off my handiwork while I watch, warm and dry, sipping something hot.

Gone to a Better Place:
A Wood Stove Memoir

O ur old wood stove is gone. It still had a good five years left in it, maybe more, but, like so many of us, it fell victim to red tape. The first sign of trouble had come two summers ago, when a small car halted halfway up our lane. I stopped hoeing to see who it might be. The driver, a young man in shirt and tie with an officious look, rolled down his window and asked was it okay to take some Polaroids of the house. When I politely asked what for, he said he was from our insurance company, Portage la Prairie. As this was the first time the Winnipeg-based company had bothered to check what they were insuring, I said okay and resumed hoeing. That he'd come was reassuring in a way.

A year later, a second Polaroid chap showed up. This one was in coveralls and more likeable. He said my insurance company had hired him to inspect the heating systems of clients in the area. More worried now than reassured, I again said yes — but this time stopped what I was doing and led the way. I would answer questions and, if need be, defend my castle.

He took pictures of our hot-air furnace, of the fireplace (unused and sealed), of the two chimneys, of the oil furnace's indoor fuel tank. Clipboard in hand, he asked the age and condition of that furnace (five years, good), whether the chimneys were lined (they were — the new stove flue with ceramic tile, the old furnace flue with flexible galvanized pipe). Finally, he examined our hot-water heater and dryer (both electric, good).

But clearly his main interest was the wood stove. After snapping it from several angles, he measured from chimney to stovepipe, from firebox to floor tile, from stove perimeter to hearth perimeter. All this went into his notes. After all, he was only doing his job. Yet I had a sense of foreboding. Something told me my faithful stove was doomed. It wouldn't matter that in twenty-five years we'd never had a chimney fire. That the only time we'd had to use a fire extinguisher was when lightning struck the house; that our flues were cleaned regularly; that we all knew not to stuff the stove with paper or cardboard and open the drafts; that the stove's several seams were routinely checked and promptly sealed. That nothing flammable was ever left near the stove, especially overnight; that hot ashes were always put in an iron pot and put in a safe place to cool; that I'd just installed a sixty-dollar stainless steel oven liner guaranteed for ten years.

The inspector, to his credit, passed no immediate judgment. And he patiently answered my nervous queries, no matter how cleverly phrased, with a noncommittal "You'll hear from the company in a few weeks." And he did note that my stove wasn't CSA approved.

While awaiting word, let me give you some background. In the early 1970s, alarmed by the rising cost of furnace fuel and the frequency of winter power outages, we bought a second-hand wood stove. It was a step stove of the type made by several firms in Atlantic Canada years ago, stoves with names like Maid of Avalon (St. John's, NL), and Queen Cook (Sackville, NB, where ours came from). Low to the floor, it had a two-door oven wrapped around the flue at the back. The top was broadly guitar-shaped with four lids in two sizes, a swinging side hob for the teapot, a wide front fender to warm your feet on, a sliding front draft and a drying rack underneath.

Of course those stoves weren't airtight; back then none were. Yet thanks to the crosswise frontal firebox, a long fire path, their heavy cast iron construction, and their nearness to the floor, they worked much better than a tall box stove. Often on winter mornings I found enough live coals to light kindling without matches.

Our Queen Cook, though needing frequent repairs with stove cement, served us well for several years. We decided to get a new stove just like it. By then its maker had discontinued that model, but we found a look-alike in the Perfect Cook made by Nova Scotia's Lunenburg Foundry and Engineering, next door to where the original *Bluenose* schooner was built.

As it happened, we had to wait two years. The company wrote an apologetic letter saying their master fitter had died suddenly, and they had to train a new man, a slow process. Would we mind waiting? We minded, but after all, we still had the Queen, plus the oil furnace, so it was no hardship. Finally the big crate arrived. A shiny new stove! We sold the old one, had a tinsmith make a new flue pipe, and installed it. Thus began a pleasant winter routine that lasted for decades. Around 6:00 a.m. I'd fire it up. Soon after my paper and kindling caught, a bright blaze would seethe in the open fender. Over time the lids warped enough to throw crescents of golden light across the ceiling, cheering to see on bleak winter mornings. Within ten minutes the kettle would be singing.

On school mornings I'd wake our several children at around 7:00 to be ready for the bus at 8:45. We all preferred sleeping in a cool house. Come morning, they'd flock round the stove like chicks round a mother hen. On really cold mornings they'd eat their cereal there while warming their coats and boots. At bedtime too the younger kids liked to have bedtime stories read there. To this day they associate *Wind in the Willows*, *Winnie-the-Pooh*, and *Chicken Little* with that wood stove. As teens they crammed for exams beside it.

We cooked porridge on it, dyed cloth on it, thawed frozen clothes off the clothesline beside it, dried wet socks, mittens, and firewood under it, roasted pumpkin seeds in the oven. And since the oven, when fitted with a tin temperature gauge, proved fairly reliable, we also baked beans in it, and sometimes bread. And of course we cooked on it when the power failed. At different times various pets slept under or near it. Sidney the retriever-spaniel liked the heat so much he regularly scorched his back. To watch his panicky backpedalling was worth the stench of burning fur. In short, our Perfect Cook was like a member of the family.

Until, that is, we heard from the insurance company. On July 23, the day before our household policy was to expire, an envelope bearing the company logo arrived in our mailbox. Inside was a form letter requesting my signature on a "No Solid Fuel" clause. It also pointed out that with older homes like ours they couldn't guarantee full replacement value. Annoyed at the short notice and the perfunctory tone, I went to see my broker. On seeing the form letter, his secretary apologized and explained that the insurance company was really supposed to send it to her first. So that *she* could give me bad news, I suppose.

Her boss, son of the man I'd dealt with for years — had it been that long? — pulled up my account on his computer. He explained why insurance companies had to be especially careful these days, what with new environmental regulations and all. Moreover, old country houses like ours were so full of irreplaceable mouldings, pine floors, and stuff that it wasn't always possible to find the proper materials or skilled tradespeople to replace them.

As for the stove, well, CSA or equivalent certification was the law now. While he conceded that my stove-manship might indeed be exemplary, it was no longer good enough. When I hinted at taking my business elsewhere, he pointed out that, given the stove's age and type, no other company would accept it either. However — and here he flashed a smile — should I buy an approved modern airtight stove, the offending clause would be removed forthwith. Otherwise it must stay.

Oh, well. It wasn't as if we had to do it right away. With two months of warm weather ahead and an oil furnace downstairs, we could budget around this. And so, muttering under my breath that insurance companies and stove-makers must be in cahoots, I swallowed my pride and signed. Meanwhile the family was warned not to use the stove until further notice. This wasn't easy on frosty mornings or rainy nights when we needed the heat and comfort. There was never much doubt that we would replace it come winter. It wasn't like getting rid of a TV; it was more like doing without a freezer or a bathtub. Stove-keeping is a country way of life. Besides, we had five cords of good hardwood split and stacked.

Before long we were shopping for an airtight. On one hand, we didn't want a high-tech model so finicky you needed a physics degree to run it, or one that would gum up the flue with creosote if you looked sideways at it. We wanted a minimum of catalytic converters, primary and secondary draft controls, and other high-tech gismos. On the other hand, we didn't want a $300 monstrosity that looked like someone had torched it together from discarded truck hubs. All we wanted was a proven model with plain good looks and some built-in forgiveness.

It should surprise no one that we found such a model in *Rural Delivery*, a Maritime magazine. Made in the West but assembled in the East, the Spectrum offered dealerships in the Maritimes, including our nearest town. It was in our price range too, $1,300 with pull-out ash drawer and a frontal Plexiglas sunburst. So we ordered one and made a down payment.

After taxes, delivery charges, installation (with precautionary double stainless steel pipes) and the safety inspection, the job cost $1,800. It seemed a ridiculous sum to pay for a thing of sheet metal, especially compared to the $800-plus-shipping we'd paid for a cast iron Perfect Cook in the 1970s. And, if we could believe the company brochure, it would save us money by making more heat from less wood. By October, the Spectrum stood in the Perfect's spot, looking capable and taking up far less space. We were in the stove business again.

But I'm ahead of my story. All summer, while we debated what to do, the old stove stood there as usual, handsome in its shiny summer polish, topped with a bouquet of whatever flowers were in season: peonies or sweet peas or irises, unaware that its days with us were numbered. Of course it's foolish to imagine a stove, even a member-of-the-family stove, harbouring such thoughts. Still, after three decades one can perhaps be forgiven for deeming it a pet. What if over time, like the Tin Woodman in Frank Baum's *Wizard of Oz* or the Velveteen Rabbit in Margery Williams's lovely tale, it somehow embodied the life of the humans around it? And supposing it did, surely it would know we had discussed getting a new stove? And how I had dragged my feet? If so, would it not be impatient with this idleness, with silly vases of flowers, and eager for the first hard frost that would remind the Saunderses to light the winter fires again? Something like an old draft horse eager to be in harness when autumn came.

But I had this terrible secret. Padding past it each morning on my way to bathroom and kitchen, I saw it as a Thanksgiving turkey with an axe in its future. Surely it knew we must retire it? For the first time our family room, our happiest room, bore an air of melancholy. What to retire it *to*, that was the question. Couldn't heat the garage with it; the insurance company wouldn't go for that. Couldn't put it in our woodlot camp; it already had a stove. I *could* lug it to the scrap dealer who took my empty beer bottles and such, but one hundred kilograms of cast iron wouldn't fetch much over ten dollars. One day I jokingly suggested to Beth that we put it in the garden to grow flowers in, like they do with old dories. She shocked me by saying it was a great idea. But the thought of it rusting away out there summer and winter was too much for me. Better to park it in the woods for the porcupines to play with! By September its fate was still unresolved.

As often happens, the solution came out of the blue. We got this phone call from a woman in New Brunswick's Albert County. Kathleen, a nurse who works in Amherst, is the wife of the brother of the woman who was my wife, Beth's, maid-of-honour at our long-ago wedding up Richibucto way, New

Brunswick. The two women had met at Normal College in Fredericton. Beth's friend later married this brother, who got a job in Truro, which is only ten minutes from where we live, so we got to know them, and through them the New Brunswick couple, and kept in touch with both couples over the years. You know.

Anyway, Kathleen called to ask did I know where she might find an old kitchen stove like the one they had admired at our house. She and Paul were planning a local museum to honour a relative of hers who had been one of the Fathers of Confederation, and...

One, two, three...Bingo!

Within two days, she and her husband arrived in their station wagon to collect the free stove. They'd lowered the back seats and a tarp was already spread. We'd dumped the ashes by the forsythia bush. Half an hour later we'd dismantled pipe, elbows, oven, doors, lids, fender, rack and all, vacuumed its innards, and stowed the parts in the wagon. Seeing me fetch the camera, Paul plucked a late rose from the white rugosa and stuck it in a lid hole. I snapped the picture and they were off. That evening they called to say the stove had arrived safely, and to assure us we'd be invited to the museum's pioneer kitchen exhibit.

Do we miss the Perfect? Of course. It could do lots of tricks the airtight can't. It boasted twice the cooking surface and had a wide range of temperature options, anywhere from tea to toast. When you fired it up from a cold start it didn't bong like an oil drum, did not utter radiator noises while cooling. Because it loaded from the top, there was less need to bend over. Though it sometimes sent sparks flying, it never spilled hot coals onto the hearth tiles like the airtight when one rakes too fast. It didn't have a spring-loaded ash cleanout flap that sometimes stuck open.

But the new stove seldom needs those ashes emptied. For that matter, it seldom needs to be relit. Luckily, it was deep enough to take our sixteen-inch-long wood. Thanks to its firebrick interior and catalytic design, it ekes a lot more heat from each load of wood, staying hot for nearly two days. And it throws its heat forward, not sideways or up, and circulates the room air better. Best of all, its sunburst window lets us enjoy the play of orange and gold flames, a big improvement over the Perfect's meagre wicket. All in all, the Perfect's retirement was a good thing. The fact that the old stove found a new home was an unexpected bonus. We have an open invitation to visit it there, and when the museum opens we plan to do just that.

Winter Woodchuck Woes

Half the fun of rural living in an old farmhouse is the wildlife you meet within and without — preferably without. Of course everyone's outdoor favourite is wild birds: chickadees dangling upside down on the suet feeder, downy woodpeckers tapping you awake, distant crows mobbing an unlucky owl. Only last September an irate male pheasant, mistaking our porch swing's metallic creak for a rival male's challenge, came squawking through the hedge to drive us off.

Surprised bird!

There's also the furry visitors. Especially squirrels and groundhogs, a.k.a. woodchucks. Chipmunks we don't mind; they mostly stay outside anyway. But the other two, come winter, want to either move in with you (squirrels) or settle too close for comfort (groundhogs).

Squirrels go for attics, invading via eave chinks to nest in your insulation, short out your wiring, and leave smelly you-know-what everywhere. Groundhogs, poor climbers but master diggers, seldom invade the house itself, preferring to launch garden raids from under patio decks in summer and, come winter, to snuggle up to the relative warmth of cellar walls and buried septic tanks.

At least that's been my experience. Which is why, now that we're cat-less and dog-less, I'm especially vigilant. For instance, several autumns ago as I fetched morning firewood in off the deck, I saw a slight movement in the corner where our hop vine (of which more later) used to be. The mover was a handsome golden-brown woodchuck, *Marmota monax*, big as a house cat, sitting bolt upright, glaring at me like it owned the place.

But I'm getting ahead of my story. Weeks before, down cellar to fetch a dozen spuds from the cold room, I'd noticed fresh brown dirt fanning out from between two boulders in the field-stone wall. No sign of tracks, which ruled out rats. So, a ground-hog tunnelling close by?

A worrisome coincidence, because the disturbed earth was directly beneath the sewage outlet pipe to our septic tank buried just metres away in the upper lawn. What if *M. monax*, liking the frost-free zone between house and tank, chose to winter there? Chose, if male, to excavate its usual maze: sleeping area, eating area, toilet area—unlike squirrels, woodchucks are very neat—and, if female, maternity ward? Never mind several escape exits. Kneeling there in my dim rock-lined cellar, I pictured at best a leak and at worst a collapsed wall, followed by a raw sewage backup. And this at a time when the earth overhead was frozen rock-hard.

Next day, rather than wait for the worst, I'd hoisted the outside deck hatch above the pipe and checked for holes in the dirt. Found only one, a rat tunnel; jammed it full of small rocks and broken glass anyway. Then, to keep the ground dry and more diggable over winter, I raked and sloped the surface evenly away from the house, and sheeted it with heavy plastic. Beyond that, it was wait and see. No sense disturbing the ground for nothing.

Later that winter, sure enough, didn't I smell sewage down cellar? And one mild day didn't I meet the culprit on our deck, chattering at me with its yellow teeth. Investigating the earthen floor around the septic pipe, I found it soaked in grey-water. An urgent call soon brought our local backhoe guy, who found outside, one and a half metres down, a sagging vinyl septic pipe with a broken rubber seal. The digging plus repairing cost me only $250—but could have cost much more. To my surprise, our insurance didn't cover water mishaps. Now it does. Still, the best insurance is prevention. And since peaceful coexistence was no longer an option, and my saucy morning woodchuck must be taught a lesson, I reverted to sterner measures.

Years ago I would have shot him with my son's .22 target rifle. But that was no longer strictly legal, since only bona fide farmers were now licensed to do that. A kinder, quieter expedient was needed. Not to kill, just to stun. As a long-time archery buff, I had the gear and knew how to use it. So when *M. monax* challenged me again, I was ready. Possibly the creature was innocent. But the circumstantial evidence said otherwise, pointing to this rodent as the underminer of our septic line, the compromiser of our health. He or she might even be the grandson of the beast who gnawed our lovely hop vine to death decades ago.

The next day, as I collected another armful of firewood, we met again on the deck. There it sat, bolt upright mere metres away, again cursing me. Slowly withdrawing indoors, I eased my armful of split maple into the woodbox, lifted my ironwood target bow from its overhead rack, strung it, nocked a blunt-tipped arrow to the bowstring, opened the back door a hand's breadth and took careful aim. Not at full draw, mind you, just enough to thump the intruder, warn it off.

Twang! Hit squarely in the chest, the 'chuck keeled over and lay still. Fully expecting it to recover and skedaddle, I fitted another arrow. But no, the poor thing was dead. Heart must have stopped. Maybe, like me, it was elderly? Or, like so many, overweight with BP issues? (It weighed nearly ten kilos.)

The news must have spread in Marmotville. A few more years passed with no more rodent trouble. Until a recent spring. Returning by a different way from my evening walk, I discovered, close to home, between cornfield and gravel road, a heap of fresh red dirt, sure sign of someone's new den.

Parting the roadside tangle of brambles and pin cherry bushes, I saw a groundhog-sized entrance hole. So, not a fox den. Feeling oddly relieved, I thought, "No problem, Miz

Monax. Stay hereabouts, eat all the dandelions, clover, and wild carrot you want, even raise a family; you'll have no trouble from me! Live and let live! Détente from now on!"

Then there came a flicker of doubt. What if, a year or two from now, Mother Monax's three or four offspring, now full-grown and scouting winter quarters, likewise move in with us? Then we'd be back where we started, only worse off.

At this point I recalled two books I'd read years before. The first was Farley Mowat's 1963 *Never Cry Wolf*, in which he claimed to repel wilderness wolves by drinking lots of tea and pissing around his "territory." The other was Carol Deppe's excellent 2010 book *The Resilient Gardener*, in which she touted one's urine as an otherwise wasted nitrogen source. Not for salad greens of course — though pee from a healthy human comes out sterile. No, she applied her liquid gold, morning-fresh and strong before bacteria set in, diluted it 1:10, and sprinkled it on heavy nitrogen feeders like squash and corn. The power of pee, she called it. Impressed, I'd been trying her method and incidentally had a supply on hand. Why not repurpose that power? The older and ranker the better? To prepare my *coup de urine*, I did a midnight den check. Fresh diggings under my flashlight beam told me the occupant was in. Next morning before dawn, gallon juice jug in hand, I crept close, parted the bushes and poured my liquid thunder down the hole.

Seconds later, up came sounds of urgent scuffling. This was followed by a brownish blur that hurtled between my legs — never knew groundhogs could run so fast — bounded east along the road slope, barrelled past my garden, scurried across our lane, and vanished into the cross-road culvert.

One totally pissed groundhog! Haven't had that problem since. Now it's raccoons raiding my grape arbour. Will Farley's method work on them? Time will tell.

Fire from the Sky

The summer we were struck by lightning, our youngest child Joyce was about five. Not that the exact date is important. Our house wasn't demolished. We weren't cooped up in a motel for weeks while repairs were made. It's just that every other detail of that day is branded on my brain. And the bolt did set fire to a basement beam. Afterwards the fire chief said that if we'd been away at the time, the house wouldn't have lasted half an hour. Half an hour! You don't soon forget a thing like that.

Like most nineteenth-century Maritime farmhouses, ours was and is eminently combustible. Framed with hemlock, floored with resinous pine, finished inside with plastered spruce laths, clad outside with spruce clapboard, it was lucky to get past the century mark unscathed. The 1940s addition of asphalt roof shingles only increased the risk.

An attic blaze would have been bad enough; the basement fire could have torched its way up through all that tinder in minutes. For weeks afterwards, I'd snap awake at 2:00 or 3:00 a.m., heart pounding from another flaming nightmare. At last I understood why Coleridge's Ancient Mariner kept telling and retelling his tale of woe to any who would listen:

> Since then, at an uncertain hour,
> That agony returns:
> And till my ghastly tale is told,
> This heart within me burns.

I was like that for months. Telling the tale seemed to calm my fears. The lightning strike itself was nothing much, just a blinding flash and an ear-splitting overhead *crack!* without a pause between. We ourselves weren't hit, so I figured the house was okay too.

That particular thunderstorm had been building all afternoon. Joyce and I were indoors, busy at this and that, while the rest of the family was in town. Because such storms are common here beside the Bay of Fundy, we didn't pay much heed. The converging shores of Cobequid Bay seem to funnel storms through here.

One can watch the process any sunny afternoon from July through October. As the sun warms the south-facing slopes of the Cobequid Hills to the north, it lofts balloons of moist warm air. Cooling, they become visible as towering white cumulus clouds. When their tops bump against freezing air five or six kilometres up, they flatten into the familiar anvil shape. Should an influx of cool air slide under several of these columns, a thunderstorm can be born.

We noticed nothing unusual until around 4:00 p.m., when we heard a distant mutter and saw the light through the windows darken. It was just a distant thunderstorm doing its thing. We stopped what we were doing anyway. First there was a sudden muting of birdsong. Then a brisk wind thrashed the birches and hitched the weather vane from west to southwest. Next, strobe-like flashes grew brighter. Then we heard the first raindrops rattling the metal eavestroughs, to be drowned out moments later by the escalating racket: snare drum, kettle drum, bass drum, and finally the full orchestra.

Half an hour later the rain slackened, the thunder ceased, the trees straightened up and fixed their hair. Now sequins of sunlight glistened from every leaf and blade of grass like brush-strokes in a Constable landscape. Songbirds resumed their conversations. Overtaxed downspouts gurgled and spat out gobs of what looked like coffee grounds but were really bud scales and twigs from spring leaf-out. The air was perfumed with earth and ozone.

Like I say, we paid little heed. Apart from fetching some things inside, we just watched and listened, walking hand in hand from room to room, enjoying the fireworks while keeping a safe distance from the windows. At one point she said proudly, "Daddy, I'm not scared of lightning anymore!" Still, when that awful blast shook our roof, her fingers suddenly tightened on mine. Ten minutes later we resumed our window tour.

We were near the north kitchen window, watching the retreating flashes twinkle against the far blue hills, when she turned to me and said, "Daddy, I smell smoke."

So did I. But how could that be? In fourteen years of living here, we had weathered many such storms, some much worse. Even though our farmhouse sits on a broad drumlin-like hill, one of the highest around, with two tall trees nearby and a giant elm shading the main roof, it had never been struck by lightning. Nor had our neighbours' houses. And we hadn't lit a fire in the wood stove since May, or used the oil furnace in weeks.

A quick round of the rooms revealed nothing amiss. The odour seemed to have vanished — or maybe our noses got used to it? Telling Joyce to stay put while I checked the basement, I flicked the cellar light switch on. Oh-oh. Our power was off. Grabbing a flashlight, I was halfway down the cellar steps when I again smelled smoke, woodsmoke. But seeing no flames, I took it for ozone from the blast. And, not wanting to leave my little girl alone upstairs too long, I gave the cellar a cursory glance and jogged back up. "There's no fire," I told her.

However, I did check the landline phone. It too was dead. Strange, for it had never failed during other storms.

Fifteen minutes later the smell of smoke was undeniable. Nervously, we checked the whole ground floor. Nothing unusual in the kitchen. Everything normal in the family room, our old wood stove cold and innocent in its coat of summer polish. And nothing amiss in the central hallway, its high windows green under their elm canopy.

But the living room! Its beautiful pine floor was ankle-deep in white smoke that unfurled in slow motion from the furnace registers like the poisonous gas it was.

My mind raced. Something down below *was* burning after all. Likely a tiny flame, or I'd have seen it the first time, even with the flashlight on. However, by now it could be well along. With the cellar door open, we listened for a telltale crackle. Still nothing.

Firefighters always warn you to flee a building the moment fire is detected. But how could I abandon our home without being sure? My spouse was ten kilometres away with the car, at a church meeting. She might not be back for an hour. The other five kids were at school. For me to run next door with a little girl in tow would waste precious time. Especially if their phone was also dead, as it might well be if a transformer had been hit.

No. First I had to know for sure what we were up against. And if there *was* a fire, the least I could do was try to slow it down.

I told Joyce we'd be okay (about the house I wasn't so sure), and stationed her near the porch door where we could grab stuff and run. I took the big ABC fire extinguisher from its bracket and made for the basement again. It's funny how a person's mind works at such a time. On the surface my thoughts veered between dread and excitement, yet at a deeper level I was coolly listing what to rescue: personal papers, albums, silverware, yes; paintings, books, clothes? Maybe.

Below deck again the acrid odour of burning wood was unmistakable. This time I headed directly to the windowless, low Old Part where the oil furnace sits on an earthen floor. Overhead the flashlight's beam lit up more white smoke. Like billowing cotton wool it blanketed the ceiling joists and beams, coiled around the heating pipes, and dangled tendrils that weaved to and fro.

Still seeing no actual flames, I clicked off the flashlight. As my eyes adjusted to the dark, a flickering orange glow appeared behind the furnace. Keeping my head below the fumes, I approached. The fire was now about a metre wide, silently licking along two rough-sawn joists that nearly touched. It was barely burning because the trapped smoke was starving it of oxygen. I ripped the safety pin from the extinguisher, took aim, and sent a blast of foam along the joists. Instantly the glow winked out and darkness swooped back.

Throat and eyes burning, I hurried back upstairs, consoling myself that at least the fire was out. I found Joyce and considered how to rid the house of the smoke. We were congratulating ourselves and getting ready to open windows and doors when I noticed an ominous new black oval in the living room's varnished floor. About the size of a hen's egg, it was charcoal black in the middle, shading delicately to toast-brown around the edges. And it was hot to the touch.

So the Enemy Below was still alive. I recollected that when we renovated the house, the carpenters had left some old joists to spike the new ones onto. Those old three-by-eights, exposed to dampness in the years before we bought the place, must have developed dry rot. If so, by now they'd be punky and fibrous, the perfect nest for a smouldering fire. Not only that, it must have broached the thick hemlock subfloor or there'd be no telltale scorch mark.

Obviously, my ABC burst had doused only the surface flames. ABC extinguishers aren't designed to cool things anyway. Water is best for that. Without water the wood can smoulder like tobacco in a smoker's pipe for hours, bursting out the moment it senses oxygen. So the stupidest thing I could do was to throw open doors and windows. Stupider still was my wild notion of lancing that black spot with my chainsaw.

Sweating now, I grabbed our small ABC extinguisher, pounded down the steps, and sprayed the joists until the pressure faded, which didn't take long. Water. My kingdom for a pail of water! But where to get some, with the power off and our well pump dead? All I had was spit and urine.

Of course! The toilet flush tank. It held ten or fifteen litres at least. By dipping a laundry pail full I could slosh water up there and . . .

My thoughts returned to that worrisome scorch on the pine floor. What if the fire hit the varnished surface before I could douse it from below? My equipment was poor, the visibility almost nil. Better to use my puny hoard of water to soak a mat and lay it over the hot spot, and to keep on wetting it till the water gave out or Beth got home, whichever happened first.

Just in case, I unhooked the toilet float arm so we wouldn't accidentally flush our only ammo away. As I worked, muttering to myself, we heard a car door thunk. As soon as I told Beth what had happened she drove off to phone the local volunteer fire brigade. Within ten minutes their scarlet and chrome truck arrived in our yard, siren wailing. Minutes later the rest of the fire was out, and a big portable fan was vacuuming the smoke and steam away.

Poking around, the firefighters determined that the lightning bolt had entered via the telephone box mounted on our northeast wall. From there it had travelled along the thin wire until, three metres in, the wire entered a hole bored through two joists. At that point the copper strand had shorted out, igniting the dry wood.

Late that evening the fire chief, having checked the nearest transformer and turned the power back on, sent most of his crew home. Not all, for if the lightning had damaged our house wiring too, a second fire could start inside the woodwork hours after they left. Not until 1:30 a.m. were they satisfied to go.

Satisfied or no, that night I slept on the living-room floor next to that ugly scorch mark. And every half-hour, to make sure it was still cool, I reached over and fingered it.

Not until the next morning did the reality of all this sink in. A bolt from the sky had very nearly destroyed our home and everything in it. Moreover, had Joyce or I been standing in the wrong place, say under the target tree or beside the telephone box, we could have been killed.

The telephone official doubted that lightning could follow a phone line indoors like that. It was theorized that a forgotten buried wire may have carried it from tree to box. (I've since confirmed that lightning *does* sometimes follow telephone lines into buildings unaided.)

Anyway, it happened. Checking the basement ceiling afterwards, I was able to poke three fingers through the hole in the subfloor and halfway through the top board. Another centimetre and the fire would have broken free. I've since often questioned the wisdom of my playing fireman like that, especially with a child present, but in the circumstances it seemed the wisest course. The house *was* insured, but that never entered my mind until afterwards. The insurance company offered us $600 to repair the floor. But matching the other pumpkin-coloured boards was impossible. So we opted to keep the scorched board as a memento of our close shave. It's still there, with the house still attached.

The Winter House

I can see our Winter House now, its warm bulk muffled in the snowbanks of my Newfoundland childhood, its lamplit windows gleaming in the December dusk.

We called it our Winter House because it was where we wintered a year or two to keep warm. Our real house, the Summer House—actually a storage building hastily converted to accommodate my young parents-to-be, homebound to escape America's Great Depression—was too chilly for the coldest months. Drafts kept circumventing the blankets and mats my father draped over windows and stuffed under doors.

One spring, fed up, he and his brother Harold built a log cabin opposite Mom's goat barn. Late that fall we moved in. Just a log cabin, but to me it was a home, even a spacious one: kitchen–living room, three bedrooms with smoky cotton "doors," pantry, and porch. Walls cozied with thick green sheathing paper, then in vogue. An Ideal Cook stove to bake our bread, heat our meals, cheer our nights. And lamplight mellowing all.

To me, Christmas in that balsam-scented abode was magical. Memory is a fickle jade, but none were green that I recall. One year it snowed for a whole week, erasing every fence. Our only exit door was buried so deep, Grandpa Saunders had to come and shovel us out.

Back then I still believed in Santa Claus. One Christmas week I was misbehaving—something about a red sled I'd just seen in Eaton's fall & winter catalogue. This was during the Second World War. My parents were barely getting by on Dad's meagre earnings as a guide and trapper, plus Mom's part-time job as local postmistress. They told me Saint Nick gave no such gifts to naughty children; moreover, he might even then be cruising overhead, doing a last-minute check on good boys and bad.

Suddenly our snow-blanketed roof came alive with a sound like the trampling of little hooves! I raced to my bunk and burrowed deep. Next morning the hoof-prints were mostly drifted over. Of course my father, in the know and out early shovelling, saw them, saw how two (not eight) sets of (sled-less) goat tracks mounted our low roof and returned to the barn. That part he carefully erased after feeding the goats and hens. A little mystery wouldn't hurt.

Still, Mom did keep goats; she didn't trust cow's milk, said untested cows could carry TB, which was true. And even a nine-year-old could figure how the two frisky animals, finding the barn door unlatched overnight, could have used hard-packed snowdrifts to...

Believing it was the hard part.

That Christmas Eve at bedtime, feeling sorry, I wrote Santa a note saying any gift would be welcome. Toward morning I seemed to hear paper rustling close by but dared not look. Waking at daybreak, I found, tucked inside my school bag, this scrawly reply on a page from my yellow scribbler: "*Dear Gary, Your red sleigh will come on the steamer next week.*"

One week and one day later, with ice forming in the bay, the coastal steamer *Glencoe* arrived bringing freight and mail on her last trip of the season. Because Grandpa ran a general store, Dad and Uncle Harold went as usual by motorboat to fetch his goods ashore. As they neared the wharf I saw, atop the jumble of mailbags, beef kegs, and flour sacks, something glinting scarlet in the sun. Edging closer, I could make out the magic inscription: *Rocket Racer*! Santa had kept his word.

Our beloved Winter House is now long gone, yet in memory I see it still: snow-mantled, bright-windowed, in a lilac dusk.

Part Seven
Land & Sea & Sky

Two Rural Dreams

Recently, I had two dreams which still trouble my sleep. In the first, I'm walking in velvet dusk a kilometre or so down a country road somewhere in these Maritimes long ago. By the smell of woodsmoke and new-mown hay, I take the season to be autumn. Gradually, I become aware of a medley of animal sounds, some near, some far: lowing of cattle, clucking of hens, the bleating of sheep, a nicker of stabled horses, the grunting of pigs. And suddenly, from nearby, a chorus of flute-like children's voices. Their words sound English—but English blurred by half-forgotten Old World accents.

Every few hundred metres along this gravel road I pass a farmstead. Each has a house, a barn, and several outbuildings, some of them joined end to end in the New England manner. The outbuildings need paint, but all seem in good repair. Great maples and elms bend over each farmstead like hens over chicks. Hollyhocks, marigolds, bee balm, and tansy spangle the front yards. From numerous hedgerows comes the sleepy chirrupings of songbirds. From afar comes the noisy, raucous bickering of crows.

In some of the windows oil lamps already glow, amber twinklings like fireflies among tree branches as I pass. Through open blinds and curtains I glimpse women clearing supper dishes, children starting school lessons, men and boys loading woodboxes against a frosty dawn.

From the barns I can hear iron-shod hooves thud on rough-sawn hemlock planks as weary Clydesdales and Morgans take their well-earned rest. Beyond the barns spread other pastures, rolling fields dotted with brown-and-white cattle chewing their cuds in the evening breeze. Most fields are fenced with zigzag rails and quilted with the greens and golds of rye, flax, oats, and barley. Farthest back are stumpy, new-cleared pastures where frost-reddened buckwheat does battle with native hardhack and goldenrod. Behind the fields loom woodlots thick with huge white ash, beech, yellow birch, and scattered remnant white pine.

Almost every farm has a neatly fenced kitchen garden. I can make out staked scarlet runner beans and Thomas Laxton peas, rows of maturing rutabaga and cabbage, clumps of rhubarb, currant, gooseberry, and raspberry. Tomatoes are blushing scarlet; squash and pumpkin hint at dusky gold; the time for sweet corn is evidently past. Disturbed earth reveals where the season's first new potatoes have been dug.

Most homesteads have a huddle of apple, damson, and cherry trees heavy with fruit. Sugar maples, their grey trunks pocked with tap holes from sap-gathering in times past, line the lanes. Here and there beehives hum.

On verandas, kerchiefed older women rock to and fro in the deepening twilight, knitting or embroidering as they converse about a wedding, a scandal, a sick infant, the coming harvest. One woman works a homemade churn's hand dasher up and down, thumping it rhythmically to separate the day's cream from its milk and turn it into butter. In a nearby kitchen, younger women introduce a newlywed to the secrets of cucumber pickling.

I pass circular wells lined with local stone and covered to keep out children and animals. A few boast cast iron hand pumps from T. Eaton Co.; most are topped with a wooden crank from which dangles a homemade wooden bucket. Most yards have a big pile of dry maple and beech firewood.

At each small farm, sequestered behind lilac or mock orange bushes or relegated to a barn wall, stands an outhouse, its unpainted door graced with a carved star or crescent moon. Despite liberal liming against flies and odour, the nearest announce their business on the evening breeze. The smell is no worse than that from ubiquitous pig sties.

Other tilt-roofed structures I recognize as smokehouses. Safely distanced from barn and house for fear of fire, they harbour smouldering hardwood chips or turf to smoke-cure dangling eel and shad and salmon. Soon they will preserve sides of beef and hams of butchered pork instead.

Now I seem to see a creek with a wooden bridge. Upstream is a dam, and above that, mirrored in a millpond, is a weathered gristmill. The creak and rhythmic *plash* of its slow-turning, over-shot waterwheel is strangely restful. Upstream, a little beyond, where two roads meet, stands a blacksmith shop. Through the open door I see the orange glow of a forge and hear the clank of iron on iron. Beyond the creek is the small whitewashed schoolhouse and, farther along the gravel road, a church with a belfry.

Downstream I see a lattice of high scaffolding. Silhouetted against the evening sky, dark shapes of men move like beetles along a wooden ship's hull. From snatches of conversation I gather they expect this three-masted barque to be ready for a neap tide launching this fall, in time to ship salt fish to Havana and bring back rum and molasses before winter plugs the tidal bay with ice.

Beside the church is a small cemetery. Hand-carved stones bear names like Belliveau, MacDonald, Crowe, and Blake. The inscriptions tell of women dying in childbirth, of men lost at sea, of others taken by TB and typhoid, and of many children taken by whooping cough and diphtheria.

In the farthest house several old men are playing a boisterous game of cards. As one of them knuckles a winning hand onto the pine table, I wake with a start. It's just the night wind rattling a loose window pane.

In my second dream, I'm walking the same road, long since paved, in a winter dusk some two centuries later. Now the landscape is open, almost treeless, mostly stubble fields without intervening woodlots and hemmed in by suburbs. In my hour-long walk I see only three farms. The original homesteads have vanished, their place barely indicated by cellar holes and rock hedges.

One farm is enormous, the others fairly small. The big farm is a complex of tall and short silos, tanks and vats. In the glare of tungsten yard lights, it is more like a petrochemical plant than a farmstead. Also there seems to be no farmhouse, only vast barns with offices or sleeping cubicles attached, as if a small crew of custodians camped here, tending various machines via computer hookups.

Through the windows I note long ranks and files of pale cows under curious lighting that seems to mimic sunshine. The cows themselves seem unable to stand. They are mostly udder, the rest of their huge bodies supported by wide slings and straps. Batteries of tubes and sensors make them look like terminal heart patients.

The rolling fields of my earlier dream have largely been flattened, perhaps to facilitate automated seeding, fertilizing, and harvesting? Many hectares lie under inflated plastic bubble blankets, inside which I can see what look like tropical vegetation but which instead are strange new forage crops under natural spectrum fluorescent tube lights. Other structures seem designed for hydroponics. Any fields not so enclosed are protected by a fibre mesh laid over corn stubble. Even so, drifting soil has coloured the snow patches cocoa-brown and deep gullies are still bleeding the ditches full of silt.

Though I pass a few unpruned old apple trees, there are no hedgerows. Also the factory surroundings are devoid of gardens or berry bushes. Along the road I see no church or school, nor shipyard, gristmill, or smithy. The millpond has become a Plexiglas-domed storage vat for liquid manure. The creek has been straightened and seems to be a conduit for liquid fertilizer. The cemetery seems to have been plowed under.

Now I come to two smaller farms. It surprises me that one of them retains not only the original home, but traces of the former vegetation. However, again metal tanks and towers have replaced the outbuildings. Clearly these holdouts are destined for absorption by the giant agri-factory down the road.

So changed is everything, so transformed, I wonder whether families with children still live here. It being late afternoon, I half expect a yellow school bus to squeal to a stop, disgorging knots of book-laden students. But all I see are caretakers' children who, having done their lessons by interactive video at home, are relaxing here and there with Virtual Reality headphones. Meanwhile their parents are nowhere to be seen, probably programming supper in subterranean bunkers nearby.

I trudge on. At the farthest farm, another surprise awaits me. An old man is vigorously shovelling snow. It's a welcome sight in that otherwise surreal environment. I'd have thought anyone over fifty would have been replaced by a robot. We exchange greetings and I ask why not.

"Oh no," he says, "these days we live to be one hundred and twenty and work till eighty. We do have robots for such menial tasks — but I prefer the old ways." Unlike his peers, Victor has resisted mandatory retirement to an Urban Work-Home. After all, he says, this was his great-grandfather's farm. "Though I hardly recognize anything but the snow," he says with a chuckle.

"Why," he continued, "these days they pipe the milk directly from udder to dairy!" Manure and urine, he explains, never touch the floor; they are siphoned off via rectal and urethral tubes into vats for on-site methane and nitrate recycling. Sensors not only monitor the animals' health, but transmit soothing video and audio impulses directly into the bovine brain. "Far more effective than primitive growth hormones and antibiotics," he assures me. Images and sounds of summer meadows work best, he adds.

"But now our chemists have substitutes for all dairy products," he snorts. "What I'd give for a taste of real cheddar cheese!

And soon I suppose everything will change again." With a dismissive wave he returns to his shovelling.

Beyond the third farm, columnar apartment buildings soar like giant lighted toadstools. Fields of colour-coordinated suburbs stretch away into the deepening winter night. I wake. It takes two cups of strong, hot tea to halt my shivering.

Bonavista Traverse

It was no big deal, no epic Cormack-style trek through un-charted Newfoundland wilderness. All we did, Hans and Al and I that last week of August in the mid-1950s, was paddle and portage across the Bonavista Peninsula from Southern Bay to Popes Harbour. The straight-line distance is scarcely thirty-four kilometres. For us, counting the zigs and zags of a forest survey, maybe fifty.

Yet for me it felt somehow grander. I've often wondered why. It wasn't only that we misjudged the difficulty or brought too little grub, or that Al got sick or that I screwed up near the end. No, I think it was a coming of age thing. I was nineteen, a University of New Brunswick sophomore due back at Upalong in a week. More importantly, I was a riverman's son raised in a river-haunted place where my childhood dream was to become a big-name guide like my dad. But my Fogo-born mother wanted none of that for me — hence my career change. The Bonavista jaunt, I now see, was an old dream revisited.

Luckily for me, Hans Mandøe, our Danish party chief, shared that dream. At age thirty-four he'd left a good forestry job tending manicured beech in his native Denmark because he hankered for wilderness. An adviser recommended British Columbia, but he chose Newfoundland.

As for Al, he was a bright St. John's teen, graduate of St. Bonaventure Catholic high school, who'd come to us straight from clerking in a St. John's bank. Aloysius didn't know a spruce from a fir, yet someone had recommended him as a UNB BScF candidate. Bonavista would be his boot camp. The pimply boy would need help to survive. Hans rolled his eyes and willed him on to me.

Fortunately for me, neither of them felt safe in a canoe. By default I became boatman to the expedition. But why the Bonavista traverse? I guess because we'd already cruised and mapped the other east coast parts and this would round out our summer's work. Along with our recent Avalon survey, it would give the province's Department of Mines and Resources (M&R) an up-to-date inventory of those woodlands in case Premier Smallwood, pursuing his "Industrialize or Perish" mantra, decided to plant a pulp and paper mill there.

His rhetoric portrayed the project as a *big* pulp and paper mill, a *huge* paper mill, perhaps dwarfing Corner Brook's, a grand imperial enterprise guaranteeing jobs and Liberal votes for generations. But I digress.

Before leaving our Lethbridge base, Hans quizzed the locals about our canoeing prospects. He knew one can't always trust aerial photos, even recent ones, because beavers can quickly transform a landscape. "Oh aye, good prospects, b'y," the locals told him. "Ye's can paddle all the way." He should have known better than to ask saltwater men about inland canoeing. Also, I suspect the locals misunderstood his German-sounding accent and mistrusted us.

In any case our first leg, from Lethbridge to Southern Bay on the Bonavista Branch railway, went smooth as silk. M&R's area supervisor Wallace Diamond had arranged for a "speeder," the stand-up trolley railway workers used for travelling from job to job, to transport us and our gear. Away we went, pumping the see-saw T-bar and praying not to meet a train. Two trips in drizzling rain and we had our eight-metre Peterborough Freighter canoe in the water and loaded. With Hans in the bow, me back aft steering, and Al hunkered with the gear, we launched the traverse.

Was it the boat's launch and loading that now glows so in memory or the fiery, rain-washed late August sunset? Or the pond itself, darkening to bronze and violet as the evening breeze cat's-pawed toward us? Whichever, that moment is forever etched on my brain. More than once I've tried to paint it. In one of the watercolours my late dad appears, paddling solo into the sun, the hill behind him lit up with maple reds and aspen yellows.

Dip and stroke, dip and stroke, the laden green canoe glides along the pond's outlet. The brook is shallow, but by careful wading we soon reach a second pond. Now only a short portage separates us from Ocean Pond on the height-of-land. Over fifteen kilometres long and half as broad, by rights it should be called a lake—but this is Newfoundland.

At sundown we decide to camp. The sky is clear, so we just spread our tent on the wet ground, unzip our sleeping bags, and flop. Don't even light the lantern. Soon we're snoring. Waking to bright sun and robinsong, we breakfast on tea and toast, reload the canoe and head for the big water. Two of us take turns portaging the canoe with tent and tin stove and grub box inside it. By nine o'clock that morning our gear is parked in a heap on the lake's north shore.

This handsome sheet of water lies northeast-southwest by the compass, widening southward within in a trough of rolling hills clothed with tall untouched fir and spruce. Untouched, that is, except for a narrow island near its western shore that looked suspiciously ragtag.

We landed—to find M&R's illegal operation. Someone had stolen scores of prime butt logs, leaving the studwood- and pulpwood-sized tops to rot. Red boughs told us the wood had been taken the previous winter and hauled away over the ice. Hans took notes and measurements. Then Hans, pointing ashore, said, "We'll split up now as agreed." He and Al would compass the woods west and south, and I would ferry our gear across to a dam site he'd picked on the opposite shore. Landing, I steadied the canoe while they stuffed lunches, rain gear, and tea kettle into a day pack. Then with a farewell wave they vanished into the wilderness.

What luck! I thought. A whole day, canoeing—and getting

paid for it! With the lightened canoe riding higher and the wind breezing up, I decided to re-trim the load with more weight forward. This boat, designed for freight, was too long to manage in waves while kneeling amidships. Paddling to the island's lee shore, I could just make out the dam about a kilometre southeast. Already, whitecaps were forming down the middle.

Should I go now, before the wind worsened, or wait for a lull? My load was still hefty, with little free-board to spare. I made a fire, had a mug-up, catnapped, took another look. No better — in fact worse. Already it was past three o'clock. The crossing would take at least half an hour — longer, since to avoid taking waves broadside, I'd have to run them on the quarter, slantwise. Luckily the craft had enough of a keel to hold a course in high winds.

It was time. Adrenalin pumping now, I lashed our sleeping bags and other gear to the cross-brace. Pulled off my heavy logans and tied them by their laces under the seat. Stowed the spare paddle handy. Then, none too soon, shoved off. Now I knew why they called it Ocean Pond. With a fetch that long, the wind had ample room to raise metre-high waves in minutes, enough to swamp a laden canoe. There was no turning back, no turning — period. No time even to think, only time to anticipate and execute. Totally in the moment. Wild, almost erotic elation. Boat and I one. When at last — an hour? two hours? — we touched the far shore, I hardly noticed. My paddle-weary right arm felt numb as I hauled the craft up to safety.

By now the sun was slanting westward. Soon the boys would be back. Time to unload, make camp, hustle some grub. To avoid the flies I chose a space on the windy point. Cut and limbed five slim and slender spruce for tent poles. Spread the tent, roof side up. Laid the ridge pole midway down the four crossed end poles. Wrestled the windward end off the ground — the stiff breeze helping — and tied it to a rock. Raised the lee end, tied it to a tree and pegged the sides. Makeshift, but with our packs ballasting the floor it would do for now. I set up the tin stove, rigged the flue pipe, fetched birch rind and dry wood, and thought of supper.

Below the dam was a deep pool with fat brook trout lazing about. I always carried hook and line on these trips, but had neither lure or bait, no bacon or anything. A tuft of red wool from my socks did the trick. Trout were soon racing each other for it. Soon I had half a dozen gutted and rolled in flour, ready to fry.

"Halloo!" Out of the westering sun came Hans and Al, delighted to find things so homey looking, treating me like a hero. While recounting our day's adventures we ate and drank, then set the tent to rights and took our rest. It was to be our last rest for a while. That night it turned cold, and sometime after midnight I woke to see Al fumbling with matches, trying to relight the fire. Next day he was racked with nausea and the runs. I fed him tea and toast and watched our bread run out. A second day in camp depleted our remaining beans and spuds. Now all we had was tea. I eked it out with brook trout.

Back on the traverse, we soon gave up paddling. Even without the packs on-board it was no use. So they waded and I dragged. Then came the over-falls, sharp-toothed runs where only careful roping gets a boat safely down. You tie it just aft of the bow and gingerly pay out rope while trying not to fall in. The boat and I were doing okay until the land fell away in rolling chutes of amber foam. At one point, the pull getting too strong for me, I braked it by looping the painter twice round a tree.

Bad idea. Halfway down, the rope pinched. Brought up short, the canoe went belly up and wallowed. Too late, I loosed the rope. Because this time I'd tied nothing down, tent and stove, bags and grub box went tumbling. I hollered. At last they came. Wordlessly we fished the stuff ashore. While beaching the boat to drain it, I noticed Hans still out there, wading and poking.

"What is it?" I said.

"My camera," he grunted.

Oh, I felt lousy then. Finally he found it. But even if the camera still worked, his pictures were ruined. "I'll send you extra prints of mine," I said sadly. He took it well, considering.

We slogged on, Al feeling much better. Toward sunset—another breath-taker, looking like scrambled eggs I was so hungry—we finally reached Popes Harbour Pond, a freshwater fjord with an ocean outlet. At the pond's head we found a clearing occupied by a small horse barn and a sawmill with year-old sawdust. So the purpose of the dam was to flush sawlogs down to it in the spring. Likely they'd run out of upstream wood and were now horse-logging second-growth trees hereabouts.

There, hanging from a tree limb, was a denim jacket bleached powder blue. I was trying it on when the left sleeve began to hum. I tossed it and ran, with hornets on my tail and the boys bent over with glee. That night we slept miserably in sodden bags on damp sawdust. I'd checked the barn's hayloft, but found in the rafters several active hornets' nests. The only good things about that mill site were the morning sun that dried our gear, and the family of curious otters that followed us partway from shore, breaching and chirping as if to cheer us on.

At the harbour village we needed a passenger boat to take us to the rail line at Clarenville.

"Gary," said Hans, suddenly shy, "you go ask those men on the wharf, please; I don't speak the language."

The boat trip down the Smith Sound fjord, like our whole trip, was unforgettable. And the hotel's fine fare and crisp white sheets felt heavenly. Sometimes the worst trips end up the best.

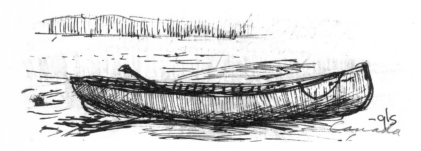

Sailing Bloody Reach

Oct. 16: North Sydney ferry terminal: Foggy morning. Lots of truck & car motors running. A bored driver in a black-and-yellow Sudbury, ON, vehicle steps out on his running board to comb his hair in the truck's side mirror. Line by line we peel off, inch up the stern ramp into the ship's echoing belly, get parked, grab stuff, find an upstairs exit, climb to main deck. Outside we've a 30-knot wind, grey seas, whitecaps, limited visibility. Best to stay inside, read, think, write.

In April of the mid-1990s, as mentioned elsewhere herein, I underwent radical prostate cancer surgery. All went well, except I happened to be among the 5 per cent of patients who suffer post-op urinary strictures (blockages) caused by overactive scar tissue. When that happens one must, to avoid pain and possible kidney damage, promptly have the urethra dilated to empty the bladder of stale urine and if necessary to install a catheter and leg bag. Over the next six months I endured such dilatations every few weeks, plus three corrective surgeries. Frustration multiplied!

Then in October, when I'd all but given up hope, I ventured to make my annual two-week painting pilgrimage to The Rock, specifically Twillingate, Newfoundland. While there I visited family in nearby Gander and a friend in Glovertown who took me sailing on Bonavista Bay. After that I never had another stricture. Coincidence? All the rum we drank? All the pictures I painted? Possibly. But I can't help but credit my native landscape with the cure.

By 8:30 a.m., with the *Clara and Joseph Smallwood*'s hoarse departing bellow still echoing round North Sydney's harbour, I'm settled in with a book. Normally on day trips to The Rock I'm outside, rain or shine, taking in the scenery, watching for marine life, exercising my legs, escaping the cigarette smoke. Today, vaguely distracted, I stick mostly to the lounge. Then I remember why: today, back in Nova Scotia, my long-time Lands & Forests secretary Carol is retiring. Retired four years myself, I meant to call before I left. At the purser's office I hand-print a fax message, pay the fee, and feel better. Reaching Port aux Basques by mid-afternoon, our motley motorcade is soon creeping bumper-to-bumper down the yawning bow-ramp and jockeying up the hill to the Trans-Canada, the open road.

Halfway up, passing the tourist chalet, my heart skips a beat as the seven hundred-metre-high Long Range Mountains heave into view on my right, their purple ramparts still patched with the previous year's snow. Of course some of their beauty is in my eyes, but the rest is in my heart. After my first year away to college Upalong I used to kneel and kiss the ground here; no need of that now, but the feeling's just as strong. Snacking in a gravel pit near Crabbes River, I wrote:

Oct. 17: As an experiment I slept in the car. Heavy rain during night + noisy truck traffic only 100 m away, but otherwise okay, sun peeking thru. From Deer Lake to Birchy Lake a rainbow rode with me — good omen. Six hours later, after lunching at Goodyears Cove in Halls Bay — the roadside spring still flows; refilled my water bottle there — I arrived in Twillingate about 4:00 p.m., dog-tired but happy.

In fact, I drive right past my destination, the Minty's vacant house they've lent me. The new paint job fooled me. They're away on vacation, but neighbours Austin and Doreen Rogers,

GOODYEARS COVE, HALLS BAY, NF
OCT 16/95

— g.l.saunders

seeing me double back, fetch a key and see that there's hot water.

The next day dawns sunny with light winds, perfect for outdoor painting. Twillingate town straddles two lofty islands enclosing a harbour that's linked at its narrowest tickle by a short causeway and bridge. For my first expedition I drive northeast up the island a ways. Settling on a cove overlooking Durrell Arm, I start a watercolour. But the complex cliff planes and muted colour baffle me, so I switch to pen-and-ink sketches of houses, wharves, and boats. Then, driving to nearby Sandy Cove, I tackle a small oil sketch of Long Point lighthouse and Wild Cove across the outer harbour.

Again the cliffs are challenging. But oils are more forgiving than transparent watercolour; they let you retouch. This time my lights and darks work better — tricky in outdoor painting with its varied light. Almost any colour will work if you nail the tones. Anyhow, I'm not copying — that's for the amateur photo-realists — I'm *interpreting*. As modern art pioneer Paul Cézanne put it, "I have not tried to *reproduce* nature but to *represent* it." Re-present — that's the ticket.

Trying and failing, for the outdoor painter, are by no means wasted effort. Even if the picture never gets exhibited, the intense concentration forever burns the scene into one's brain. Back in Nova Scotia years later, I can still see those basalt cliffs, all mauve and ochre in the autumn sun, their cast shadows mysterious in blue and purple.

The next day, in search of motifs, I cross the bridge into North Twillingate. Motifs abound, every view paintable. That day I complete two small oil sketches, first a small panel of Back Harbour fish sheds, then after lunch a larger one of the inlet's long beach and sheltering headland. Working there, I'm conscious of the brooding presence of Others. For in pre-settlement times this harbour was a favourite Indigenous summer haunt. Each spring, the Beothuk's hungriest time, they'd paddle out here from distant Red Indian Lake to catch the spring smelt run and gather seabirds' eggs to boil and dry for winter use.

On October 21, Day 17 since my last urethral reaming, bladder still behaving, I drive to Gander to revisit my brother, Calvin, and his wife, Cathy, meanwhile stopping en route at Clarkes Head to see several uncles and cousins. The next day, Calvin and I drive to Glovertown for supper with a mutual friend, a lawyer by trade and a sailor by avocation.

Bustling in his kitchen, our host soon served us a fine supper of baked salmon with white wine. After an hour or so of talk, laughter, and rum, we walked down to the jetty to see his beloved sloop. Hearing a sudden low hum below deck, I asked what it was. "Bilge pump," said he. "She's pretty tight, but all boats, even wooden boats, hanker for the ocean bottom. So when the bilge-water reaches a certain level the pump cuts in." Back at his place, he invited us for a sail on Bonavista Bay next day. Calvin couldn't stay, but I could and would. Next morning being sunny with a light westerly, we hoisted sail and headed northeast out the arm past Culls Harbour and Saunders Cove. The shouldering hills, recently aflame with maple, witherod, and blueberry, were now brocaded in the mellow golds of rowan-berry, aspen, and birch.

The winds staying light, no motoring needed, we conversed without shouting while he steered and I painted. Then, on the back of the same watercolour sheet, my last, I sketched his boat from back aft. Near sunset, we tacked about and headed back in velvet dusk to the jetty, motoring the last leg. At the dock, in near darkness now, he had some trouble finding a spot among some new arrivals, but at last got safely moored.

Next day, before leaving, I gave him the two-sided water-colour. It wasn't much, but all I had. My gratitude wasn't only for our wonderful *East-Viking* voyage; it was also because I felt finally healed. After all, it was now Day 19 since my latest ream job. Granted, my waterworks might seize any time. But something — was it the name Saunders Cove for a nearby inlet? — assured me otherwise. Even the name of the fjord we'd sailed seemed symbolic: Bloody Reach. Likely the name cele-brated some bumper seal harvest, or, possibly, a half-forgotten slaughter of Beothuk. Whichever, my marathon of bleeding and blockages seemed, if not fully run, then close to the finish line.

When, as we shook hands, I mentioned this to my host, he cocked one eyebrow in mock seriousness and said, "Well, I *am* a shaman, you know." Shaman or no, like I said, I never had another urinary blockage.

Sable Island: Ultimate Shunpiking

No other bit of land . . . is so fully exposed to the fury of north Atlantic storms. It stands near the outer edge of the banks, with 100 fathoms [600 ft/183 m] of water close to its eastern end. Rich in romance as well as tragedy—on its shores and hidden reefs countless vessels have been wrecked during the last three centuries—inhabited by a flora which curiously resembles that of New Jersey rather than Nova Scotia, and by birds which are not known to breed elsewhere . . . it is at once the loneliest and the strangest spot in the Maritime Provinces.

— J.W. Goldthwait, *Physiography of Nova Scotia* (1924)

Road maps seldom show this bit of Nova Scotia, for it lies far out to sea, 290 kilometres east of Halifax, Latitude 44° North, Longitude 60° West. Its nearest neighbour is Canso Head, 160 kilometres to the northwest. Sailors called Sable "the graveyard of the Atlantic." Over 240 ships have been wrecked there to date, not counting those whose remains have washed away. The survivors of those wrecks stayed no longer than they had to. Or, if it was winter, they likely died there. The sandbar island offers no trees or cliffs or caves for shelter, only dunes and grasses. Yet people *have* lived here. Apart from Indigenous Peoples visiting from the mainland—the Mi'kmaq still go there today—you need a good reason and a hard-to-get government permit. There's a risk of being stormbound, but those who can afford the cost and risk feel it's worth it. The ultimate in shunpiking, really.

From the air, Sable Island (French *sablon* = sand) looks vaguely like a thin-lipped smile on a face aligned north and south.

Between the twin sand ridges that form the lips, rainwater lakes and marshes flash in the sun. Until 1833, a lagoon separated the ridges, with an opening on the north side. That year a storm reclosed the gap, and the lagoon became a body of water called Wallace Lake, which persisted until the mid-1950s.

Despite these changes, despite the constant onslaught of wind and tide, the island's perimeter has remained surprisingly stable over time. By comparing old sailing charts with aerial photographs taken between 1952 and 1965, researchers found that in two centuries the west end had lost 15 kilometres, while the east end had gained 18 kilometres. Since 1900, there has been little real shift. But one big hurricane could change all that.

The island proper is about fifty kilometres long, more if one includes its underwater extremities. Its maximum width used to be almost three kilometres; now it's more like one. Trudging up and down dunes and around marshes, a good half-hour's walk. The highest dunes flank the north beach, where they attain about twenty-five metres. The sand itself is a whitish quartz flecked with pink garnet and traces of magnesium. It is very soft. Even on the wet beach one sinks ankle-deep. In high winds the sand drifts like snow, filling old buildings and burying fences. Rocks are absent, pebbles rare.

Geologically the island is a relic of the last Ice Age. It lies near the outer edge of a vast rumpled plain of glacial outwash, which the melting Wisconsinan glacier dumped beyond its eastern front. Fishers call it the Sable Island Bank. In the glacier's last stages nineteen thousand years ago, when the sea was at its lowest, the bank was mostly dry land. When the glaciers finally melted, raising the sea level more than 100 metres, all but the highest part went under. Shaped by wind and a great clockwise system of ocean currents, it became Sable Island. Long Island in New York State had a similar origin.

Botanically the island owes much to the last Ice Age too. Its most common plants are marram or beach grass, plus two varieties of beach pea as well as goldenrod, yarrow, creeping and common juniper, cranberries, and a few bog and marsh plants. Botanists often remark on how much its vegetation resembles coastal New Jersey's. There's a reason. As the expanding ice sheet drank down the seas, continental shelves hove into view around the globe. At first the continent's eastern shores were a soggy expanse of marshy islands. Later the continent became a wide coastal plain stretching from the Grand Banks to the Carolinas, bisected by the ancestors of today's St. Lawrence, Hudson, and other rivers — including one that flowed south across central Nova Scotia and out through today's Halifax Harbour.

Meanwhile, plants and animals that had survived south of the ice cap began to inch north again. By the time the ocean returned, the tide of temperate flora and fauna had reached future Sable Island. Offshore draggers have fished up intact mastodon teeth and still-rooted pine stumps. The rising ocean stranded many eastern seaboard species there and the hardiest survived.

Sable Island's climate fluctuated over time. Borings in fossil five-thousand-year-old sods reveal the shells of warm-water mussels and oysters. Climatologists think a temporary westward shift of the Gulf Stream may have brought milder weather. (A pleasant thought for next February.)

Today Sable's fauna is dominated by its wild "pony" — actually a horse. Galloping along the gleaming strand, tail flaring in the salty wind, it has become an icon of the Wild and Free. Its ancestors probably swam ashore in the 1600s from shipwrecked vessels, perhaps those of French entrepreneur Isaac de Razilly, who settled the mouth of the LaHave River near today's Riverport in 1632. Cattle have been pastured there too, but only temporarily. The only other large land mammals are grey seals, which mate and whelp on the beaches each autumn. The Ipswich sparrow has been there so long it has evolved a sand-coloured plumage noticeably paler than that of its Massachusetts cousin.

More than three hundred years of human contact have irrevocably changed the face of this giant sandbar — especially the arrival of horses. Even if their manure is helpful, the incessant tromping and chomping of some two hundred hoofed animals can't be good for the vegetation. Yet the herd seems to be in balance with its environment. The 1901 construction of a life-saving station seemed to upset that hard-won balance. Dune blowouts came oftener. That year, in an effort to stabilize the sand, the federal government undertook a massive tree-planting program: 69,000 evergreens, 1,000 willow cuttings, 600 fruit trees and shrubs. To this they added 12,500 deciduous plants and many rhubarb roots. As well, 2.5 kilograms of native pine seed was broadcast over likely areas. However, by 1913 only 13 plants survived; by 1927 only 1 was left.

The willow cuttings especially were a big disappointment. Set out on France's coastal Landes dunes they had done well — but the Landes had no wild horses. No one thought to fence the cuttings; the wild horses had a feast. This was supposedly remedied in a second willow plantation, until the winter gales sand-blasted their bark away. Of Sable's current flora of two hundred plus plant species, seventy were introduced. Among the survivors was tussock grass from the Falkland Islands. The late forester Ralph S. Johnson thought that New Jersey wild plum should fare well there too.

Recently, the greatest threat has been from industrial development. Wind speeds here average 29 kilometres per hour year-round, and a scuff mark in the wrong place can trigger a major blowout. In the 1980s, Mobil Oil and other firms discovered quantities of both oil and gas under the island; fortunately (some would say), low prices hampered development. Now an undersea natural gas pipeline is being built from Sable to Country Harbour in Guysborough County. Road-building and even footpaths are discouraged, and dikes have been built to prevent ocean flooding.

Recent studies of the island's ecosystems have led to more sophisticated attempts to control blowing sand. Predictably, the native plants do best. But they need help. Since the late 1980s, plantings have focused on native colonizing species like marram, sandwort, and beach pea. Snow fences have been erected and over seven thousand surplus Christmas trees stuck in the sand. Results look promising.

But the late Nova Scotia naturalist J.S. Erskine was less optimistic. While he believed the island to be self-renewing, he pointed out that it is merely the crest of a large but steadily shifting and dwindling undersea bank, and in the 1950s had this to say: "when the bank is worn down, the island must go with it, and all the sand-binding plants in the world will not stop it." He gave it two centuries at the outside.

Sky Stone

The sight of shooting stars is common in the country, away from city lights, as the nights close in; yet, it's rare to have one drop in one's lap, so to speak. That happened to me a year ago. The strangeness of it still teases me like a half-remembered dream. Indeed, if an actual meteorite wasn't sitting on my window sill, substantial as a hockey puck, I'd swear it *was* a dream.

By rights such honours should accrue only to devoted backyard astronomers or to space buffs, not to someone who hardly knows the Big Dipper from Orion, who's more at home with hayfields than star fields. My sole credentials are a love of night walks and a fascination with all things planetary. Especially with the notion that "empty space" is far from empty, but cluttered with bits of leftover universe ranging in size from dust motes to mountains. It gives me goosebumps to think that every few million years one of those mountains could slam into us, causing earthquakes and tidal waves and mass death, and leaving scars like eastern Quebec's vast Manicouagan astrobleme (star wound), now a semicircular lake.

This fascination naturally leads me to collect space trivia. Did you know that Planet Earth daily sweeps up roughly a thousand tonnes of interstellar dust? That "shooting stars" seldom exceed sand-grain size but owe their brilliance to sheer velocity, hitting our upper atmosphere at up to ninty-five kilometres a second? That Earth's orbit yearly intersects a whole series of celestial dust trails, thereby producing meteor showers named for the zodiacal sector whence they appear: Perseids in July-August, Leonids in November, Geminids in December, and so on? That, of the estimated five hundred biggish meteorites that plunge intact to earth and sea each year, only five are ever found—usually the metallic 10 per cent, which is why ancient peoples called iron "the metal from the sky"—while the rest pass for ordinary stones? That worldwide only about 2,200 fallen meteorites are definitely known, of which Mecca's revered Black Stone is one?

Fascinating—yet remote compared to the first winter bird at one's feeder, or snow for Christmas. Maybe that's why, for all my night walking, I'd never made a date with a meteor shower, let alone expected to own a meteorite. Until last November.

I don't recall what changed my mind, though spending time in my friend Reg's homemade new backyard observatory must have played a part. Whatever the catalyst, there I was on the seventeenth (normally the Leonids's big night), trudging east (supposedly the best direction) on our gravel road sometime after 12:00 a.m. (said to be the best time), eyes glued to the starry vault.

The night was perfect for star-gazing: frosty, clear, no moon, no clouds, the town-glow dim. *Una nostra estrellada*. Perfect or no, in half an hour not a single meteor had shown up, or down. Rubbing my stiff neck, I reluctantly turned homeward—then faced about and began walking backwards...just in case.

Suddenly, halfway between Duncan's farm and Andrew's, the meteor appeared. Trailing purplish sparks, it rocketed straight down our Shore Road, arched overhead—I nearly fell over—and vanished behind the next hill. So low did it seem, so big, my body instinctively braced for the fiery crash. Instead—a deafening silence. The possibility of finding a meteorite (as fallen meteors are properly termed) had never seemed so real to me. I later learned that meteorites are not known to fall during meteor showers.

In any case, that was it for the night. Apparently that year's Leonids arrived forty-six hours behind schedule. The next night, Reg counted fifty-six in-falls in one hour. Ah, well.

Then, in early December, my odd coincidence occurred. Beth and I had gone to a rural Christmas craft fair as we often

do, and there, among the booths of bright woollens and home-made fudge and wooden toys, was a display of semi-precious stones. And amid the purple amethysts and pearly geodes, like ET among the stuffed toys, sat a stone that did not fit.

"Hey," I blurted to the booth person, "that looks like a meteorite!"

"It is," she said, smiling.

"How do you know?" I said.

"A geologist told me."

"Okay if I pick it up?"

"Sure."

Picture a small bran muffin studded with glass raisins and heavy as lead. It was a meteorite all right. As calmly as possible I put the thing back, and, seeing no price tag, asked if it was for sale.

"Oh, I don't know," she said. "I just put it there to look at." My hopes sank. "Still, it's been kickin' around home for a good while now." My hopes rose. At last she named a reasonable amount and we closed the deal. Walking away, my jacket dragged down to starboard by its iron content, I couldn't wait to get home and examine my prize.

The meteorite weighed 198 grams. Its composition was mostly iron and nickel, hence the rusty hue. Its pitted surface came from gas bubbles bursting and lighter elements vaporizing during the incandescent fall. The raisins were melted crystals of purple garnet, a magnesium-rich silica, probably $Mg_3Al_2(SiO_4)_3$.

Such a rock is good to have around. Never mind crystal power or astrological gyres; I keep it near for other reasons. First, in gratitude that it wasn't an asteroid the size of Vancouver Island. Second, because it's older than anything on Earth. Though some scientists believe our planet is an accretion of such meteorites. Third, because this stone on its elliptical path around the sun has journeyed farther than any human being, likely out beyond Mars, perhaps even beyond Jupiter. Fourth, because it speaks of another incredible journey, a saga unfolding here and now on this emerald globe as it turns like a Christmas bauble in the void. From crystal to colloid, from prokaryote living cell to twenty-storey, from crawling trilobite to leaping humpback whale — it was around for the whole show. And now to us, *Homo sapiens*, apparently in charge — another thought that gives me goosebumps, but also hope.

Of such things my sky stone whispers, glinting with purple fire as the Season of Good Will bears down upon us.

Plastic Ocean Blues

Recently I read a book that rattled me. Me, with a raft of doomsday books already, books ranging from James Lovelock's *Revenge of Gaia* (2006) to Naomi Klein's *This Changes Everything* (2014) to Al Gore's *Inconvenient Sequel: Truth to Power* (2017), and a dozen in between.

Scary books all—but this one was different—and oddly comforting. While the others catalogued our crimes against Mother Earth and offered scant hope, Alan Weisman's book *The World Without Us* (2007) began where they left off, with humans extinct and the Earth left to heal on its own.

Apocalyptic though it was, the book won a slew of awards that year: *Time* #1 Non-Fiction Book, *Globe & Mail* Best Book, *National Post* Best Book. Glowing reviews followed. To my mind Heather Mallick's review on *rabble.ca* said it best: "Weisman has an Atwood-like talent for describing the terrifying derelict structures we will leave behind."

I read the book anyway—then tried to forget it.

Until this summer. On July 20, as I strolled a garbage-laden Newfoundland beach, Weisman's chapter on ocean pollution came crashing home to me. Hitherto my environmental worries were centred onshore: genetically modified (GM) crops, stripped forests, melting permafrost, fracked drinking water, dead birds, dead bees. Now I saw an even greater threat looming offshore, mostly out of sight, mostly out of mind.

The most arresting chapter was titled "Polymers Are Forever." Forever? Aren't we taught that nothing in Nature is forever? That everything recycles? Worm eats grass, bird eats worm, bird dies to grow more grass? Water becomes mist becomes snow becomes glacier becomes water?

But Mother Nature has other dimensions, among them the microscopic and molecular. Down there we meet true permanence. Like, for instance, those long-chain hydrocarbon molecules which constitute natural polymers such as spider silk, lac bug shellac, cellulose, lignin — and human fingernails. By fiddling with those long-chain molecules we've managed to create things which *are* well-nigh indestructible. Doctored and spiked with various chemicals — a dash of sulphur, a whiff of chlorine — they also become infinitely shape-able (the literal meaning of "plastic").

True, plastics exposed to sunlight and heat and air soon become brittle and shatter. However, submerged in cool, dark ocean depths they last much, much longer. Try this test: tie a new plastic grocery bag to an underwater wharf piling and leave it for a year. Likely it'll still be usable.

But here's the hidden menace: at the micro level, plastic's *ultimate particles persist.* How long, no one yet knows; modern plastics have only been around fifty years or so. (In my childhood the only plastic thing we knew was the post office telephone.) Some scientists say for centuries, perhaps more.

So now I knew what Weisman meant. How could we have let this happen? As he explained it, the polymer revolution began when nineteenth-century British scientist Alexander Parkes successfully turned wood cellulose into celluloid film. Then in 1907, Belgian-American chemist Leo Baekeland, seeking something better than insect glue for coating electric wires, invented the hard, mouldable substance he called Bakelite.

Bakelite made him rich — and changed the Western world. It unleashed a cascade of new synthetics such as PVC, Styrofoam, and nylon-based artificial silk — which re-invented the fashion industry. Things once lovingly hand crafted from clay, wood, paper, or glass could now be poured and mechanically moulded, putting artisans out of work.

The Second World War let loose another cascade. With Japan threatening access to Asian rubber tree latex, the Allies desperately needed a substitute. Again, long-chain molecules, this time from crude oil, came to the rescue. Synthetic rubber was soon followed by Plexiglas, polypropylene rope, foam rubber, polyurethane toys—not to mention marine net floats, see-through packaging, toothbrushes—and the ubiquitous grocery bag.

The list has kept growing. Only last month, buying a large tin of house paint, I discovered the "tin" was mostly plastic. Lugging it up a ladder the next day, I feared it wouldn't survive a bump.

Thankfully, most plastics are recyclable—even Styrofoam, once banned. The problem is, most North Americans don't bother. Unlike Europeans, we toss. That's why many cities are banning plastic grocery bags outright. And it's why stores are finally training staff to ask, "Do you need a bag for that?" (And, if we say yes, charging us five cents for the privilege, or five bucks for a logo-stamped cloth bag.) But don't complain; it's for a good cause.

Back to my beach and the seas beyond. The thing is, oil-based plastics, unless colonized by mussels or algae, seldom sink. Instead they float on top, or hover in the water column, mobile as fish. How do they get there in the first place? Dumped from ships? Yes. Weisman says the world's merchant marine alone contributed over half a million plastic items in 2005.

But most plastic garbage still originates onshore. Yon grocery bag dangling from yon tree or blowing across yon landfill will eventually end up in a lake or brook that will ferry it to sea. As a consequence, we have, in the Great Pacific Gyre (that vast oceanic whorl between North America and East Asia), so much plastic that it's being called the Great Pacific Garbage Patch. Roughly the size of Texas, it dwarfs five other floating garbage dumps circling other seas. A US researcher who sailed the patch found its garbage to be 90 per cent plastic. And most of that, claimed a Los Angeles scientist, came from faulty local landfills. And now we're letting summer cruise ships into the Arctic Ocean.

How does all this impact sea life? Well, for starters, sea turtles commonly mistake plastic grocery bags for jellyfish and choke on them. Likewise, many ocean fish mistake the smaller plastic items for legitimate prey—and die from constipation. Smaller still are flushable *microbeads* found in body wash—"Designed to scrub and freshen your skin!"—and toothpaste, and the microfibres found in unfiltered grey-water from laundered synthetic clothing lint and especially from polar fleece.

Worse, at the penultimate particle size, which plastic makers call *nurdles*—mere needles—they become food for microscopic zooplankton, free-swimming organisms that not only underpin the entire oceanic food chain but also *supply a third of Earth's atmospheric oxygen.* When they go, so perhaps will their immediate consumers and so on up the food chain to capelin, herring, cod, dolphin, whale—and humans. And the lost oxygen? We've already lost immense stretches of oxygen-producing tropical forest. And the world's oceans already exhibit dead—anoxic and acidic—zones. Who knows?

The latest bad news is that plastic water bottles routinely shed microscopic slivers, which we ingest. Our kidneys filter all liquids, but no one yet knows what harm these slivers may do. The worst news of all is that micro-plastics bond to existing waterborne toxins like metallic copper, creating aquatic poison pills.

With all this micro talk, let's not ignore large-scale fishery artifacts like legal nets and trawl lines. Traditionally made from natural fibres like silk, cotton, and hemp, now they mostly consist of coloured plastic monofilament, all but invisible under water. Cod-jigging off Twillingate last summer, I was amazed at how quickly the meshes vanished down there. It's no secret that such nets, some of them hundreds of metres long, routinely drown seals and whales. Worse, storms sometimes tear them adrift, floats and all, to keep on fishing, untended and untendable, indefinitely.

BEACH DUMP, NS

Might all this edible ocean garbage poison entire ocean ecosystems, the way carbon acidification is wrecking coral reefs? Again, no one knows. Maybe recent stock declines aren't *all* due to overfishing and climate change. Can our fish stocks handle this triple threat?

"But," some may object, "the oceans cover two-thirds of the globe! Surely they can handle our puny dumping?" Well, yes and no. Yes, the world ocean is vast. But no, most plastic pollution happens in shallow coastal waters where many fish congregate and breed. And even the deepest ocean deeps, 8 kilometres down, are shallow compared to the Earth's diameter of roughly 13,000 kilometres—more like the skin of an apple.

Back again to my cove and beach. Lacking time to comb all its detritus, and mistrusting my subjective eye, I chose to sample a single metre-wide strip straddling the high tide flotsam line. From cliff to cliff my strip measured 71 metres. So, a fair-sized sample, and likely fairly typical.

What I found astounded me. Every conceivable plastic artifact was there but a telephone, from tampon applicators to corrugated beach signs to toothbrushes. There were so many empty 12-gauge shotgun shells I decided to count them: 295 — including one still loaded! They alone made a small pile. The rest I sorted into four much bigger piles: containers (mostly pop and water bottles but also "green" detergent sprayers), rope and netting, toys, miscellaneous. After photographing each pile I bagged them (in plastic, what else?) and set the five sacks out for the town's Tuesday pickup. Within the hour, hungry herring gulls had ripped open the bags. Only my weighted tarp kept the contents from returning to the sea before dark.

And those shotgun shells? Let's not be too hard on our seabird hunters. Picture them out there in a boat, huddled in oilskins against a sleety nor'easter, eyes peeled for the next fly-past of eider, turrs, or bull-birds. All they're after is a few meals of healthy winter meat that doesn't come shrink-wrapped on white styro trucked from Toronto. And such shooting takes real skill. Pivoting with each wheeling flock, taking a bead against the boat's roll and pitch, firing without hitting other gunners, downing a few birds, hurriedly ejecting the spent shells before the next flight. It's simply a seasonal harvest of low-cholesterol meat provided free by Nature. And the plastic fallout is by comparison minuscule.

No, they have every right. What's our excuse?

Part Eight
Remembering

Neil Van Nostrand, Ecologist

My good friend Neil·is gone. On October 6, 2016, on a sparkling blue-and-gold afternoon under the giant oaks that shade the Gaspereau Valley cemetery west of Wolfville, Nova Scotia, some four dozen of us — family, friends, and colleagues — saw him into the good earth.

His plain pine coffin was graced by home-grown flowers and a grey-and-tan coyote skin. Coyote skin? Yes. For Neil Van was a professional wildlife biologist. Ontario-born, he'd studied agronomy at the University of Guelph — farming ran in his large family — then took a master's degree in wildlife management at nearby Acadia University. This led to his long-time job as small game biologist with the province's then Department of Lands and Forests out of Kentville in the Annapolis Valley.

That's how we met. I'd recently been hired by L&F's Extension Division in Truro to manage its education and information programs — print and audio-visual, exhibits, signage, advertising, queries — for staff and interest groups such as teachers, hunters, trappers, and Christmas tree growers.

Though I had a forestry degree and a rural background, I needed more first-hand information about my adoptive province's wildlife management efforts. Besides, I was planning a quarterly wildlife mini-magazine and needed material. So when Neil got permission to introduce willow grouse (aka ptarmigan) from Newfoundland to Cape Breton in 1969, I asked to join the expedition.

Neil picked me up and together we drove three hours from Truro to North Sydney, there to board an RCMP Marine Division cutter bound for Brunette Island in Fortune Bay on the island's south coast. Once there, we'd collect the ptarmigan chicks and/ or eggs to bring back across the strait. During the three-hour car trip, we talked ourselves hoarse about everything under the sun.

Neil also brought along, besides Acadia's graduate student Al Godfrey, two trained bird dogs (Pete and Shots, to locate the grouse nests), and six custom-made wire cages (to house the chicks' broody bantam hen foster mothers). Our other gear included a long-handled bird net and a cassette tape player/ recorder (to lure nesting chicks).

Ptarmigan, a cyclic northern species, which likely lived here-abouts in post-glacial times, are no longer native to Nova Scotia despite the province's wealth of berry-rich bogs and barrens. (They especially love cranberries.) So Neil had persuaded his superiors that populating those uplands with a new game bird was a good idea.

Boating everything ashore from the RCMP cutter, wading the last few metres in surf—no wharf on Brunette—we stacked the cages beside the Newfoundland Wildlife Service's green plywood cabin in Mercer's Cove, a fishing village depopulated twelve years earlier under Premier Joey Smallwood's grandiose relocation scheme. The island already boasted imported woodland caribou, Alberta bison, and Arctic hare.

That week, using the dogs plus recorded mother ptarmigan homing calls, and helped by NWS staff and two more dogs, we collected over ninety brown-and-ochre, week-old chicks, which the bantam hens quickly adopted. These the RCMP, whose regular task was nabbing rum-runners from nearby St. Pierre and Miquelon islands, ferried with Neil, Al, and me to two thousand-hectare look-alike Scatarie Island off Sydney. (To up his odds of success, Neil had earlier hired a veteran Nova Scotia trapper to reduce the island's booming red fox population.)

Nothing like such an expedition to cement (or ruin) a budding friendship! In Neil I found a naturalist like myself, a reader, an innovative thinker, a dreamer, but also a man of foresight and action. What he found in me, six years his junior, he never said—men are reticent about such things—but we hit it off and never looked back. Oh, we had some differences—but what friends don't? True friends care enough to make up and move on.

The ptarmigan transfer seemed a surefire winner. Alas, in the end, for unknown reasons, likely illegal hunting, the introduction fizzled. He'd even picked a high-population year for collecting. Perhaps the climate had already warmed too much? A major disappointment.

By contrast, his study of beaver population dynamics and his follow-up work on trapper education were crowned with success. Nineteenth-century over-trapping and twentieth-century habitat losses to logging, hydro flooding, and urban encroachment had decimated their numbers. To him—vocal urban critics aside—legal, humane harvesting by trained trappers with proper gear was a valuable source of seasonal rural income and an honourable and historic trade. Selecting western Nova Scotia's protected Tobeatic Sanctuary population for study, he demonstrated that judicious harvesting can actually stimulate the remnant rodents to produce more and healthier kits.

However, to succeed—and to have the public onside—the province's hundreds of trappers must be educated. This meant preaching conservation and having them adopt more humane methods. To this end, working with them, he developed courses and workshops. These covered beaver ecology, proper pelt preparation, and above all switching from primitive leg-hold traps to the modern conibear system. My files still contain his 1974 "NS Trapper Education Course," which my shop printed for him, outlining techniques for humanely capturing each of our native furbearers.

In 1968, he'd also helped found the Trappers Association of Nova Scotia, for which, at his request, I'd designed the original crest. Neil and I also upgraded hunter safety coordinator Bert Crowe's mimeographed "Wildlife Notes." Ably illustrated by

Bridgewater artist Don Pentz, they became our popular ninety-four-page *Notes on Nova Scotia Wildlife* (1980). Unfortunately it covered only mammals and birds, a defect Julie Towers remedied with her *Wildlife of Nova Scotia* (Nimbus, 1980). Another teaching tool was his annual *Trapper's Newsletter.* In 1986, with stories from Neil's Kentville colleagues Art Patton, Fred Payne, Pete Austin-Smith, and others, we launched the aforementioned full-colour magazine, which we called *CoNServation.* Modelled on a similar Ontario magazine I liked, it eventually reached some twenty thousand hunters, anglers, and the general public. Biologist Bob Bancroft edited it for a time; later so did Tony Duke and Sandy Anderson. In 2014, to honour Neil's pioneering work, the Fur Institute of Canada gave him the North American Furbearer Conservation Award.

With wildlife issues well represented, we needed a periodical for woodlot owners and the general public. Under editor Jim Guild, this was our illustrated bimonthly tabloid *Forest Times,* which by the 1990s reached some ten thousand subscribers. Like our two other periodicals, it went to every public and institutional library in the province

After retirement we both kept busy, he in organic farming and I in artwork and writing. And we kept in touch. New books, new research, new ideas were grist for our mill. Actually, Neil unwittingly goosed my writing output. Since the early 1960s, on my own, I'd been writing and illustrating general articles for the old *Atlantic Advocate* based in Fredericton, New Brunswick. Driving back from Cape Breton in 1969, we had both vowed to do more, do something beyond our day jobs, something for the planet. As a retiree he chose organic farming, I nature writing.

Both vows were kept — and rewarded. For his farming he won the coveted Acorn farming award, while I won the Evelyn Richardson Award for Non-Fiction for *My Life with Trees.* Far as I know, where Neil now is they don't farm. As for me, I'll keep writing and drawing while I still can — for the both of us. He'd want that.

Hezekiah and the Pine

Most families, somewhere in their past, harbour a tree story. Ours is about a man who in youth made a solemn bargain with a pine tree and in his old age kept it. Hezekiah Gillingham was my father's mother's brother and by all accounts a "character" among characters.

In my childhood memories he is sixtyish, tall, and gaunt, wearing blue coveralls and smelling of pine sawdust and plug tobacco. His stork legs bear him along so fast, we kids have to jog to keep up. We follow him because he is whimsical, musical, funny—and enjoys our company. He hums a lot, sometimes breaking into songs of his own instant making: "Oh, I wants a stick a' tabaccy, hoot te tootle te toot!" In my childhood memories, Uncle Hezekiah looms like one of the towering white pines so common along our Gander River before the lumberjacks arrived.

The architect of that flurry was J.W. Phillips of Maine, USA. After the White Pine State's best timber had been picked through, Phillips came sniffing around Newfoundland. Finding a modest supply on both the Exploits and Gander watersheds, he secured leases and built a big steam sawmill near tidewater at the mouth of each.

Something of J.W.P.'s drive emerges from the tale of his courtship. On a visit to St. John's years before, he spied this pretty maiden in a store. Months later, still haunted by her face, he set his mind on marriage. This was some years before our trans-island railway was completed, let alone our Trans-Canada Highway, and the east coast was plugged with drift ice. Undaunted, he trekked a hundred rugged miles across the island to its ice-free South Coast, caught a boat to St. John's, and asked for the lady's hand. They married soon after.

The Phillips' Gander Bay mill stood across the half-mile-wide estuary from Clarkes Head where Uncle Hezekiah and my family lived. In my childhood years, early 1940s, nothing remained of the mill but a sawdust knoll, a rusty beached tug, and a name—Georges Point. (George was J.W.'s son and foreman.) All the boilers, shafts, crown gears, and pulleys had long since been sold for scrap to make stoves, anchors, and such at a St. John's foundry.

Even as a boy, Hezekiah had what people called "a good head for ciphering." It was he who later surveyed the route for the wooden flume that delivered water to run Grandpa Saunders's small water-powered sawmill across the Bay in Clarkes Head. This flume marched downhill on timber stilts a quarter mile through woods and bogs from a dam on Clarkes Brook. Sloping precisely 1 inch in 48, it cleared the public road by 20 feet, high enough that its miniature waterfall, entering a vertical turbine's spiral cups, cranked the mill up to 27 horsepower. For years Grandpa sawed lumber, laths, and shingles to supply the northeast coast's small but steady market. Uncle Hezekiah performed this engineering feat with only a carpenter's spirit level and a ball of twine. My father as a boy sometimes walked that flume with the worker who opened and closed the dam. Dad claimed you could roll an orange all the way without a nudge.

Good head or no, Hezekiah got little schooling in our remote village. By the time its first teacher, James Rowsell, arrived from England, he was a young man. Though he'd already taught himself to read, to please his parents he attended school for a winter or two, his lanky frame taxing the small seat and vice versa.

Then he went to work in the big steam mill across the bay. Phillips soon made him chief log scaler and lumber tallyman. All summer the mill sawed six days a week on two eight-hour shifts. Hezekiah was, in Mr. Rowsell's apt phrase, "kept on the hop." It was a phrase he himself liked. Moreover, living on the wrong side of the estuary as he did meant that he rowed to and from work in all weather. Wintertime, as log scaler, he snowshoed from camp to camp, measuring the season's cut before the spring breakup whisked them downstream to the mill. It was a tough way to make a living.

Even so, as a forester I envy him those years. For as a boy he witnessed the construction of one of The Rock's first steam-powered sawmills, saw the growth of a small village of workers' homes, a general store, a post office, and school where nothing but cliffs and woods had been before. And because the mill had a steam generator (run off slabs and edgings), he saw the bay's first electric lights gleam across the estuary seventy-six years before the government made it commonplace. Plus he measured logs the size of pilot whales—logs from ancient trees, which were young when Shakespeare was a lad. He had seen them hauled up the green chain, heard them clunk onto the carriage and rumble through the wailing band-saws to emerge as pumpkin-coloured planks and deals for export. He got to breathe the resiny fragrance of acres of stacked lumber drying in the sun, of sawdust steaming in the rain. He could run his long fingers over silken wainscoting that was two feet wide without a knot. His sister Mary, a domestic in Phillips's home, marvelled at a thirty-inch parlour door sawn from a single pine board.

Hezekiah also saw trolleys laden with such lumber screech and clank to dockside where schooners wearing patched brown sails and women's names ferried it to places like Fogo, Joe Batt's Arm, and Greenspond. Once in a while, he saw a great Danish windjammer ghost up the bay under a cloud of canvas, anchor in midstream, open cavernous bow hatches, and swallow thick pink deals as fast as two chuffing steam tugs could tow them out.

Unfortunately, no reliable data on the mill's annual output seems to exist. Certainly it was less than that of Lewis Miller's big operation on the upper Exploits. But it's likely that from its start-up in 1890 to shutdown in 1905, the Georges Point mill put out at least several million board feet a year.

Uncle Hezekiah, scaling the logs each winter, tallying the mountains of export deals week by week, watching the sawdust rise up and overflow into Barry's Brook, must have wondered how long it could last. In fact the good pine was nearly all gone from the Gander watershed. Newfoundland is near the northern limit of *Pinus strobus.* At best only sheltered river valleys like those of the Gander and Exploits could yield the timber such mills demanded. Already by 1900, J.W.'s sawyers were running into heart rot, small logs, and "wind-shook" timber — trees whose annual rings had parted and filled with pitch.

As profits waned and woes mounted, foreman George sought solace in rum. Finally, Phillips's two mills shut down and their leased woodlands were sold to the Harmsworth pulp interests of England.

One summer's day long before all this happened, Hezekiah was boating down the river with a load of supplies. Feeling hungry, he stopped to boil the kettle. The beach he picked was overshadowed by a great white pine too windblown to tempt a lumberman. The young man noted that river ice had gnawed its trunk, triggering a bumper crop of cones which now lay strewn along the bank. Gathering firewood, he found a knee-high plume of silvery green, healthy offspring of the matriarch. "Little one," he murmured, "you're after growing in a bad spot. Next spring's ice will likely carry thee away."

With a chunk of blue-grey for trowel, he filled his hat half full of the rich coffee-brown loam, teased the seedling into his hat, covered the roots with damp soil and placed the result in the canoe's bow. Lunching on bread and tea and jam, Hezekiah had an idea. Back home, he chose a sheltered back corner of his father's pasture, made a little fence to keep out free-roaming ponies and sheep, and planted the seedling. Then he made a vow: "Little pine, when you are grown and I am old, you shall be my coffin."

Down all the years of marriage and work and child-raising with his beloved Carrie, Hezekiah nurtured and protected that tree. At last it grew so tall that in haying time he could lodge his scythe against its trunk and sprawl in its shade. People who saw his faithful pony Joe standing guard knew the old man was taking a noon nap.

And when the time was right, this gentle man felled and limbed and bucked the sizable tree and took its logs to his brother-in-law Frank to saw. Grandpa, as kinfolk will, protested such a request. But Hezekiah merely chuckled. He built coffins for others, why not for himself?

Grandpa sawed the logs into suitable planks and planed them smooth. Hezekiah left half the lumber in payment — "sawing on the halves" they called it in those nearly cashless days — shouldered the chosen boards and toted them back to his workshop near Point Head. Humming, he measured and sawed and planed them to a perfect fit. Securing them with copper boat-building screws, he printed his initials on the casket's bottom in blue lumber crayon and told his family where to find it. Hezekiah lived for several years after that, secure in the thought that, when the time came, his long pink eternity box was ready.

Donald Culross Peattie, in his delightful *Natural History of Trees*, tells how the American frontiersman Daniel Boone likewise crafted his own coffin, using in his case black cherry wood. It comforts me to think that those two pioneers, so different in gifts and temperament, could think of no finer way to depart this life than in a fragrant wooden shell of their own making. Except Hezekiah went the great Kentuckian one better: he grew the tree himself.

A Rose for Mary Matilda

I am longing for the Bay ice to be good for crossing so I can take a run over for a few days to help pass the time.
— Mary (Gillingham) Saunders, age eighty-four
(Letter to the author, January 7, 1966)

One Sunday when I was eight or nine and the bay was flat calm, I was down by the landwash dreamily skipping small, flat, rounded stones as Newfoundland boys have always done. You try to make them hop as far as possible before they turn, tilt, and sink. It takes practice. And Sundays back then, with no boats stirring, were perfect for that.

Suddenly a woman's voice whispered in my ear, so close it made me jump: "Do you know that every rock you throw on Sunday must be picked up in the next life?"

"No-o," I stammered, craning to see her face.

"'Tis true," said Grandma Saunders with a sigh as she took the next stone from my hand. "And you're old enough now to know better."

"I—I'm sorry, Grandma," I said, slinking away. For by then I must have slung hundreds. That warning was one of the first of her many attempts to save my immortal soul.

'Twasn't that she was hard-hearted or legalistic. On the contrary, she was generous and fun-loving. In my earliest memory of her, she's beckoning to my cousin Frank and me, busy digging a snow cave outside her kitchen window, to come in for 'lassy buns hot from the oven. No, except for her Sunday policing, she was the best of grandmothers, much more fun than her husband, Grandpa Frank. She teased, she told funny stories, she made up songs, she wrote poems:

The hands were moving round the clock,
The hour was getting late;
The wind was howling fiercely,
And the storm did not abate.

And she was a gracious hostess. She and her merchant husband, devout Anglicans, often hosted the bishop on his seasonal Gander Bay rounds. She had learned such courtesies as a servant girl to Mr. Chapman, manager of the big J.W. Phillips's sawmill over to Georges Point across the bay.

But on the matter of Sabbath-breaking she was adamant, almost Jewish. The fact is, her whole generation was raised to revere the Lord's Day, the Christian Sabbath. Thus housewives commonly prepared their Sunday vegetables on Saturday evening. Men would leave new-mown hay to go mouldy rather than gather it on a sunny Sunday. Sunday was for Bible study, for teaching children their catechism, for reading John Bunyan's *The Pilgrim's Progress* (if you could afford the book), for singing hymns, going to church, visiting, writing letters.

Above all it was for *resting*. Postmoderns who've never made bread for a hungry family twice a week, or felled trees for a living, or tended acres of salt fish through sun and rain, or harvested a cellar-full of potatoes or turnips can scarcely comprehend their utter need for rest. In the words of ninety-year-old cod fisher Eddy Hamlyn of Twillingate, "We worked from daylight till star-dark. Aye, and the womenfolk worked even longer."

"A man's work's from sun to sun," quoted Grandma, "but a woman's work is never done!"

Nor was the Sabbath only for the well-to-do. It was also for the powerless and marginalized: the scullery maid, the field hand, the stranger in your midst, even the sled dogs and horses. It was scriptural, in fact one of the world's first labour laws — the right to an earned rest from honest toil. Apart from a promise of rest, it was an outward and visible sign of humble submission to the Eternal, a public badge and banner of godly intent.

Practice that, teach it to your children, and thy days would be long in the land which the Lord had given thee. In contrast, all else in one's religious life — alms-giving, charity, personal prayer — was to be done in private lest vanity and pride rear their ugly heads.

I can see her now, above average height with mirthful brown eyes behind round-rimmed spectacles, her oval face framed by bobbed, greying hair. I hear the soft accents of her Poole ancestors — "medder" for meadow — her cadences informed by years of reading the 1611 King James Bible, her speech salted with the homely Anglo-Saxon words of Archbishop Thomas Cranmer's even older *Book of Common Prayer*, words still recited at weddings and funerals across diverse Protestant faiths: "*With this ring I thee wed... Ashes to ashes, dust to dust... And there is no health in us.*"

All of which begged the question — why me, a mere boy? What did I do or not do to make her fret so for my spiritual welfare? I wasn't even her first grandson. That was my brother, seven years older. Was I really that bad?

Well, yes and ňo. Boys will be boys; she knew that, having raised four of her own. But when my brother was little, her two youngest were still at home, keeping her busy. By the time I arrived she had more leisure, time to milk her cow, tend her rose garden, do church work, watch over me.

Speaking of which, my parents weren't regular churchgoers. That may have troubled her — though my mother, Winnifred, did fill in as organist now and then. As for Dad, he never liked church and anyway was often busy making a living: guiding sports or hunters on the Gander River, ferrying passengers by motorboat to and from Twillingate Hospital, trapping in the wintertime. A dollar here, a dollar there.

Mom was also part-time postmistress. When both our parents had to be away, her teenaged sister, Beatrix, came from Fogo to look after us. Back then, Newfoundland children mostly started school at seven. Homebound, I was getting to be a handful.

My curiosity about the world was intense — especially about water and fire. "You're always coming home soaking wet," Aunt Beattie would cry. And matches fascinated me.

These tendencies my grandma, living just across the meadow, must have noticed. "The Devil finds work for idle hands," she always said, and resolved to keep a sharper eye on me. It wasn't meddling. It was her duty as my only living grandmother. Mom's mother, Prudence (Waterman) Layman of Fogo, had died eight years before I was born.

One day when no one was about, I climbed up on the woodbox and stole some matches from behind the stove. They weren't safety matches, but the colourful strike-anywhere sort. I'd often watched my parents light the morning fire and I had a Plan. By the time Mom found me in the nearby woodshed, I had a nice little fire of shavings going on a workbench. With a terrifying screech she yanked me away and beat out the flame with her apron. It was a near, near thing. We could have lost not only the shed and our winter's firewood but the house as well. Dad gave me a lacing — a few stinging swipes about the legs with an alder switch — and I never stole matches again.

But now I was a marked lad. Oh, the waywardness of boys. Hadn't King Solomon himself warned parents against us in Proverbs 22:15: "Folly is deep-rooted in the heart of a boy"? And I was a little hypocrite. Around grownups butter wouldn't melt in my mouth. "Such a nice boy," purred the church ladies, "a minister sure when he grows up." But I wasn't minister material and Grandma knew it.

She didn't know the half of it. Some of it was just curiosity, a love of science. Baiting hens with crusts of bread tied to a fishing line to make them regurgitate. Spooning sugar into a glass of water on the sly to watch it dissolve, then guzzle it down unbeknownst to Mom. Or acts of revenge, like taking a jarful of angry bumblebees next door to Aunt Kathleen's and dumping them on her kitchen floor to get back at her son Frank for something or other. Or, a few years later, just plain disobedience: taking a canoe without permission to steal goose-berries from the Hodder property on Salt Island across the bay. Or singing blasphemous doggerel:

I don't care if it rains or freezes,
I am safe in the arms of Jesus;
I am Jesus's little lamb,
Yes by Jesus, yes I am!

Then there was the Sunday ice-sledding episode. Frank and I never meant to go so far. But heavy rain and bitter cold had left the bay coated glass-smooth with irresistible ice. Because once we cleared Grandpa's wharf, a westerly gale grabbed our coasters—each equipped with a small fir for a sail—and blew us willy-nilly northeast. Laughing and yelling above the hollow din of our metal runners, we were halfway across the bay before we capsized on a drifted-over rent (crack).

In the sudden quiet we heard a wind-baffled sound. The church bell! We'd forgotten church! And played hooky from Sunday school! Struggling home against the gale, slipping and sliding, took us forever. Yet that time—they were so glad to see us—we went unpunished.

It was the innocence of angling that finally cured me of my juvenile Sabbath-breaking. Mom and Dad never much minded my fishing, even on Sunday, for they loved fresh brook trout. So, come springtime, after Sunday school, I'd dart behind the wharf sheds where Grandma couldn't see, then skulk along the shore to nearby Clarkes Brook. Below the bridge lay a dandy pool. Hidden (as I thought) behind the steep bank, I began to fish.

On a rising tide the brook changed its whole personality. All its talkative rills and ripples flattened and fell silent. This was my moment. Riding the incoming tide were sea trout returning to spawn. Here they rested before tackling the rocky upstream run to Clarkes Pond. As they lazed in the dark current, their plump flanks flashed silver and bronze. Sabbath or no, how could I resist?

Yet somehow—from an upstairs window?—Grandma spotted me, came and confronted me, counselled me again to mend my ways.

Ah, Grandmother, were you afraid our little brook would drown me, the way the Gander had drowned your young brother Stanley in 1924? Or that my inordinate love of trouting would woo me away to roam the woods like your four sons, especially my father? I was older now, knew my catechism, had recently been confirmed by the bishop, was supposed to be more mature.

For the first time, genuine remorse smote me for aggrieving this wise woman who wished for me only good. I thought it over and sincerely promised to do better. Well I might. Only a year or so earlier, I had planned and carried out a petty theft to which she was sole witness. Worse, I'd cajoled cousin Frank into helping. Had anyone but she caught us, or had she handled it differently, I might have become a genuine delinquent.

It happened this way. I was by now a sugar in love with sugar —hence the sugar-water trick. My every earned penny went for candy at Grandpa's shop. In his big shop window sat a glistening jar of rainbow-hued "common candy": red-striped white peppermint knobs, satiny pink "chicken bones" with chocolate marrow, glossy jelly beans, succulent molasses kisses.

Choosing a moment when no customers were inside and Grandpa was busy in his back office, I stationed Frank on watch outside, ducked behind the counter and grabbed the jar. Then we carried it between us up the lane past Grandma's windows to a firewood tepee out back. We had just begun to share the loot when Grandma's face appeared.

There was no escape, no excuse. As we stared at the ground she leaned in, lifted the half-empty jar, put back the candies one by one, and stood regarding us. Then, to our astonishment, she gave us each one candy, ordered us never to steal again, and was gone.

This was far worse than any tongue-lashing. We dragged ourselves home to face the punishment our parents would surely dish out. But there was none. She never told on us. That was Grandma for you.

In June 2007, vacationing in Newfoundland long after she had died at age ninety-seven, I parked in Clarkes Head near where her rose garden used to be. The 1966 road widening had buried most of it, but I hoped to find some remnant to plant elsewhere. In the ditch I found a single rugosa seedling. Taking it to our summer place on Twillingate Island, I planted it under the south window, out of the wind but close enough for us to catch its fragrance on a summer evening. Despite the salty gale, it has prospered. Every summer, while its bright pink blossoms last, I keep one in a wineglass on our windowsill. A rose for Mary Matilda, who also wrote:

So now my song is ended,
We have no more to say;
We'll go upstairs and say our prayers,
And pray for a better day.

Remembering Lucy and Helen

Lucy. Her very name means light-bearer. And whenever I think of her, even now, more than a decade after her death, the image that leaps to mind is light. I see light prismatic and velvety, a sculptural shimmer, a palette glowing in lemon, mauve, and cerulean. For Lucy was a painter.

And I hear her voice. It is a cultivated voice, modulated and expressive, at times throaty, prone to laughter and to staccato bursts of words followed by silences as she waits with raised brows, eyes dancing, lips half-parted in a smile, for my response.

"Art is communication, yes," she exclaims, "but not of *values*. Art is the communication of *discovery* and *experience*. D'you know what Kokoschka always said? 'Make me see what *you* see.' Yes, *that's* the thing." Sometimes in the heat of debate she lisps. This lends her a curious air of innocence, like that of a little girl wearing dental braces. Sometimes her words overflow in helpless stuttering.

"Care for a rum toddy? Some grog?"

That was her standard welcome on my infrequent visits to the grey-shingled cottage she shared with painter Helen Weld outside Yarmouth, Nova Scotia. Their lane being too narrow for a car, visitors parked in a turnout between shore and lily pond and ascended a short path hedged with tall red rugosa rose bushes. Nearly always there was the rhythmic applause of surf along nearby Pembroke Beach. And in heavy weather one heard the distant bellow of Cape Forchu's foghorn. Salt water, seaweed, wild mustard, timothy hay, pink roses, alder pollen, bayberry, goldenrod, aster: these were the seasonal fragrances.

Turning right at a woodpile, one entered a narrow porch crammed with stovewood, dry kindling, garden tools, and pails of fresh well water. A hand-decorated door opened on a kitchen as snug as Badger's underground den in *The Wind in the Willows*.

Entering now, I note again how the kitchen's east window overlooks the lily pond and cove, how a south window faces Chegoggin Point and the North Atlantic. How overhead, decades of woodsmoke have seasoned the white spruce wood ceiling to toast-and-honey hues. Again I inhale incense of stove heat, candle wax, turpentine, kerosene, recent cooking. To the left, a squarish iron cookstove commands the north wall, from which hang a dozen blackened saucepans, skillets, and utensils. Under each window a wide quilt-covered bench serves as seat by day and bed by night. Between the benches is an oil-clothed table with a lamp, salt and pepper shakers, some books and mail, a marmalade jar of cutlery, and a sugar bowl with a purple mussel shell for a spoon.

From ceiling to table level, pine shelves glint and glow with china, pottery, mugs, and candlesticks. There are two full spice racks, their contents alphabetically arranged by Helen, the tidy, sensible one. Every available cranny and niche displays memorabilia of their countless painting expeditions: pencil sketches, yellowed photos, sand dollars from the beach, a bracket fungus from the woods, multi-hued pebbles from Newfoundland.

"I'd love a toddy." (*Will it taste of turpentine?* I wondered that first time. It didn't.) Smiling, Lucy pokes the fire, grabs a battered saucepan, pours in grapefruit juice and hot water, adds a splash of rum, a spoonful of honey, a couple of cloves. While the toddy is heating, I fetch fresh garden produce from my vehicle and move my bag to the guest's alcove. Wandering into the adjoining living-room-cum-studio, I savour again its prints and paintings, its fieldstone fireplace and chimney, the admirable homemade floor-to-ceiling bay window crowned by a half-cone of triangular panes. North light glimmers coolly on a square wooden dining table. A paint-daubed easel holds work in progress.

In the kitchen we sit and sip, and talk and laugh until the day darkens from lemon to indigo, and it's time to light lamps and think of supper. Lack of electricity and indoor plumbing have never bothered Jarvis and Weld. Overnight guests quickly learned to step back in time. Hadn't these two women tented for months at nearby Markland in 1930? Spent the whole year of 1934-35 painting in Doane's uninsulated cottage at Yarmouth Bar? Forty years later, they still preferred that gypsy simplicity, even to using a hand-flushed basement toilet. For years they wouldn't hear of putting in a furnace — why do so when there were no pipes to freeze and burst? No, stove and fireplace suffice for us, thank you. They did install a telephone.

When I first met Lucy Jarvis at the University of New Brunswick in 1957, I was a sophomore forestry student and she'd been there, teaching and painting, for over twenty years. Born in Toronto in 1896 of Maritime Loyalist stock, she had come east as a child when her father, a branch manager for the Bank of Montreal, was assigned first to Chatham and Woodstock in New Brunswick, then to Yarmouth. In those days, well-bred young ladies whose parents could afford it were sent to finishing school to learn to cook and comport and to sew a fine seam. Lucy, after graduating from Toronto's Havergal College in domestic science in 1915 and taking a commercial art course, was unsure what to do. Her father suggested art school, and in the fall of 1925 she enrolled at Boston's School of the Museum of Fine Arts.

It was here, standing in line for lockers the first day, that she met lifelong friend Helen Weld of Lowell, Massachusetts.

When an instructor named Thompson asked Lucy if she had ever studied drawing, she replied, "No, but I took some commercial art."

"Well," he said, "you're doing pretty well in spite of it."

Although the museum gave her a solid grounding in classical art, in time she would renounce the school's conservatism for an exuberant impressionism that would evolve into a mild expressionism. In 1929, she withdrew, trading a diploma for a scholarship. Helen also withdrew, and they spent the summer camping and painting around Yarmouth, where Lucy had lived for a time as a child. Afterwards she painted in Toronto and Brantford, Ontario, undertook portrait commissions, and exhibited with the Royal Canadian Academy. For a year she taught art at King's Hall in Compton, Quebec. Another year was spent painting at Yarmouth Bar. From 1935 to 1940 she was a cataloguer and draftsperson for the Royal Ontario Museum.

Then two events brought her east again. Her father died and her mother (née Kate Harris of Moncton) moved to Fredericton. Lucy soon gravitated to UNB. I might never have met this remarkable woman had I been fonder of statistics and mensuration, two courses required for the BSc in forestry. As it happened, a five-year forestry bursary had brought me to UNB, but I was a half-hearted student who, since high school, had dreamed of attending the Ontario College of Art, indeed was saving my meagre earnings as a checkout boy for it.

Late one afternoon, after a gruelling statistics test, I ventured into the Arts Centre. My classmates considered the place "artsy," no place for a would-be forester or engineer. Despite the place's stark military exterior — it was a former Quonset hut — the inside was pleasant. Lucy greeted me warmly and we struck it off. Here one could relax and browse full-colour reproductions of Giotto or Matisse (and rent them for pennies a month), could attend live poetry readings, music, and drama, even take art lessons. It was UNB's first student centre. For me it opened a new window on life.

The Arts Centre notion grew out of a chance meeting in 1940 between Jarvis and artist Pegi Nicol MacLeod at, of all places, a Toronto swimming party. When Pegi came to UNB that year, they took the idea to Margaret MacKenzie, wife of UNB's progressive new president. That December the pair set up shop in the vacant old Observatory beside the Old Arts Building. On opening night, thirty-five people showed up in a minus 35°C blizzard.

The following year, Lucy took over the winter art classes from Pegi, who returned to teach summer school until 1948. In 1946, to accommodate returning soldiers, the centre moved downtown to makeshift quarters at Alexander College. Five years later, it was back on campus.

For Lucy those war years had been busy. From 1942 to 1944, she travelled rural New Brunswick as a National Film Board projectionist for the War Information Service, doing her bit to combat what she termed "all those totalitarian countries trying to clamp down on creativity." For two years she also taught part-time at the Provincial Normal School.

Meanwhile, the centre had become a respected institution. Said Professor Alfred Bailey at the time, "Its humanizing influence radiated far and wide." Lucy conducted art classes for adults, juniors, and children both on and off campus, arranged exhibitions, and organized discussion groups. Her Saturday morning children's art classes helped shape many talents, including that of Fredericton native Mary Pratt. "She believed not in catchy art," recalled Pratt, "but the real thing." In 1946, the university named her full-time director. She also taught aesthetics and cultural history. Erudite professors were glad to tap Jarvis's wide knowledge of culture, her gift for lively synthesis and exposition.

My favourite Jarvis image from those days is that of her pedalling around campus on her sturdy English bicycle, floppy purple beret jammed down over unruly reddish hair, front basket piled high with paraphernalia. To me this icon of independent thinking rebuked the aridity of calculus and stats, and for that I loved her.

Dr. and Mrs. MacKenzie treasured her too. In 1955-56, UNB awarded her a sabbatical, which she and Helen spent painting at Montparnasse, Paris. When she retired to paint full-time at Pembroke Dyke in 1960, the university named her a lifetime faculty member. The Canada Council awarded her an unsolicited senior artist's grant, which, augmented by friends' donations, allowed her to buy a car and tour England and Europe for nine months. She studied at the studio of André Lhote, at Paris's Grande Chaumière, and at Oskar Kokoschka's School of Seeing in Salzburg. In 1966, 1967, 1968, and 1973 she returned to France. Always she came back to the studio-cottage that Vernon Thompson had built for her in 1948.

Meanwhile Helen Weld had kept in touch. Herself a wise and gifted — though less flamboyant — painter, she had been cited in newspaper reviews for the strong and colourful work she exhibited in group shows. Most of her time, though, Helen devoted to helping other artists. After her mother's death in 1971, she came to live with Lucy full-time. The pair quickly became part of the Yarmouth community. They hosted Hallowe'en and Christmas parties, staged children's puppet shows in their living room, and skated with local kids on the duck pond out front.

Their Pembroke years were very productive. In scores of landscapes and portraits, mostly oils, they celebrated men hauling nets and scraping boats, the annual Fisherman's Parade, the upturned faces of children. In bad weather they might work on still lifes or self-portraits, but both preferred painting outdoors. To resist the seduction of the picturesque scene, they'd set an alarm clock, drive until it went off, and paint whatever they saw.

Surrounded by prettiness, Lucy never painted prettily. Like Cézanne she did many versions of the same beloved scenes: ducks on the pond, lobster pots on the beach, cows belly-deep in August meadows, winter seas blossoming above the cliffs called The Churn. In oils she liked to glaze and scumble, to lay on buttery daubs with a palette knife, to squeeze water lilies of titanium white and cadmium yellow directly from the tube.

Yet the touch was delicate. In her best works, a mother-of-pearl iridescence at once defines the form and delights the eye. "Carving with colour," she called it, echoing old Kokoschka. This formal solidity flowed mostly from a mastery of drawing. Her line, like that of Frederick Varley, was nervous and elegant, especially when exploring the nude.

Except for occasional local exhibits, she took few pains to promote herself at large. Instead she lived and worked in simplicity and relative obscurity, content with the untutored praise of neighbours and children, scorning "the Art Racket" and "art fakers" who go commercial. "I don't *sell* paintings," she once said, "people *buy* them." When, in the winter of 1972, she let me mount a Truro, Nova Scotia, show of two dozen paintings — matched by an equal number of Helen's — I was surprised. But then our small public library was the sort of homey venue they liked.

Jarvis and Weld supported the whole spectrum of Yarmouth's creative endeavour, from pottery to music to theatre. Their views of Art were libertarian and eclectic. When her catalogue for an exhibit of students' work came off the press with the title mistakenly edited to say "Art is Communication," Lucy corrected it to "The Arts as Communication," and had it reprinted. Self-effacing, she said, "I don't teach, people learn!" In the foreword she wrote, "Who can say what ART is? Even the Oxford Dictionary, in desperation, defines Art as Skill. We all know skill that is not Art." Contemporary Yarmouth painters Alex Gigeroff, Ruth Rideout, Margaret Chipman, and Hugh Eamon all acknowledge their debt to her honesty and vision. So do I.

Over the years, I visited Lucy and Helen several times, sometimes with my family, sometimes alone. I recall one time when Lucy, then about seventy-five, came hurrying down the lane to meet our car, her stocky, firm body encased in a black one-piece swimsuit, eyes alight with mischief. When she failed to entice our three shy children to kiss her or to join her in the chilly water, she jogged on down to the ocean, plunged in, and romped like a seal. She certainly challenged their notions of "old lady." Both women continued to squaredance well into their eighties.

She could be crotchety, sharp of tongue. A lively sense of humour saved her. When a nervous UNB student named Hans Forestall accidentally introduced her as "Miss Juicy Larvis," she whooped with glee. At our Truro art reception, an awkward silence followed the opening remarks. Suddenly one of her paintings escaped its homemade barnboard frame and clattered to the floor. "Just the thing to loosen everyone up!" she whooped. Children instinctively warmed to her wit and skill. Predictably, she loved the zany philosophy of James Stephens's book *The Crock of Gold*. She liked men, but remarked, "The only males who were ever interested in me went to war and got themselves killed or something."

In February, four months before her death at eighty-nine, the University of New Brunswick honoured Jarvis with a major retrospective. The sizable task of assembling and later returning dozens of paintings from owners near and far, of answering numerous telegrams and letters, and of meeting visitors seemed not to daunt her. Then in mid-May her sister died in Fredericton. Lucy, the eldest, found herself the last of her family.

"Suddenly she seemed to wilt," said Helen. Around 2:00 a.m., on May 24, Helen woke to the sound of fitful coughing and erratic breathing. Unable to rouse her friend, she called an ambulance. Lucy Mary Hope Jarvis never regained consciousness. The doctor diagnosed a massive stroke. Mourners thronged the funeral. Tributes poured in from the Maritimes and beyond. A group of local students playing *Tom Sawyer*, though they barely knew the woman, dedicated their earnings to her memory.

Last October, as I left the pavement and turned toward Pembroke Dyke, a new green-and-silver highway sign announced

"Helen and Lucy Road." Helen, ninety and nearly blind from an unsuccessful cataract operation, greeted me as of old. We found some rum, stoked the fire, and made a toddy. On Lucy's easel Helen had placed her friend's last picture, a vertical landscape of beach vegetation swirling up to a pastel sky. It reminded me of Van Gogh's scarlet vineyards, a faded print of which hung near the fireplace. "The only painting he ever sold," Lucy liked to say. Brushes and palette lay nearby. It was as though the painter had just stepped outside. In a sense she has. Godspeed then, light-bearer, mentor, friend of fishers, carpenters, children, carver with colour, seer.

NB: In 1995, the Art Gallery of Nova Scotia honoured Lucy and Helen with a joint retrospective that drew over three thousand people before moving on to Yarmouth and Wolfville. Helen died a year later.

Lloyd S. Hawboldt, Bug Man

Born in 1916 in New Glasgow, of Lunenburg parents, he was raised in Halifax. He lived for years in Dartmouth and died there in 1997. But really he belonged, as we say in Newfoundland, to Truro. And he was the best boss I ever had.

Anyone heading east along Truro's West Prince or Duke Streets early on a weekday morning between 1950 and 1969 might have met him walking briskly to work, a smartly dressed, wavy-haired man of medium build wearing rimless glasses, smoking a pipe, and carrying a leather briefcase. He might have been a university professor or a banker.

In fact, Lloyd Stanley Hawboldt was a kind of physician. He was Nova Scotia's provincial forest entomologist. Spruce budworm, birch dieback, forest tent caterpillar, Armillaria root rot, Dutch elm disease: these were his daily concerns.

As he unlocked Lands and Forests' rented premises at 523 Prince and climbed the creaky stairs to his office, such topics occupied his mind. This well-read, down-to-earth man with a Master of Science degree from McGill University was known for his professionalism, his wry wit, and his excellent communication skills. His opinions were sought and valued from the department minister on down.

When he hired me for the summer of 1964, he was also director of the province's fledgling forest extension service. Its primary mandate was to deliver technical help to producers of lumber, Christmas trees, blueberries, and maple syrup. Fire prevention, forest conservation, and hunter safety were the service's responsibility too.

His team of foresters and technicians had established demonstration forests such as the Giants Lake Sugar Bush and the New Germany Christmas Tree Illustration lot. They had set up a hunter safety program, a junior guides school (an early version of Junior Forest Wardens), a sawmill efficiency program, and a province-wide school motion picture program.

He was researching and writing numerous technical bulletins, often illustrating them with photographs he'd taken and developed himself. The province's first Christmas tree and blueberry growers' manuals came out of his shop.

Hawboldt found me a desk, a chair, and a typewriter and asked me to write a guide to native trees, a conservation storybook for children, and a woodlot owner's manual. *Trees of Nova Scotia* and *The Brook and the Woodcutter* are still in print; the woodlot manual was to grow into something grander.

This boss's motto, "Head and Heart," should be engraved on every office manager's door. Hawboldt knew how to delegate and how to support. One day, to my co-workers' amusement, he found me reading a stack of children's picture books. "I'm, ah, researching your children's story," I explained.

"Good!" said he. "One could do worse than read Hans Christian Andersen."

When I left in late August to return to university, he presented me with a gilt-and-morocco-bound copy of *The Forest Resources of Nova Scotia*, which he had helped the late Richard Bulmer compile. Published in 1956, it summarized the province's first scientific forest stock-taking. I mined its wealth for years and still treasure it.

In 1965, I joined Lands & Forests full-time and stayed twenty-six years. Of these, the four with "LSH" were the best. In 1969, when Bob Burgess succeeded Wilf Creighton as deputy minister, he went to Halifax as his assistant. That left a vacuum in Truro, but Lloyd had built well and we took it from there.

Nova Scotia owes this modest native son more than it perhaps realizes. It was he who charted the course that made the province Canada's leading exporter of balsam fir Christmas trees. As a Maritime Lumber Bureau director, he worked tirelessly to upgrade regional lumber standards so our lumber could compete on international markets. To simplify woodlot cruising, he commissioned expatriate Russian forester Simon Kostjukovits to develop standard yield tables. He pushed for more accurate log scaling and dreamed of a standardized woodlot management system.

Most far-sighted of all, he supported the controversial 1965 Forest Improvement Act. The act was modelled on Sweden, where half the forest land was likewise held by small woodlot owners who did pretty much as they pleased, while steelmakers demanded more and more wood for charcoal. Thanks to saner laws, a timber famine was averted, and the country became an exporter of wood.

Hawboldt knew that in a province where over twenty thousand owners controlled the best and most accessible forest land, laws alone could never guarantee good stewardship. That required a critical mass of informed voters who would hold politicians and landholders accountable.

He saw in the act's proposed network of politically neutral local committees, each answerable to government, a platform for preaching good forestry while restraining abusers. It seemed to him that the FIA might succeed where the 1946 Small Tree Act had largely failed.

Robert Stanfield's Progressive Conservative government was enacting the new act in stages: owner registration first, then regional forest practices boards, then green belts along streams and major highways. Green belts soon became a hot issue. Timber barons and woodlot owners alike feared losing the right to cut where they chose. Predictably, industry lobbied against the act and killed it in its crib.

Meanwhile, as Hawboldt and others had predicted, a massive spruce budworm epidemic ravaged the aging fir and spruce forests of eastern Nova Scotia. The province, mindful of New

Brunswick's seemingly endless spray program, dismissed aerial insecticides. Because the outbreak destroyed half the fir on Cape Breton Island, reforestation—always popular with voters and politicians—became the watchword, whether planting was needed or no.

On the positive side, a series of cost-shared federal-provincial agreements helped woodlot owners update boundaries, build roads, dig fire ponds, and practise silviculture. On the negative side, costly media and court battles were fought over supposed links between Reye's syndrome in children and the use of farm-registered herbicides to protect forest plantations from competing vegetation.

Lloyd at least had the satisfaction of using his expertise to help salvage millions of cubic feet of budworm-killed wood through a debarking and underwater storage program. And as editor-in-chief of *The Trees Around Us* he played a key role in producing the comprehensive forest practices manual he'd always envisioned.

Lloyd Hawboldt died in April 1997 at Dartmouth General Hospital. His life's work made it a little easier for lumbermen, Christmas tree growers, maple syrup producers, and woodlot owners to earn a fair wage for a good product. His pioneering hunter safety program made the woods a little safer for hunters and the rest of us. His film program gave hundreds of teachers and thousands of students a glimpse of how forests and wildlife and people interact.

Scientist, writer, photographer, communicator—he was a true conservationist, and the world needs more like him.

Afterword
Mars, Anyone?

Would you sign up for a one-way trip to Mars? Yes? No? When a group of Americans was asked recently, over two hundred said yes. We all have escapist days — but Mars? Yet space tourism is suddenly real. Several companies are gearing up for it.

Virgin Galactic, brainchild of flamboyant UK transport mogul Sir Richard Branson, was out front until his mother ship VSS *Enterprise* crashed. SpaceX, owned by Elon Musk of Tesla, hopes to reach Mars within a decade. And non-profit Mars One envisions a permanent colony on the Red Planet by 2025; over two hundred thousand have volunteered to go.

These private ventures, unlike NASA's publicly funded $400 million-a-pop missions, will rely on reusable rockets — a huge cost saving. At first it'll be short sallies to the stratosphere and back. (Virgin Galactic envisions a flight of under ten minutes, just long enough to experience zero gravity, see the Earth's curvature and return — for $240,000.) Next, the International Space Station. Then the Moon, a three-day voyage each way.

But Mars is one-way. Its elliptical orbit never brings it closer to Earth than 58 million kilometres. That's at least a six-month voyage using current technology. Without a Martian refill depot, or a spaceship big enough to handle the round trip, no one comes back.

Knowing all this (one hopes), why did so many sign up? Well, curiosity, for one thing. Mars, our nearest outer neighbour, has always fascinated humans. Now you see it, a glimmering reddish dot on its two-year circuit round the sun, now you don't. Greeks and Romans revered it as their god of war. The Romans even named a month (March) after it.

Boredom is another motive. They say travel is equal parts pursuit and flight. Mars should deliver on both. First the thunderous lift-off, then the spectacular panorama of the country, the continent, and finally of Planet Earth turning in the starry vault. And then Mars itself, looming larger by the month.

Today, thanks to NASA's various probes, especially its current Curiosity rover and Reconnaissance Orbiter, we know Mars much better. On the plus side there's spectacular scenery: massive impact craters, the solar system's biggest known volcano, and a gorge dwarfing our Grand Canyon. We also know that its day/night cycle matches ours. That it has seasons like ours — but about twice as long. That it once had rivers, lakes, a huge ocean, and recently revealed muddy seepages apparently kept semi-liquid at minus 25° Celsius temperatures by dissolved magnesium chlorate and sodium perchlorate (think road salt).

On the con side, while daytime summer temperatures are livable, nighttime and winter temperatures are murderously cold. There's almost no air. Months-long, planet-wide dust storms are common. The soils are chemically reactive, possibly carcinogenic, and perhaps even caustic enough to eat through spacesuits or to corrode metal. And since Mars lacks an Earth-type electromagnetic shield, lethal solar radiation makes surface life improbable. Underground? In ice? Possibly.

Questions, questions. I have one: How did ancient Romans and Greeks, lacking telescopes, know that Mars/Aries has two fast-moving moons — asteroids, really — which we only discovered in 1877? Calling them the god's sons, the ancients named them Deimos (= terror) and Phobos (= fear).

Curiosity and boredom aside, is Mars madness really about science and exploration? Canadian astronaut Julie Payette thinks not. "They're not going to put anyone on Mars," she recently told *Maclean's.* "They don't even have a vehicle. It's a marketing ploy."

Yet we're signing up in droves. Could guilt and fear be the real reason? Guilt that we may have doomed life on the planet? With the one-percenters cashing in on our dread?

For the climate news *is* grim. Last summer northeast Newfoundland had more icebergs than lifelong residents had ever seen. I counted a hundred in one sweep of ocean, most from the sped-up Arctic calving during 2012's sultry summer. One sheet was kilometres long. Tourists jostled to ogle and snap. I painted those ice castles but with a heavy heart. For this was Greenland melting. Good for tourism, bad for the planet. What next? Cross-polar shipping, free-for-all drilling and unfixable spills, polar bear extinction?

Meanwhile, scientists at the South Pole declared West Antarctica's vast ice sheet "past the point of no return." Antarctica holds 90 per cent of the world's ice. In local terms that's enough water to make Nova Scotia an island and submerge downtown St John's.

Statistics may lie but not the view from space. Canada's Steve MacLean, orbiting Earth aboard *Columbia* in 1991 and *Atlantis* in 2006, saw a "huge" drop in mountain glaciers in that period.

In 2014, US scientists concluded that climate change had "moved firmly into the present." And Pope Francis, speaking at UN headquarters recently, called this a moral issue because the hardest hit are the world's poor. And for this he blamed corporate greed and our "throwaway culture."

Canada's author-activist Naomi Klein agrees. In her acclaimed 2014 book *This Changes Everything: Capitalism vs The Climate,* she fumes: "Climate change isn't an issue to…worry about, next to health care and taxes. It is a civilizational wake-up call…spoken in the language of fires, floods, droughts, and extinctions." Blaming unfettered capitalism's "Grow or Die" mindset, she thinks we've already passed NASA's 2° Celsius tipping point into runaway warming. "Only mass social movements can save us now," she warns, singling out First Nations activists and youth for special praise. Significantly, the pope gave Klein an hour-long audience but allotted our prime minister only eleven minutes.

Of course, we're all to blame. Canadians' per capita carbon footprint now rivals America's twenty tonnes a year. (A typical East Indian peasant produces one tonne.) Yes, we're a big, cold country with a huge road net. Yet, we think nothing of jetting off to a birthday party in Australia, spewing half a tonne of CO_2 per passenger-kilometre. (Half the cost of flying is fuel.) While our federal politicians mouth green slogans abroad and push for more pipelines back home, tiny Denmark is getting rich selling excellent wind turbines to the world.

We haven't even mentioned food and fresh water. At seven billion and counting, how shall we cope with wobbly weather? Especially now that China and other Asian countries crave more red meat? (Raising one kilo of beef takes roughly five thousand litres of water.) Already we're seeing crop failures and groundwater shortages in arid regions, California included.

Doleful British cleric Thomas Malthus (1766-1834) foresaw our dilemma. Population increase being exponential (two, four, eight), he taught that over time it will, all things being equal, outpace food production, which is arithmetical (two, three, four).

He was right—in the wrong century. For he overlooked the Industrial Revolution and New World largesse. The first goosed food production and distribution; the second opened new pastures to exploit. And how could he foresee the 1950s Green Revolution? Thanks to breakthroughs in plant breeding, synthetic fertilizers, and pesticides made from leftover Second World War poisons, we dodged a second Malthusian bullet.

Now, to echo seed-saving advocate Dr. Vandana Shiva, we need a new miracle. Some say GM food is it. Others cite issues like health, contamination of conventional crops by accidental cross-breeding, and Big Food's tightening grip on global food supplies.

Anyhow, even GM crops need fertile soil and reliable weather—both in short supply. Decades of deep plowing have decarbonized (oxidized the humus) across vast tracts of US cropland. Meanwhile long-term fertilizer use without adequate liming is acidifying topsoils. In sun-baked California, increased irrigation is raising soil salinity.

Drip irrigation must replace wasteful spraying.

"Not to worry," say the climate change deniers. "More CO_2 in the air will grow crops faster." True—but more CO_2 overhead means more trapped heat below, further reducing yields. Since the 1980s, global wheat production has fallen 2 per cent per decade. Corn and soy show similar declines.

Undeterred, deniers point to our rapidly warming North. Yes, the ranges of some crops *are* creeping north. Northern Manitoba is now a major soy producer. But you can't grow soy on tundra.

Solving the global food crisis must include curbing population growth. Short of war, disease, or starvation, this comes down to birth control. And since Western birth-death ratios are basically stable thanks to education, prosperity, and the Pill, the onus falls on so-called developing nations.

China led the way in 1980. Its family planning policy restricted 36 per cent of its population to one child and 53 per cent to two if the first were a girl; minorities were exempted.

Iran too, alarmed at its unsustainable fertility, made a brave start around 1990, lugging birth control kits up mountainsides by donkey. And it was working—until Ayatollah Khomeini, needing child soldiers to fight Iraqis, axed the program. It has remained axed. Meanwhile, India is overtaking China as the world's most populous nation.

But there's hope. Famine isn't inevitable. There *is* enough food and water to go around. It just needs to be conserved and distributed fairly. In the developing world vast tonnages are lost to spoilage, pests, and rodents. In the industrialized West, up to a third is wasted every day. (Ask any restaurant server.)

And women in the developing world are increasingly chanting: "Two is enough." Education, incentives, penalties help. So do Canada's non-profit agencies such as the Foodgrains Bank and Seeds of Diversity, the latter of which saves and distributes weather-hardy heritage seeds. Then there's private donors like America's Bill Gates and the Clinton Foundation. Some of their money comes from dirty oil stocks, but nothing is perfect.

The wild card is still climate change. In December the developed nations will meet in Paris to party and hammer out yet another carbon-curbing deadline. Ho hum. Big promises, poor delivery.

In perilous times it helps to recall past successes. The 1970s ban on ozone-eroding chlorinated fluorocarbons (CFCs) was one. In a rare display of unanimity and resolve, international delegates met in Quebec, hammered out the Montréal Protocol, sold it back home and—so far—have made the ban stick.

That deal likely saved our skins, our eyesight, perhaps even the biosphere. And our ozone shields have been healing ever since—though new gases pose new threats.

Taming climate change will take that level of co-operation and resolve.

Which brings us back to Mars. After the longest bus ride in human history (researchers are exploring chilled-gas hypothermic sleep to pass the time), our feckless pioneers will finally arrive. As noted, some things will look familiar. Other things, not so much.

The sun will look much smaller. The midday sky will be pinkish white—all that dust. There'll be nothing green. The air will be unbreathable CO_2 with a pinch of argon and nitrogen. With so little air to carry sound, an eerie quiet will prevail.

Water? So far it's either BYO fresh water or make your own (no pun intended). If as some think, the North Pole's seasonal water frost conceals a thick icecap, problem solved. There'll be water to drink, to extract oxygen, even to produce hydrogen to heat greenhouses and to fuel rockets and rovers.

Still, bulky spacesuits and cramped quarters will be a constant drag. "You'll live in a tin can," said one star-trekker. Luckily, Mars's gravity is only 62 per cent of Earth's.

Still, not much fun. Phoning home will help, but soon the pull of Mother Earth—scary weather, rising seas, terrorists, and all—will mute every joy. Compared to colonizing Mars, life on Earth is sweet and infinitely worth saving. I say invest the money and time and human lives here. Mars can wait.

Acknowledgements

American Forests
"Tough Little Trees of the Fringe," May/June 1994

Atlantic Forestry Review
"Chaga Saga," November 2017
"Lloyd S. Hawboldt, Bug Man" August 1997
"Ticked!" September 2018

Atlantic Salmon Journal
"Part Surgeon, Part Seamstress: A Fly-Tying Memoir," Spring 1999

Breakwater Books
"The Winter House," from the author's *September Christma*s 1992, with permission

Discover Nova Scotia: The Ultimate Nature Guide, Nimbus/NS Museum, 2001
"Sable Island: Ultimate Shunpiking"

Nature Canada
"God's Dead Dog & Other Roadkills," Autumn 2001
"The Hornet Dilemma," Autumn 1999
"Leaf Thief II," Autumn 2001
"The Lovely Duckling," 1998
"Of Mayflies & Millennia," 2002
"Meditating in the Country," 2002
"Sky Stone," Winter 2000

NQ (formerly *Newfoundland Quarterly*)
"Bonavista Traverse," Autumn 2011
"Caribou Caper," Spring 2012

Earthkeeping

"A Rose for Mary Matilda," Spring 2013
"Of Seals and Cod and Us," Winter/Spring 1998
"So Excellent a Fish: Capelin," Winter/Spring 1998

Rural Delivery
"Bumblebee Hotel," November 2016
"A Calendar of Roadside Flowers," July/August 1999
"Cold Room Capers," Winter 2004
"Cornsequences," March 2000
"Down to Earth," May 2004
"Fire from the Sky," October 2000
"Getting to Know You, Old House," December 2004
"Gift from the Sky," December 2002
"Gone to a Better Place: A Wood Stove Memoir," September 2002
"Hezekiah and the Pine," September 1996
"Leaf Thief I," October 2001
"Mars, Anyone?," November 2015
"Nature under Glass," April 2020
"Neil Van Nostrand, Ecologist," December 2016
"Oatmeal Shenanigans," January/February 2004
"Peeper Spring," June 2017
"Plastic Ocean Blues," Spring 2018
"Potato Bug Waltz," July 2001
"Rural Dreams," November 1996
"A Salmon for Supper," June 1997
"This Old House: Honeymoon & After," September 2003
"Tree Frog Moment," June 2017
"Turtle Tale," September 2010
"Two Rural Dreams," November 1996
"Window Talk," September 2005
"Winter Woodchuck Woes," December 2013

Truro News
"Catediquette," December 2021
"COVID-19 Moment," June 14, 2020
"I Miss My Barbers," June 2021
"Robinsong" (as "Birdsong"), 2021
"Spider Love," January 2021

Gary Saunders is a forester, painter, educator, and writer. Born in Clarkes Head, Newfoundland, Saunders worked as a forester in Newfoundland and Nova Scotia, along the way studying fine arts at the Ontario College of Art and Mount Allison University. A contributor to periodicals such as *Atlantic Advocate, Saltscapes, Canadian Geographic*, and *Canadian Living*, Saunders is the author of twelve works of non-fiction including *Earthkeeping, Alder Music*, and *My Life With Trees* (winner of the Evelyn Richardson Award for Non-Fiction). He lives in Clifton, Nova Scotia.